CANADIENS LEGENDS

MONTREAL'S HOCKEY HEROES

MIKE LEONETTI

FOREWORD BY JEAN BÉLIVEAU

WITH PHOTOGRAPHS FROM THE HOCKEY HALL OF FAME, BRUCE BENNETT STUDIOS,

THE DENNIS MILES COLLECTION AND THE LEGENDARY HAROLD BARKLEY ARCHIVES

ADDITIONAL ESSAYS BY DAVE STUBBS, AND HALL OF FAME JOURNALISTS RED FISHER AND FRANK ORR

RAINCOAST BOOKS
www.raincoast.com

This book is dedicated to all the Canadiens players who were members of Stanley Cup winning teams, who were named NHL all-stars or award winners, or were elected to the Hockey Hall of Fame

Raincoast Books gratefully acknowledges the ongoing support of the Canada Council for the Arts; the British Columbia Arts Council; and the Government of Canada through the Department of Canadian Heritage Book Publishing Industry Development Program (BPIDP).

Raincoast Books
9050 Shaughnessy Street
Vancouver, British Columbia
Canada   V6P 6E5
www.raincoast.com

In the United States:
Publishers Group West
1700 Fourth Street
Berkeley, California
USA   94710

Library and Archives Canada Cataloguing in Publication

Leonetti, Mike, 1958-
Canadiens legends : 95 years of Montreal's hockey heroes / Mike Leonetti.

Includes index.
ISBN 1-55192-731-4

1. Montreal Canadiens (Hockey team)–History. I. Title.

GV848.M6L45 2004   796.962'64'097i428   C2004-901960-0

Library of Congress Control Number: 2004092415

Designed by Teresa Bubela

Printed and bound in China.

1 2 3 4 5 6 7 8 9 10

Title page: *A battered and bloody Maurice Richard shakes hands with Boston goalie "Sugar" Jim Henry after defeating the Bruins.* [HHOF]

Page 5: *Maurice Richard laces up his skates.* [HB]

Contents

Foreword by Jean Beliveau 6

Introduction *The Montreal Canadiens: Hockey's Greatest Team* 8

The Early Years 1909–1939

Introduction 17

Sprague Cleghorn 22 • George Hainsworth 23 • Joe Hall 24 • Aurel Joliat 25 •
Edouard "Newsy" Lalonde 26 • Alfred "Pit" Lepine 27 • Joe Malone 28 • Sylvio Mantha 29 •
Howie Morenz 30 • Buddy O'Connor 34 • Didier Pitre 35 • Albert "Babe" Siebert 36 •
Georges Vezina 37

The Voices of Montreal Hockey: A History of Canadiens Broadcasters by Frank Orr 38

The Powerhouse is Built 1940–1960

Introduction 41

Emile "Butch" Bouchard 45 • Floyd Curry 48 • Bill Durnan 49 • Bernie "Boom Boom"
Geoffrion 51 • Doug Harvey 55 • Dick Irvin 59 • Tom Johnson 60 • Elmer Lach 62 •
Gerry McNeil 64 • Dickie Moore 65 • Ken Mosdell 69 • Bert Olmstead 70 •
Jacques Plante 71 • Ken Reardon 75 • Maurice "Rocket" Richard 76 • Frank Selke 81

The Richard Riot by Red Fisher 82

The Quiet Dynasty 1961–1973

Introduction 85

Ralph Backstrom 90 • Jean Béliveau 92 • Hector "Toe" Blake 96 • Yvan Cournoyer 100 •
Dick Duff 104 • John Ferguson 106 • Terry Harper 108 • Ted Harris 110 •
Charlie Hodge 112 • Jacques Laperriere 114 • Claude Larose 118 • Jacques Lemaire 119 •
Frank Mahovlich 123 • Claude Provost 125 • Henri Richard 127 • Jimmy Roberts 131 •
Bobby Rousseau 132 • Serge Savard 134 • Jean-Guy Talbot 136 • Gilles Tremblay 138 •
J. C. Tremblay 140 • Rogie Vachon 142 • Lorne "Gump" Worsley 144

Scotty Bowman — One-of-a-Kind Coach by Red Fisher 148

The Second Great Dynasty 1974–1984

Introduction 151

Ken Dryden 156 • Bob Gainey 160 • Rejean Houle 164 • Doug Jarvis 165 • Guy Lafleur 166 • Yvon Lambert 170 •
Guy Lapointe 171 • Peter Mahovlich 175 • Sam Pollock 176 • Doug Riseborough 178 • Larry Robinson 179 •
Steve Shutt 183 • Mario Tremblay 186

Happy New Year! — The Canadiens Host the Russians by Frank Orr 188

Return to Glory 1985–1995

Introduction 191

Guy Carbonneau 196 • Chris Chelios 198 • Vincent Damphousse 199 • Eric Desjardins 201 •
John LeClair 203 • Claude Lemieux 204 • Kirk Muller 205 • Mats Naslund 206 • Stephane Richer 207 •
Patrick Roy 208 • Denis Savard 212 • Bobby Smith 213

The Battle of Quebec: The Great Canadiens-Nordiques Rivalry by Dave Stubbs 214

Decline and Rebirth 1996–2003

Introduction 217

Patrice Brisebois 222 • Saku Koivu 223 • Craig Rivet 225 • Sheldon Souray 226 •
Jose Theodore 227 • Richard Zednik 231

A Change of Venue: The Forum and Bell Centre by Dave Stubbs 232

Conclusion 234

Index 238

Acknowledgements 240

Foreword

BY JEAN BÉLIVEAU

IT WAS THE DREAM of every boy growing up in Quebec in the thirties and forties to one day put on the uniform of the Montreal Canadiens. I was no different from anyone else who loved playing hockey during that era. We would practise for hours after school in the rink we had in our backyard. By playing outdoors we learned to stickhandle and develop other skills that might one day allow us to play for the Canadiens. When I was 12 years old, Maurice Richard played his first full season in Montreal. One year later, he scored 50 goals in 50 games. The "Rocket" soon became everyone's hero, including mine.

In 1948–49, while playing junior hockey in my hometown of Victoriaville, I scored 48 goals in 42 games. That performance got me noticed, but our team didn't survive financially, so the next season I had to find another junior club to play for. A few teams in the province were interested, but I decided to go to Quebec City to play for the Citadelle. I was treated very well there: when my junior days were over, they gave me a car! I decided to show that I appreciated all that was done for me by staying two more years in Quebec City and playing in the Quebec Senior Hockey League for the Quebec Aces. I gained valuable experience playing for the Quebec Aces with veterans like Herb Carnegie, Gaye Stewart and Ludger Tremblay. The club was well coached by Punch Imlach. I was 22 years old, and the salary was as good as I might have earned playing in the then six-team National Hockey League. However, after two seasons I knew it was time to try playing for the Canadiens. About to get married, I decided to pack up everything and move to Montreal.

Playing in the NHL wasn't a new experience for me, since in the two previous seasons I had had a couple of tryouts with the Canadiens. I got into two games in 1950–51 and scored my first goal against goaltender Harry Lumley. I played in three games the next year and scored a total of five goals, three against Charlie Raynor in one game against the New York Rangers and two versus "Sugar" Jim Henry of the Boston Bruins. Injuries made my first two years a little difficult, but in my third season, 1955–56, I added some toughness to my game and that little edge in my play gave me some more room on the ice. I had a good year with 47 goals and 88 points, and I was awarded the Hart Trophy. Best of all we

won the Stanley Cup, the first of five in a row. A group of new players joined the Canadiens that year, including Henri Richard, Claude Provost, Jean-Guy Talbot, Bob Turner and a first-year coach in Toe Blake. Our new coach was an honest man who could be tough on you, but he was usually right. Toe was a former player himself, so he knew how to handle a team of stars. He was able to get the players to understand that it was the team that came first and that personal achievements were second. It wasn't an easy task for Blake to coach this team, but every player loved playing for him.

We had virtually no changes on the team between 1955 and 1960. But then the Rocket retired, and gradually stars such as Doug Harvey, Dickie Moore, Bernie Geoffrion and Jacques Plante left. We started to add new players to the club. Two major additions were John Ferguson and Ted Harris, both big and physical men. Teams like the Toronto Maple Leafs were tough for the Canadiens to handle, but now we had the size we needed. By 1964–65 we were ready to challenge for the Cup, and we beat the Chicago Black Hawks in seven games during the finals. I had the honour of being named the first ever winner of the Conn Smythe Trophy, but I was much more pleased that we had regained the Stanley Cup.

We then went on to win four more Cups. It would have been another five in a row had it not been for the opposing goaltenders Johnny Bower and Terry Sawchuk in 1967 when the Leafs beat us in six games. But I have a great love and respect for the players who were on the so-called "Quiet Dynasty." We had a group of young guys — J. C. Tremblay, Jacques Laperriere, Bobby Rousseau, Yvan Cournoyer, Terry Harper, Gilles Tremblay, Claude Larose, Rogie Vachon — who were learning to work together and blending well with veterans like Dick Duff, Ralph Backstrom and Gump Worsley.

I wanted to retire after the 1969–70 season, but general manager Sam Pollock asked me to stay one more year. He told me the team wanted to add new players — the Canadiens had missed the playoffs for the first time in my career — and Sam wanted me to provide the group with some leadership. I was concerned about whether I could play to the level I was comfortable with, but I agreed to stay while making it clear that 1970–71 would be my final season. I scored my 500th career goal that season. Backed by the great

goaltending of Ken Dryden in the playoffs, we won the Stanley Cup. The Boston Bruins were favoured to win it all that year, but we beat them in the first round. I can still see Phil Esposito shaking his head after Dryden robbed him with an incredible save!

The Stanley Cup win in 1971 was the 10th of my career. It also marked the fifth time I accepted the trophy as team captain. Being named captain of the Canadiens was the greatest personal honour I have ever received in all my years in hockey. I couldn't believe it when they told me I won the players' vote in 1961. It was an honour. I was also very happy to join the front office when my playing days were over. I stayed there until 1993 when I decided it was time to retire after 40 years with the organization. The Canadiens

have always been very good about how they treat their former players. The alumni group they established serves as an example for all other teams in the league.

Although I am retired now, my association with the team continues in my role as one of the Canadiens ambassadors. I still enjoy going to the games. I have faith that Bob Gainey will set the team on the right course and help the Canadiens produce many more memorable moments. This book profiles many great Montreal players who have earned a special place in history by wearing the Canadiens sweater.

—Jean Béliveau

Introduction

The Montreal Canadiens:
Hockey's Greatest Team

F rom the first day in 1909 that the Montreal Canadiens came into existence, playing hockey for the team has always been special. Putting on the red, white and blue sweater with the famous CH logo seems automatically to make any player work harder to become worthy of the uniform worn by many legendary performers. As hockey's oldest franchise, the Canadiens organization, through both players and management, has inspired and sustained a tremendous sense of public responsibility that is the envy of other teams. Naturally, demanding fans — in Quebec but especially in Montreal — keep that responsibility in constant view by expecting nothing but the best from their hockey team.

Senator Hartland Molson, one of the most prominent team owners in hockey history, ran the Montreal Canadiens from 1957 to 1968. (HHOF)

All of Canada follows hockey religiously, but in Quebec the most successful franchise in hockey history also carries the flag for a nation within a nation — the proud Québécois. It isn't easy to carry this burden for representing, not just a city, but an entire people. As champions in every sense of the word, the Montreal Canadiens can look proudly at their achievements. The Canadiens have thrilled hockey fans with their great accomplishments. They have shown that people from different backgrounds — mainly French and English — can work together as the best team in hockey and one of the best in all of professional sports.

The success of the Montreal Canadiens is rooted in quality management. From the days of founders like George Kennedy and Leo Dandurand to the modern-day leadership of Bob Gainey, Montreal managers have recognized one important duty: putting a winning team on the ice. Some of the most successful general managers in hockey history have worked for the Canadiens — Tommy Gorman, Frank Selke, Sam Pollock and Serge Savard being the most notable. They were astute developers of talent with a keen sense for a good deal.

Enlisting good people for support roles, these managers knew that their most important hire was the coach. With multiple Stanley Cups to their credit, mentors like Cecil Hart, Dick Irvin, Toe Blake and Scotty Bowman have patrolled from behind the Canadiens bench. (One-time championship winners include Claude Ruel, Al MacNeil, Jean Perron and Jacques Demers.) With every move scrutinized by the media and devout fans, the Canadiens make for a difficult club to manage. The men in charge have always had to focus on what's best for the team. The pursuit of excellence explains why the Canadiens replaced some winning coaches and traded away some good hockey players. Over the years the Canadiens organization has developed many quality managers (among them Cliff Fletcher, Ron Caron, Doug Risebrough) and coaches (among them Jacques Lemaire and Pat Burns) who went on to succeed elsewhere. The Canadiens know that this pattern of change is the price of a winning team.

Good managers and coaches also recognize the need for top players. The Canadiens have been fortunate to have more than their fair share. It all started in 1923 with the acquisition of Howie Morenz, hockey's first superstar. A slick, superbly talented performer, Morenz could lift fans out of their seats. He sold tickets in the early years of the NHL and turned the Canadiens into a formidable club. Once Morenz left the team, the Habs struggled on the ice and at the gate for a few years. But then a young man with fire in his eyes and an incredible drive to score goals joined the team, and the Canadiens took off once again.

From 1942 to 1960 Maurice "Rocket" Richard led the team to unprecedented heights — winning eight Stanley Cups — while scoring at levels once considered unachievable. The first French-Canadian superstar was as exciting a player as the NHL has ever seen. He became the ultimate success symbol for French Canada, the hero to an entire province. When Richard retired, a young Jean Béliveau was ready to assume the leadership mantle: he took the team to another five championships between 1965 and 1971. An elegant man both on and off the ice, Béliveau became the Canadiens' greatest spokesman, not only while he played but also long after he retired and moved into the front office.

Right: Jean Béliveau's first full season as a member of the Montreal Canadien was in 1953-54. (HB)

Vezina Trophy on six occasions. Very capable netminders like Gump Worsley (a future Hall of Fame member), Charlie Hodge and Rogie Vachon filled in the next few years. Each of them won (or shared) at least one Vezina Trophy and at least one Cup.

Ken Dryden came out of Cornell University to take the Habs to another six titles between 1971 and 1979. He became known for making the big stops the team needed. By 1985–86 the Canadiens were still searching for the next great player when suddenly Patrick Roy took the league by storm (much as Dryden did in 1971) and brought the Canadiens back to glory on two occasions before he left the Habs in 1995. Even though Roy didn't finish his playing days with Montreal, by the end of his illustrious career many observers considered him the best goaltender of all time.

As much as the Canadiens depended on their best players and goaltenders to take them well into the playoffs, they also realized the need for top defencemen. Great blueliners like Sylvio Mantha, Doug Harvey, Tom Johnson, Emile Bouchard, J. C. Tremblay, Jacques Laperriere, Serge Savard, Larry Robinson, Guy Lapointe, Chris Chelios and Eric Desjardins were all instrumental in Montreal championship teams. No team can win as many championships as the Canadiens without great defencemen. Since the Norris Trophy for the NHL's top defenceman was first awarded in 1954, the Habs have taken it 11 times.

Shrewd management, top forwards, excellent defencemen and top-notch goaltending have allowed the Habs to be the most dominating team in NHL history with three dynasty periods to their credit. The first dynasty may have been the greatest: five consecutive titles between 1955 and 1960. No NHL team has matched the five in a row (a few have come close) and no organization has had as many stars on one team. Built carefully by Selke, the Montreal clubs of those years boasted Hall of Famers like Henri Richard, Dickie Moore, Bernie Geoffrion and Bert Olmstead. In 1960 the Habs won the Cup in eight straight games. Blake said that the 1960 team might have been the best he had ever coached.

It took the Canadiens five years to climb back to the mountaintop. Pollock built a solid if unspectacular club that would win four

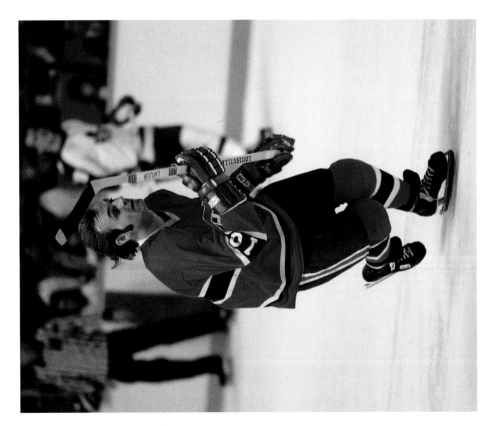

Guy Lafleur was selected first overall by Montreal in the 1971 NHL entry draft.
The Canadiens acquired the first draft selection in a trade with the California Seals. [DM]

The Canadiens landed their next great French-Canadian star during the 1971 NHL entry draft: Guy Lafleur. Pollock's wheeling and dealing got the Habs the number one pick of the draft, despite the fact that they had just won the Cup! It took a while before Lafleur hit his stride, but once he gained the necessary confidence, he was unstoppable. A tremendous skater with a hard shot and a determination to score, Lafleur was the top player on a team loaded with great performers. The Habs won five more Cups during Lafleur's best years with the team. As he slowed down, however, the Habs wondered about the next star who would galvanize the team.

It took years before a new star emerged in the position that the Habs always understood required the very best. Throughout the years that the Canadiens dominated the NHL, they usually had the league's best goaltender. In the early years it was Georges Vezina and George Hainsworth, while during the forties Bill Durnan was the league's supreme netminder. Jacques Plante was superior to any NHL goalie in the fifties when he was on six championship teams. While with the Habs, he was named the winner of the

Cups in five years (1965–1969). Had it not been for the upstart Toronto Maple Leafs in 1967, they might have matched their previous mark of five straight. The third dynasty between 1976 and 1979 was also directed by Pollock for all but one season. A powerful team that could play the game any way the opposition chose, the Habs of the 1970s boasted three great defencemen — Savard, Lapointe and Robinson — plus future Hall of Famers like Yvan Cournoyer, Jacques Lemaire and Steve Shutt. The Canadiens were again denied a fifth straight Cup, but a strong case can be made for the four consecutive winners as the best dynasty of all time.

Taken together the three Montreal dynasties show that the Canadiens have provided some of hockey's greatest moments and produced some of the game's top stars. The Canadiens management wanted a flamboyant and entertaining team that put on a good show for the fans, even when they played on the road. Confident that their attack meant that no game was ever out of reach, they realized that offence sold tickets. The Habs beat the opposition with style, skill, speed and lots of colour. Winning with such flair made the team well-known, especially in the United States, to those unfamiliar with the game. Even those not well-versed in hockey knew that the Montreal Canadiens were hockey's best team. It's no accident that the Canadiens have appeared on the cover of *Sports Illustrated* magazine more than any other hockey team. This publication hasn't often given hockey its due, but it has recognized the importance of the Habs. Montreal's commitment to hockey excellence has preserved the best of the game north of the border even as the game's power base was shifting to American interests.

As effectively as Habs management has worked over the years, it's never easy to appease a critical public. The media in Montreal are often the centre of attention and the agent of change, capable of running the unwanted owner out of town. The Habs know they must face at least one controversy each season. Good managers like Serge Savard understand that the problems are usually temporary. Dealing with issues they would rather avoid comes with working in Montreal for the most famous team in hockey.

Controversies have erupted over the French-English issue. The team has done its best to respect the two solitudes. It has been said that the Canadiens have gone out of their way to acquire French-Canadian players. But this is no different than Toronto seeking Ontario-born players who grew up watching the Leafs or the Edmonton Oilers and the Calgary Flames looking for Alberta natives. It's true that the greatest players who have worn the Canadiens sweater were native Quebecers strongly aware of Habs tradition. Striking the right balance between competing interests is never easy, but the team serves as a model of harmony between the two groups.

Part of the controversy centres around what the Canadiens mean to the city and province. The passion with which people follow the Habs is undeniable. The organization's high standards drive players to give that little extra that makes a champion. Newcomers understand immediately what the Canadiens stand for by looking in the dressing room at the faces of legendary Habs elected to the Hall of Fame. There's no escaping the team's rich history and the reverence inspired by great Canadiens. If that isn't enough, the Bell Centre's inscribed words from John McCrae's moving poem "In Flanders Fields" serve as a reminder: "To you with failing hands we pass the torch, be yours to hold it high."

All this has inspired Canadiens to play with great heart and a fire to succeed. Expected to carry on the tradition, players are treated well by the team in return. (Pollock used to give retiring players one more year's salary to help them avoid post-career problems.) Many players performed at a level they wouldn't have reached elsewhere. The records of players after being traded away by the Habs compare poorly with their Montreal records. Team captains are a special breed, since they are expected to take the team to the Cup. It isn't easy to lead such a high-profile team in two languages, but captains like Mantha, the Richards, Béliveau, Cournoyer, Savard, Gainey and Guy Carbonneau have all led their team to glory.

A unique team like the Canadiens needed a special building to play in. For many years the Montreal Forum filled that role in spectacular fashion. Not a beautiful building, the Habs arena was terrific. It was built — and refurbished on two occasions — just for hockey. (It hosted many events over the years, but it was mainly the home of the Canadiens.) Even on television, the Forum had a special air about it. With seats close together, there was little room to manoeuvre, but it was a magical place, especially when the Canadiens were on top of their game. At playoff time the Habs fed off the energy of the crowd and the charged atmosphere.

As time went on, the building acquired a life of its own, the ghosts of the past roaming the hallways and stands, making sure the Habs won. In a 1993 final against the Los Angeles Kings, when the Habs were about to go down two games to none, the Canadiens rallied to tie the game late on an illegal-stick violation and then won the game in overtime! It was as though the Forum had a strange hold on the events. The Canadiens would find a way to win at home, like so many times before, and take the Stanley Cup, which rightfully belongs nowhere else! The Habs' final game in the Forum in 1996 was a sad night, but the team did a masterful job of closing the building with a ceremony that left not one dry eye in the building and in living rooms across the country. The Habs had done it right again.

A victim of hockey's new economics, the Forum still stands, but it isn't the same. The Habs haven't been the same since winning their last Cup and moving into their new arena. Management hasn't been stable since 1995, and more than one coach has come and gone. Bad trades and poor selections at the draft table have compounded the problems. The great farm clubs of the past are nothing more than distant memories.

The new arena wasn't proving to be an advantage: without ghosts to haunt the opposition, the team hasn't put fear into anyone for years. Worst of all, the team's loyal following of the winning years has all but disappeared. The passion associated with the Canadiens has been missing. Only one good season — an eighth-place-overall finish in the Eastern Conference in 2001–02 — revived the city, but only briefly. Its highlight was the performance of the team's new star, goaltender Jose Theodore. When the Habs missed the playoffs in 2002–03, everyone sensed changes had to take place. When in the past upper management came to the same conclusion, the team didn't hesitate to get the best man for the job.

A new owner (George Gillett), the recently hired team president (Pierre Boivin) and the general manager (Andre Savard) all agreed on the need for drastic change. The result was the hiring of Bob Gainey, whose task was to restore the franchise to its former glory. An astute hockey executive and proven winner in management, Gainey will bring a strong work ethic to his new job. He has

Montreal Canadiens Stanley Cup Victories

YEAR	OPPONENT
1916	Portland Rosebuds
1924	Calgary Tigers
1930	Boston Bruins
1931	Chicago Black Hawks
1944	Chicago Black Hawks
1946	Boston Bruins
1953	Boston Bruins
1956	Detroit Red Wings
1957	Boston Bruins
1958	Boston Bruins
1959	Toronto Maple Leafs
1960	Toronto Maple Leafs
1965	Chicago Black Hawks
1966	Detroit Red Wings
1968	St. Louis Blues
1969	St. Louis Blues
1971	Chicago Black Hawks
1973	Chicago Black Hawks
1976	Philadelphia Flyers
1977	Boston Bruins
1978	Boston Bruins
1979	New York Rangers
1986	Calgary Flames
1993	Los Angeles Kings

the authority to make the required changes. In his first season with the team in his executive role, Gainey limited himself to observing the organization. He realized that incumbent coach Claude Julien needed a chance to show what he could do. This approach paid off when the Habs returned to the playoffs. The two men seem to have a good rapport. Stability will be the new cornerstone for the new-look Habs. The new management team even helped the Canadiens, the most decorated club in hockey history, to a first in the '04 playoffs: overcoming a three-games-to-one deficit to beat the Boston Bruins in seven games! Gainey will have to find better forwards to support a strong defence and an exceptional goaltender. If history is any indication, the Habs are in good hands with a proven man like Gainey in charge.

It's a difficult task to chronicle all the great moments of Montreal Canadiens history, even in a large book like this one. A combination of words and superb photography capture the team's illustrious history of doing the right things to win. Many times and over many years, the Canadiens have shown the other NHL teams how to build

a winner. Their overall playoff record, as of the end of the 2003–4 season — 86 series won and 391 victories in 661 postseason games, both NHL records — is the standard for all hockey franchises.

A Canadiens trademark is the new heights reached by its players in the playoffs. The Canadiens have won Stanley Cups when they were expected to win *and* when they weren't! No other team (including Toronto and Detroit) comes close to the Canadiens in championship titles. The team could rest on those laurels for a long time. However, the management, players, fans and media won't be satisfied with that forever. The next Stanley Cup win could happen whenever the Canadiens sense the opportunity. In the meantime, no other NHL team has an astounding 24 Stanley Cups to their credit. The following pages pay tribute to hockey's greatest team.

The Canadiens celebrate their 1993 Stanley Cup victory — their last championship on Forum ice. (Doug MacLellan/HHOF)

The Montreal Canadiens were born out of a desire to add a French-Canadian presence to the world of professional hockey and to the city. Most of the professional hockey clubs based in Montreal up to 1909 were English teams such as the Victorias, the Shamrocks and the Wanderers. It was firmly believed that a team made up solely of French-speaking hockey players could be very successful in Montreal.

Ironically enough, the founder of the Canadiens was neither a native Quebecer nor even a resident of Montreal. J. Ambrose O'Brien was the son of a wealthy mine owner who was interested in owning and running professional sports teams. He already had interests in hockey teams from the Ontario cities of Cobalt, Haileybury and Renfrew, and he wanted to be a part of the Canadian Hockey Association (CHA) that rejected him. However, an executive of the Montreal Wanderers who was looking for a new league to play in approached him.

Facing page: *In the 1909–10 season Jack Laviolette was the first coach of the Canadiens. A player-coach, he skated for the Habs until the 1917–18 season.* [HHOF]

O'Brien got the rights to the proposed French hockey club, and a new league was born under the banner of the National Hockey Association (NHA), which would include all the teams under his control. (Two CHA teams would also join the new league, causing the CHA to fold). T. C. Ware assisted O'Brien financially, helping to put up an initial $1,000 to form the team and an additional $5,000 to help meet payroll and pay for equipment and operating fees.

While it was thought that a French Canadian should own the newly formed team, it was O'Brien who named Jack Laviolette—a player-coach with access to the best French-speaking players because they often gathered at his restaurant—to put together the first Canadiens squad. The term "Canadien" referred to Montreal's first French Canadian settlers of New France, a hard-working people, and the nickname "Habs," as the team became known, referred to the first French settlers of New France, a tough and rugged people. The first stars of the team Laviolette put together were Didier Pitre and Newsy Lalonde, and the team earned the moniker the "Flying Frenchmen." The first NHA game was played on January 5, 1910, when the Canadiens defeated the Cobalt Silver Kings 7–6 in overtime. Some 3,000 people attended the first game at the Jubilee Rink (at the corner of Moreau and St. Catherine Street) and saw Lalonde score the first goal. The team wore red, white and blue uniforms (the colours of the flag of France). The sweaters were blue, and an ordinary "C" served as the team crest. The team was a big hit with the fans, who loved the skill and speed displayed by the Canadien players.

At the same time, a man named George Kendell (who went by the business name of Kennedy) challenged the use of the name "Canadiens," since he owned a club called the Club Athlétique Canadien. The matter ended up in court, and the settlement gave Kennedy the Canadiens NHA franchise (he had hoped to join the new circuit anyway), and O'Brien had to give up his stake in the team. It was also decided that the team could recruit English-speaking players (since French players were in short supply) and that other teams could sign French players. For the 1910–11 season the team got new red jerseys, and the next season saw the team adopt a red, white and blue sweater. In 1916 the team developed a full red, white and blue uniform with a "CA" serving as the team crest. The team won its first Stanley Cup in March of 1916 by defeating the Portland Rosebuds of the Pacific Coast Hockey League (PCHL).

In 1917 the National Hockey League was formed at a meeting in Montreal, with the Canadiens as one of the founding members. The club name was changed to le club du hockey Canadien, and the now famous "CH" logo made its debut. The Canadiens won their first NHL game at the Montreal Arena on December 19, 1917, and beat Ottawa 7–4 with Joe Malone, netting five goals, as a new scoring sensation. The Canadiens were back playing for the 1919 Stanley Cup in Seattle when the Spanish influenza struck, knocking five Habs, along with Kennedy, out of the finals. Defenceman Joe Hall died of the dreaded disease, and Kennedy died less than a year later due to complications from the illness. New owners purchased the team from Kennedy's widow in 1921 for a sum between $11,000 and $11,500, outbidding two other groups interested in the club.

The new owners were dubbed the "Three Musketeers of Sports" and included Leo Dandurand (a sports promoter from Illinois), Joseph Cattarinich (a one-time hockey goalie and all-round great athlete who had helped Laviolette manage the team in its first year) and Louis Letourneau. Cecil Hart, a man who had represented

Joe Cattarinich was a one-time goaltender who went on to help manage the Montreal Canadiens in 1909–10, their first season. [HHOF]

"We don't own the team, really.

The public of Montreal, in fact the entire province of Quebec owns the Canadiens. The club is more than a professional sports organization.

It is an institution, a way of life."

Senator Hartland Molson (former Canadiens owner)

Georges Mantha played both defence and left wing for the Canadiens from 1928 to 1941. He scored 89 goals and 191 points in 488 games as a Hab. He was also on two Stanley Cup-winning teams. (HHOF)

Dandurand during the purchase process, would serve as a team director and eventually as a coach. As for the on-ice product, the team boasted stars such as Aurel Joliat, Johnny "Black Cat" Gagnon, Georges Vezina, Joe Malone, Billy Boucher, the Mantha brothers (Georges and Sylvio), the Cleghorns (Odie and Sprague) and hockey's first superstar, Howie Morenz. The Canadiens won the Cup in 1924, beating Ottawa in the NHL playoffs and then knocking off Vancouver (PCHL) and Calgary (WHL) to take the championship. More than champions alone, the Habs were great promoters of the game, with the dazzling skills of Morenz being the most important selling feature in this hockey era. Good marketing skills by Dandurand saw the NHL rise in popularity in the United States, and soon there would be teams in Boston, Detroit, New York and Chicago. The game also grew in Canada (Ottawa, Hamilton and Quebec City all had NHL teams at one point in the early years of the circuit), and the Montreal Maroons were formed as an English-speaking club (all the previous English teams had disappeared by this time). They would play in the newly built Montreal Forum beginning in the 1924–25 season.

Since 1920 the Canadiens played at the Mount Royal Arena, which seated 10,000 fans. (Two previous homes, the Westmount Arena and the Jubilee Rink, were the victims of fires.) But in 1924, area businessmen led by Senator Donat Raymond and Sir Edmund Beatty decided to erect a new artificial ice arena that would hold 10,000 spectators. The Canadian Arena Company Limited was formed, and the Forum was built in 159 days for about $1.2 million. The new building was to house the Maroons, but it was the Canadiens who played the first game ever in the new hockey shrine. Due to problems at the Mount Royal Arena, the Canadiens switched their November 29, 1924 contest to the Forum and beat the Toronto St. Pat's 7–1 before some 8,000 fans. The Canadiens '24–'25 uniform featured a world globe for the crest, since they had won the Cup the previous season and were considered world champions. The Habs did not win the Cup for the rest of the decade, but the newly formed Maroons took the challenge trophy in 1926. The Canadiens experienced another death in the family when netminder Vezina contracted tuberculosis and died a short time later in 1926.

The Canadiens came back to win back-to-back Cups in 1930 and 1931, winning both championships in the Forum, which had become the Habs' official home starting in the 1926–27 season (they shared the rink with the Maroons). Led by the scoring exploits of Morenz and the solid goaltending of George Hainsworth, the

Habs became the first team to win the Stanley Cup in consecutive years since the NHL took control of the trophy beginning in 1926. But that was the end of the good times for the Habs for the rest of the thirties. By the 1935–36 season the Canadiens had finished last and were out of the playoffs. Morenz was traded away when the team thought he was slowing down, and even though he was brought back later, it was never the same. In January of 1937 tragedy struck the Canadiens again when Morenz suffered a badly broken leg and died suddenly while recovering in hospital. Yet another death shook the Canadiens in 1939 when Babe Siebert, newly appointed as coach, drowned before the start of the '39–'40 season. The '39–'40 season saw the Habs finish dead last with only 10 wins in the 48-game schedule. About the only good news the Habs received came in the form of left-winger Hector "Toe" Blake, picked from the Maroons in 1935. He would have a great impact on the Canadiens' fortunes for years to come in more than one way.

The team was sold once again in 1935 when Dandurand and Cattarinich (the two remaining owners) moved the team to the Canadian Arena Company that was controlled by Senator Raymond (who already owned the Maroons) for a total of $165,000. Led by Ernest Savard, Maurice Forget and Louis Gelinas, a new group of directors was appointed to manage the Habs. It soon became obvious that two NHL teams could not survive in Montreal, and the Maroons ceased operations in 1938. The folding of the Maroons left the Habs in the hands of Senator Raymond and Canadian Arena Company vice-president William Northey, who took over the club in May of 1940. Despite the change in ownership and the team's past success, the future of the team looked very bleak as the winter of 1940 approached. However, management made key moves by bringing in a new coach (Dick Irvin) and an experienced general manager (Tommy Gorman) and discovering a superstar player (Maurice Richard) who was just three years away from starting his career. Better days were just around the corner.

AWARDS SUMMARY 1909–1939

STANLEY CUP: 4 (1916, 1924, 1930, 1931)

VEZINA TROPHY: 3 (George Hainsworth, 1927, 1928, 1929)

HART TROPHY: 7 (Herb Gardiner, 1927; Howie Morenz, 1928, 1931, 1932; Aurel Joliat, 1934; Albert Siebert, 1937; Toe Blake, 1939)

SPRAGUE CLEGHORN

SPRAGUE CLEGHORN was such a mean hockey player that the opposition absolutely hated him. He was never afraid to use his stick, and after one such occasion (when he cut an opponent for five stitches over the eye) his own team, the Montreal Canadiens, suspended him because they were so upset by his tactics. But it was Cleghorn's rugged play and durability that made this 5'10" defenceman a valuable performer in the early days of professional hockey.

A native of Montreal (and a product of a very rough neighbourhood while growing up), Cleghorn played on several amateur teams around the city between 1906 and 1909. He then played eight games for the New York Wanderers for the 1909–10 season, scoring seven goals. He played the next season for the Renfrew Millionaires in the National Hockey Association (the forerunner to the National Hockey League) before returning home to play for a number of years for the Montreal Wanderers of the NHA. He led the NHA in assists in 1914–15 with 12 and added 21 goals (in just 19 games) for a very impressive 33-point total. Cleghorn liked to rush the puck even though he was a defenceman in a low-scoring era of hockey. Cleghorn would make rink-length dashes that would excite the crowds, and he once scored five goals in one game. He showed himself to be a fierce competitor and was feared because of his volatile temper. However, a broken leg suffered in an accident jeopardized Cleghorn's career. He missed the entire 1917–18 season.

The Wanderers thought Cleghorn was all done as a hockey player and let him go, much to the delight of Ottawa Senators manager Tommy Gorman, who believed Cleghorn was a great blueliner. Gorman claimed his rights (there was a dispersal draft of Wanderer players when their arena burned down), and Cleghorn told Gorman

he was ready to go. The Senators paid the $8.50 transportation charge to get Cleghorn to Ottawa! He was with the Senators for a couple of Stanley Cup wins (although he did play part of one year with the Toronto St. Pat's) but then returned to Montreal to play for the Canadiens in 1921 when a trade was arranged. He joined his brother Odie, a forward on the Habs squad.

In his first season with the Canadiens, he scored 17 times in just 24 games, and Cleghorn was named captain of the team. He was still much hated by all the other teams, and Ottawa (a team Cleghorn grew to hate because it let him go) tried to expel him from hockey after he attacked three Senator players in one game on February 1, 1922. His stick assault on Lionel Hitchman in the 1923 playoffs forced him to take an underground route out of the arena, as Ottawa fans were ready to lynch the brawling defender. Montreal manager Leo Dandurand was so upset with Cleghorn that he suspended his own player for the final game of the series against the Senators.

Cleghorn anchored the defence corps that won the Cup in 1924 (the Habs' first NHL championship). When the Habs took the Cup to a reception, the car with Cleghorn and several of his mates broke down. The silver Cup was left along the curb as the players pushed the car up a hill. Once the car was up the hill and moving again, the Cup was all but forgotten until one hour later when they realized it was missing. When they returned they found it just where they left it! Cleghorn wore out his welcome in Montreal and found himself dealt to Boston for the 1925–26 season. His NHL totals include 83 goals and 138 points in 259 games. He was elected to the Hockey Hall of Fame in 1958.

CLEGHORN'S CANADIENS STATS:	GP	G	A	P	PIM
regular season	98	42	15	57	218
playoffs	13	3	3	6	6
STANLEY CUPS: 1					

A feared defender, Sprague Cleghorn scored 167 career goals as a professional with 255 total points in 374 games. [HHOF]

GEORGE HAINSWORTH

MONTREAL NETMINDING legend Georges Vezina once attended an Ontario Hockey Association (OHA) game with Montreal manager Leo Dandurand and thought a goaltender they were observing by the name of George Hainsworth would make a good National Hockey League puck stopper. Vezina also faced Hainsworth in an exhibition contest and was impressed. In effect, Vezina was picking his own successor with his observations and recommendation. It would not be easy for the little (5'6" and 150 pounds) Hainsworth to fill the rather large skates of Vezina, but time would prove that the Canadiens had indeed made a wise choice by selecting a worthy successor for their netminding duties.

Hainsworth was born in Toronto in 1895 but grew up in Kitchener, Ontario, when his family moved there. He was a good baseball player but also excelled at hockey and played in the Kitchener area for many years. Hainsworth had a burning desire to play hockey and practised being a goalie by stopping wooden pucks he made in his father's small plumbing store. He was finally discovered for professional hockey by the legendary Newsy Lalonde, who had Hainsworth play for him in Saskatoon for the Western Canadian Hockey League. He played three seasons in Saskatoon, and Dandurand was advised that Hainsworth was a good prospect for the NHL. When Vezina suddenly died, the Canadiens needed a top-flight goalie, and Hainsworth finally got his chance with the Habs in 1926–27 at the age of 30. He quickly showed he belonged by recording 14 shutouts in his first season in Montreal and followed that up with 13 more the next year. In 1928–29 Hainsworth had a remarkable 22 shutouts in 44 games (still a record), and he then took the Habs to two consecutive Stanley Cup wins in 1930 and 1931. He won the Vezina Trophy

as the NHL's best goaltender the first three years (1927, 1928, 1929) it was awarded.

Slight and small, Hainsworth built his game around efficient moves to stop pucks. He played a smooth, calm game that appeared effortless. He was technically sound, which helped him deal with a Canadiens team that was not the best defensively. But he thrived and was soon accepted when he played one game against the Toronto Maple Leafs with an eye swollen shut (his nose was broken from a shot during the pregame warm-up). He was grimly determined to play the game and, with no backup goalie available, held the Leafs to a 1–1 tie. His play earned the admiration of the Montreal fans who had been cool to the new goalie, and his performance against the Leafs seemed to win them over. He won over 20 games in six straight seasons (they only played 44 games) but in 1932–33 he posted a losing record for the first time as a Hab. A 10–0 loss to the Leafs was the low point for the normally reliable netminder, who admitted he played poorly, and on a whim the Canadiens offered him to the Leafs. Conn Smythe accepted the deal for the Leafs and goalie Lorne Chabot was sent in exchange.

Hainsworth had three good years with Toronto, including a 30-win season in 1934–35 (in a 48-game schedule) but the Leafs let him go early in the 1936–37 season. After the Habs re-signed him as a free agent, he played in only four contests before his career came to an end. His 94 career shutouts remained the NHL record until Terry Sawchuk broke the mark in 1967. Hainsworth became a municipal politician after his retirement, well thought of in his new role, until an auto accident took his life at the age of 55. He is a member of the Hockey Hall of Fame.

HAINSWORTH'S CANADIENS STATS:	GP	Wins	Losses	Ties	Shutouts	GA
regular season	318	167	97	54	75	1.75
playoffs	31	13	13	–	6	1.70

STANLEY CUPS: 2

When George Hainsworth joined the Montreal Canadiens, he wasn't given the traditional sweater number one for goaltenders. He had to wear sweater numbers 12, and 17 before being given Georges Vezina's old sweater number one. [HHOF]

JOE HALL

When the media stick a label on someone it sometimes stays with the person no matter what happens. This isn't just a modern reality in professional sports but something that happened as far back as the early 1900s. Such was the case for defenceman Joe Hall, a hockey player known as the physical type. The 175-pound, 5'10" defenceman was willing to take on anyone, and a newspaperman tagged him with the nickname "Bad." The moniker stuck with Hall for his entire career, even though many a teammate would extol the virtues of the rugged blueliner. Attacking an official would do nothing to change his reputation (Hall claimed he was trying to get back at an opponent) but when Hall refused to pay a $100 fine (and a further $27 for ruining the man's suit), he only added to his bad boy image. It's a true shame that Hall died so young (at 38), unable to redeem himself and perhaps clear his name.

Born in England in 1882, Hall learned to play hockey in western Canada with teams in Winnipeg and Brandon, Manitoba. But he really began cutting his reputation in the rough-and-tumble International Hockey League in 1905–06 when he played for a Michigan-based team. He was an aggressive player who prided himself on being a tenacious checker, leading the IHL with 96 penalty minutes in just 20 games (his record also shows 33 goals scored, with no assists). His willingness to take on all comers got him a job with the Quebec Bulldogs in the National Hockey Association (NHA), and he was on two Stanley Cup-winning teams in 1912 and 1913. He had some offensive talent, scoring 13 goals one year and 15 in another, but his best skill was keeping the opposition honest. His penalty minute totals reflect a player who liked body contact during his seven years with the Bulldogs.

When the players on the Quebec squad were dispersed, Hall was selected by the Montreal Canadiens on September 26, 1917. Canadiens player-manager Newsy Lalonde, a one-time arch-rival of Hall's, signed the defenceman for the Habs. Hall was one of the first English-speaking players on the Canadiens, and his first year with the Habs saw him record 100 penalty minutes (in just 21 games) while scoring eight times and adding seven assists. In 1918–19 Hall and the Canadiens defeated Ottawa for the right to play Seattle for the Stanley Cup. The Canadiens headed west to play Seattle in the finals, but tragically Hall wouldn't make it back to Montreal. Seattle won the opening game on March 19 by a 7–0 count, but the Habs showed they were worthy contenders by winning the next game 4–2. Seattle bombed the Montrealers 7–2, but the Canadiens held Seattle to a 0–0 tie the next game and came back to win the next contest 4–3 in overtime. Hall was showing some of his customary flair by battling Cully Wilson of Seattle, but it was noticeable that he was having difficulties. He staggered off the ice during the overtime contest and was rushed immediately to hospital.

The flu was causing an epidemic all over North America, and Hall fell victim to the bug (several other Montreal players were sick as well). The Habs asked for permission to get new players to replace those who got sick but were denied their request. With the series tied 2–2, the Stanley Cup final was called off, and for the only time in history, there was no Stanley Cup winner. Hall died on April 6, six days after he entered hospital. Many of his teammates took the death of Hall very hard. Joe Malone of the Canadiens, lamenting the loss of his teammate, commented that Hall had no more opportunity to erase the "bad" name he had acquired years ago.

HALL'S CANADIENS STATS:	GP	G	A	P	PIM
regular season	38	15	8	23	189
playoffs	12	0	1	1	29

Joe Hall was a member of three Montreal-based hockey teams during his career, playing for the Wanderers and the Shamrocks (of the National Hockey Association) before joining the Canadiens in 1917. (HHOF)

AUREL JOLIAT

WHEN ANYONE SPEAKS of the best players of the early era of professional hockey, the name Aurel Joliat inevitably comes up. Listed officially at 5'7" and 136 pounds, Joliat was something of a dynamo who impressed all those who watched him play hockey. He understood the game very well and could dazzle with his stickhandling abilities. Joliat was quick on his skates and not the least bit afraid to use his stick if he had to protect himself.

He wore a baseball-style cap when he played and practically dared anyone to knock it off his head. The cap added colour to Joliat's game, which featured great playmaking and goal-scoring skills.

Joliat was born in Ottawa, Ontario, in 1901 and learned to skate on the Rideau Canal with boyhood chums, Bill and Frank Boucher (who would achieve their own fame in the NHL). He started out as a defenceman and played on a championship team in the Ottawa area, but he also played some football. His amateur status was in doubt so he travelled to Saskatoon and switched to left wing from defence. Montreal Canadiens manager Leo Dandurand was tipped off about the talented Joliat and made a deal to acquire the "mighty atom from Ottawa" by sending star Newsy Lalonde to Saskatoon on September 10, 1922, along with $3,500 in cash. Joliat was put on a line with Odie Cleghorn and Bill Boucher, and he scored two goals against the Toronto St. Pat's. Even though the Habs lost the game to Toronto, the St. Pat's had difficulty keeping up with Joliat's moves. During the first ever meeting between the Canadiens and the Montreal Maroons on December 10, 1924, Joliat scored four goals in a 5–0 victory. Joliat could spin and turn like few other players and showed a great sense of anticipation. He could break up plays and counterattack

quickly, knowing that he had to excel at the finesse game.

He was soon teamed with the great Howie Morenz, and the pair produced a great number of goals for the Canadiens. Joliat had 12 his first season, then 15 the next (both 24-game seasons) and then broke through for 30 in 1924–25 in 25 games. He had over 20 goals two more times for Montreal and was named the NHL's best player. When he won the Hart Trophy in 1933–34, he had 22 goals and 37 points in 48 games. Joliat was a first team all-star in 1931 and was selected to the second team on three other occasions. He helped the Canadiens to three Stanley Cups and played his entire NHL career with Montreal, retiring after the 1937–38 season. Throughout his career Joliat never lost any of his feisty nature. Even after suffering two displaced vertebrae, the result of falling some 35 feet off a roof, he was still able to play with an edge to his game. Joliat would take on the legendary Boston defenceman Eddie Shore, a much bigger man with an even larger reputation for being tough. Joliat once racked up 105 penalty minutes in 1927–28 as testament to his physical play.

Joliat considered a goal he scored against Calgary in the 1924 Stanley Cup finals to be the most memorable of his career. He skated through the entire Calgary team before rounding the net and depositing a backhander into the net's far corner. After his retirement Joliat worked for the Canadian National Railway in his hometown of Ottawa. Invited back to the Forum at the age of 83 when he was voted on the Canadiens all-time team, he showed the fans he could still skate and shoot. He was named to the Hockey Hall of Fame in 1945, and passed away in 1986.

JOLIAT'S CANADIENS STATS:	GP	G	A	P	PIM
regular season	655	270	190	460	771
playoffs	54	15	14	29	88

STANLEY CUPS: 3

For being one of the most popular players in Canadiens history, the Montreal fans presented Joliat with $7,500 after a playoff game at the Forum. (James Rice/HHOF; inset photo: HHOF)

EDOUARD "NEWSY" LALONDE

THE MONTREAL CANADIENS have enjoyed the luxury of great goal scorers throughout much of their history. One of the first such players was Edouard "Newsy" Lalonde. He was known as "Newsy" because as a youngster he had worked in a newspaper plant. A tough 5'9", 168-pound centre, Lalonde could score goals with ease and was an exceptional offensive player in an era without a lot of scoring. He was a member of the first ever edition of the Montreal Canadiens (for part of the 1909–10 season), scoring 16 goals in six games, and later served, being a natural leader, as a team captain. Before he left the Habs, he also coached the team for a short period.

Lalonde was born in Cornwall, Ontario, in 1888 and was spotted by hockey scouts while playing for the Woodstock (Ontario) Seniors. After he turned 18, he began playing pro hockey in Sault Ste. Marie. He arrived in the Soo by train at 8:00 p.m. and was in uniform for an 8:30 game. He was supposed to be an extra for the game, but when another player got hurt, Lalonde got into the game and scored two goals in a victory over Pittsburgh in an International Hockey League (IHL) contest. He was in professional hockey to stay and scored 29 goals in 18 games for the Soo squad. He bounced around a little for the next few years before settling down as a regular with the Canadiens by the 1912–13 season. He became a consistent 20 or more goal scorer (leading the NHL with 22 in 1918–19), also winning two scoring championships. Lalonde's best goal-scoring years saw him record 37 and 33 goals to help the Habs win their first ever Stanley Cup in 1916. He once had a six-goal game (against the Toronto Maple Leafs on January 19, 1920), and he also scored nine in a contest when he

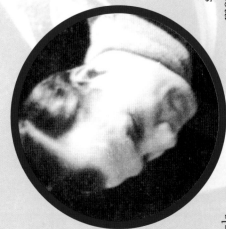

played for Renfrew for part of the '09–'10 season before the formation of the NHL.

Lalonde's style earned him great popularity with hockey fans (and much disdain from the opposition) and a loyal following. He was such a good athlete that he was able to earn more money playing lacrosse than playing hockey. Lalonde was named the best lacrosse player in Canada for half a century. But it was hockey that gave Lalonde his fame, as he used his great determination and temper to get the better of his opponents. He had many great battles, especially with Joe Hall of the Quebec Bulldogs. These two warriors weren't afraid to use their sticks on each other, but later Lalonde welcomed Hall to the Canadiens and the two became teammates. Sprague Cleghorn, another tough guy, nearly ended Lalonde's life during an on-ice incident, but Lalonde pleaded with police not to press charges against his hated foe. He was a villain during the 1917 Stanley Cup finals when the Canadiens faced the Seattle Metropolitans. Lalonde was penalized five times and even slammed the butt end of his stick into the referee's stomach, for which he received a match penalty and a \$25 fine. The Habs lost the final in five games to the Seattle club.

After five seasons in the NHL with Montreal (including a stint as a player-manager), Lalonde was 35 years old when the Habs sent him to Saskatoon in exchange for untried rookie Aurel Joliat. The trade wasn't well-received at first, but Joliat proved to be a good acquisition. Lalonde played in western Canada for three full seasons. He returned to the NHL with the New York Americans for just one game in 1926–27 and was done playing hockey by 1929. Lalonde suffered a hip injury in 1971 and died in November of that year. He was elected to the Hockey Hall of Fame in 1950.

LALONDE'S CANADIENS STATS:	GP	G	A	P	PIM
regular season*	98	124	41	165	183
playoffs*	7	15	24	39	23
STANLEY CUPS: 1					

* for games played with the Canadiens in the NHL only

One of the great goal scorers in the early years of professional hockey, Lalonde scored 453 total goals in 336 career games played. (HHOF)

ALFRED "PIT" LEPINE

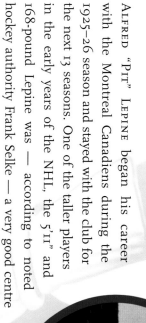

ALFRED "PIT" LEPINE began his career with the Montreal Canadiens during the 1925–26 season and stayed with the club for the next 13 seasons. One of the taller players in the early years of the NHL, the 5'11" and 168-pound Lepine was — according to noted hockey authority Frank Selke — a very good centre with a flair for playmaking and a polished approach to the game. He was also known for a sweeping poke check but ultimately wasn't as well-remembered as he might have been had he not played in the shadow of the great Howie Morenz.

A native of St. Anne de Bellevue, Quebec, Lepine gave his all to the Montreal Canadiens who signed him as a free agent on November 13, 1925. His goal-scoring abilities became evident early on when, as a rookie, Lepine scored nine times for the Canadiens in just 27 games. He followed up with 16 in 44 games the next season, but a collarbone injury forced him to miss half of the next year. Lepine recovered well enough and returned to play on a line with Armand Mondou and Georges Mantha, scoring six goals in 1928–29. However, he scored a career high 24 the next season and added another 17 in 1930–31. He improved his goal total to 19 the next season but then never again scored more than 12 for the Habs.

He played a very prominent role on the Canadiens' Stanley Cup winning squads of 1930 and 1931, scoring many key goals. In 1930, the Habs defeated Chicago and the New York Rangers before edging the Boston Bruins in the finals (in two straight games). The win marked the first time the Canadiens won the Cup on home ice. During the 1931 playoffs, the Canadiens knocked

off Boston 3–2 in games before doing the same to the Chicago Black Hawks (shutting out the hometown Chicago squad 2–0 in the deciding fifth game before 18,000 fans) to take their second straight championship. It was the first time the Habs won back-to-back Cups. Lepine played with Mantha and Wildor Larochelle during those Cup-winning years. The Habs were the underdogs to Boston in the '30 final, but Lepine was outstanding, scoring once in the opener (a 3–0 victory) and checking furiously in the second game (a 4–3 Cup-clinching victory). He had an excellent final in '31 against the Black Hawks, scoring the winning goal in the first game of the series (a 2–1 road win) and then scored a pair, including the winner, in the fourth game of the series. Chicago had the Cup within their grasp, but the Canadiens wouldn't quit, overcoming a two-goal deficit to win 4–2 and then taking the Cup in the next contest.

After Howie Morenz was traded to Chicago, Lepine became the number one centre and had the great Aurel Joliat as a winger. He led the team in scoring in 1934–35 with 31 points in 44 games. The next season saw Lepine miss many games due to a broken thumb (only six goals in 32 games) and the following year saw the return of Morenz to the Habs lineup. Lepine played for a while with Toe Blake on his line. Nearing the end of his career, he scored seven goals in 34 contests. He suffered a major leg injury, although he did play in 47 games for the Canadiens in his last season, 1937–38, scoring just five times. Lepine died in 1955.

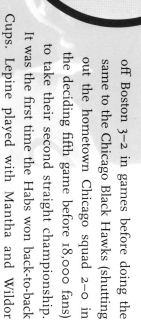

LEPINE'S CANADIENS STATS:	GP	G	A	P	PIM
regular season	526	143	98	241	392
playoffs	41	7	5	12	26

STANLEY CUPS: 2

Pit Lepine scored five goals in one game when the Canadiens beat Ottawa 6–4 on December 14, 1929. (James Rice/HHOF)

JOE MALONE

ACCORDING TO THE *Official NHL Guide and Record Book*, there are a few offensive records that Wayne Gretzky doesn't own. That Gretzky's name doesn't appear under some categories means that his contemporaries earned those few records that eluded him. But a closer look at the book shows that some marks of excellence still belong to the hockey players that starred generations ago. One such player is Joe Malone, who holds two marks of distinction: the first is a 2.20 goals-per-game average (set when Malone scored 44 goals in just 20 games in 1917–18) and the second is the record for most goals in one NHL game — 7, which Malone established on January 31, 1920, as a member of the Quebec Bulldogs. To many, Malone is just a name in the pages of history, but he deserves to be mentioned as one of the all-time best players.

Malone was born in Quebec City in 1890 and came to prominence as a professional hockey player when he joined the Bulldogs in the National Hockey Association. He joined the Quebec club in the 1910–11 season, scoring 21 goals in 18 contests. The Bulldogs also won the Stanley Cup that year and became champions again the following year when Malone had 43 goals (to lead the league) in just 20 games. Malone also led all goal scorers in the 1912 playoffs when he scored nine times in four contests. The slick centre also had seasons of 24, 16, 25 and 41 goals while he was with the Bulldogs. He also had a nine-goal game when the Bulldogs tore apart the Sydney Miners 14–3 on March 8, 1913, during a Stanley Cup final game. Malone was quick on the ice, able to find openings like no other player in his era. He had an upright skating style, and his touch around the net was marvelled at by everyone who saw him play. Malone admitted he didn't have a hard shot, but he said he always knew where the puck was going to be.

There's no telling how many goals he might have scored had they played more games.

Like many others players of the time, Malone was a good athlete who excelled at other sports like lacrosse and baseball. But his hockey skills got him noticed the most, and the Montreal Canadiens were certainly interested in his services when the Bulldogs dropped out of professional hockey before the start of the National Hockey League for the 1917–18 season. The rival Montreal Wanderers passed up the chance to select Malone's playing rights, and the Habs quickly snapped him up. He played in 20 of the scheduled 22 games and still came up with 44 goals, leading the league in points with 48. He scored a goal in 14 consecutive games that year and was on a line with two other Canadiens stars, Newsy Lalonde and Didier Pitre. Together the line chalked up 84 goals. In the next season, even though recovering from a broken arm, Malone managed seven goals in eight regular-season games, then added six goals in five playoff games.

Quebec returned to big-league hockey for the 1919–20 season, and the man known as "Phantom Joe" rejoined the Bulldogs. He led the NHL in goal-scoring with 39 goals in 24 games and also led in points with 49. The Bulldogs became the Hamilton Tigers the next season with Malone, scoring 52 times, as the player-coach for two years. He returned to the Canadiens as a substitute player for his last two seasons and was with the club when they won the Stanley Cup in 1924. Malone never made more than $2,000 in any year that he played hockey, and he was even more modest about his personal achievements on the ice. He was very proud of his achievements but felt that the modern game was different from the one he played. Elected to the Hockey Hall of Fame in 1950, Malone passed away in May of 1969.

MALONE'S CANADIENS STATS:	GP	G	A	P	PIM
regular season	58	52	6	58	35
playoffs	9	6	0	6	3
STANLEY CUPS: 1					

Between the years 1904 and 1924, Joe Malone scored 344 goals in 274 professional hockey games. [HHOF]

SYLVIO MANTHA

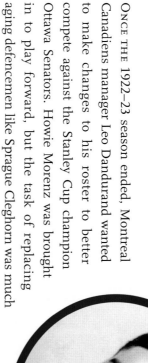

ONCE THE 1922–23 season ended, Montreal Canadiens manager Leo Dandurand wanted to make changes to his roster to better compete against the Stanley Cup champion Ottawa Senators. Howie Morenz was brought in to play forward, but the task of replacing aging defencemen like Sprague Cleghorn was much more difficult. One player given a chance to prove himself was Montreal native Sylvio Mantha. He signed a contract as a free agent on December 3, 1923. It would prove to be a wise choice that would lead to a Hall of Fame career.

Mantha first came to the attention of the Canadiens while playing industrial and senior hockey in the Montreal area. He played right wing as a junior, impressing the Canadiens with four goals in one game. Since the Montreal club had immediate needs on defence, they asked Mantha to move back to the blue line. He eventually became known as a top two-way defenceman who was very good at moving the puck up the ice while remaining strong in his end. Mantha was fortunate enough to play on a Stanley Cup-winning team as a rookie in 1924. He saw limited ice time in his first year with Montreal (one goal, three assists in 24 games) but became a regular once Cleghorn was dealt to Boston. He gained valuable experience when teamed with veteran Herb Gardiner (a future Hall of Famer himself) on defence.

He had his best years when the Habs won back-to-back Stanley Cups in 1930 and 1931, sharing blue line duties with Marty Burke and Albert Leduc. Mantha was especially good in the playoffs (contributing four goals over those two playoff years) and playing

an aggressive brand of defence when he had to. (He led all players with 26 penalty minutes in 10 playoff games in '31.) Mantha scored two important goals against Boston in the '30 final as the Habs swept the Cup in two straight contests by scores of 3–0 and 4–3.

He was good again in 1931–32 when he made the second all-star team for the second time in his career but began to slow down after that point. By the 1934–35 season, he performed a more or less backup role. When the team was sold, Dandurand recommended that Mantha be appointed as player-coach. The new owner agreed, but a poor season did Mantha in, after which Cecil Hart replaced him as coach.

Considered a very reliable defender, Mantha had the full confidence of Dandurand when he was with the Canadiens. He had an offensive side to his game (scoring 63 career goals) and his highest output of 24 points came in 1929–30. Mantha finished in first place nine times over a 14-year career. He also played with his brother, Georges, for many years on the Habs squad. Mantha was signed by the Boston Bruins for the 1936–37 season but only played in four Bruins games. It was ironic that he should play for the Bruins, since he was the first to score a goal in the Boston Garden when he led the Canadiens to a 1–0 victory in the first game ever played (on November 20, 1928) at the arena that became a shrine.

He became a linesman in the NHL and a referee in the American Hockey League. Returning to the Montreal area, he tried coaching (junior and senior teams) to stay in hockey. He was elected to the Hockey Hall of Fame in 1960 and passed away in 1974.

MANTHA'S CANADIENS STATS:

	GP	G	A	P	PIM
regular season	538	63	72	135	665
playoffs	46	5	4	9	66

STANLEY CUPS: 3

Sylvio Mantha served as a player-coach for the Montreal Canadiens for the 1935–36 season when the team went 11–26–11 (last in the Canadian division of the NHL) during a 48-game schedule. He was replaced as coach the next season by Cecil Hart. (James Rice/HHOF)

HOWIE MORENZ

HOWARTH WILLIAM MORENZ, the National Hockey League's first superstar, was born in Mitchell, Ontario, on June 21, 1902. As a youngster, he had every intention of following in his railwayman father's footsteps. But young Howie was simply too gifted as an athlete (he also liked baseball) not to become a professional hockey player, even though he once resisted the notion. Morenz loved to play hockey and would skip the piano lessons his mother had arranged for him just to go out and play on the pond. Morenz never did learn how to play the piano but was a sensation on the ice, where he displayed a great competitive spirit and lightning speed. He scored goals in bunches.

Morenz moved to Stratford, Ontario, 12 miles away, to begin his junior career. The Stratford club rejected him at first and a disgruntled Morenz was set to walk away when the team, needing new talent, called the youngster back. It was a good decision as Morenz stayed with the Stratford Midgets for the next three years, scoring 50 goals in 17 games (season schedules were very short in this era). He then played senior hockey for 14 games (scoring 25 times) in Stratford, and although he didn't think he was good enough for pro hockey, a few teams thought otherwise.

The Toronto St. Patrick's expressed mild interest in the player known as the "Stratford Streak," while Ottawa, Hamilton and the Montreal Maroons were also potential suitors. Montreal Canadiens manager Leo Dandurand was tipped about the young talent and dispatched assistant Cecil Hart to sign Morenz to a contract before any other club did. The Habs offered Morenz between $2,500 and $3,500 for the 1923–24 season and, after negotiating with Morenz's father William, included a signing bonus of $850 and assured increases for the next two years. Morenz was worried about playing pro hockey and feared he would be rejected for being too small (5'9", 165 pounds). He sent the contract and money back to the Canadiens, but the Habs refused to let him out of the deal and talked him into reporting to training camp. Morenz made the team as a centre and scored his first goal on December 26, 1923, before 8,300 fans in a 3–2 loss

to Ottawa. He beat Clint Benedict who was in goal for Ottawa. Morenz would score 13 goals in 24 games as a rookie, helping the Canadiens win the Stanley Cup with four goals in four playoff games. The Habs took the Cup with a surprise win over Boston in the finals. The Bruins had lost only five games all year, but Morenz's superb play lead to the upset.

In spite of his insecurities about playing pro hockey, Morenz owned the NHL for the next few years and scored 28, 23, 25 and a league-leading 33 goals in 1927–28 when he also led all scorers with 51 points (in just 43 games). It was at this time that Morenz became the greatest attraction pro hockey had seen to date. His spectacular rushes and brilliant stickhandling lifted fans out of their seats. His desire to win was evident to everyone who watched him perform, and his style of play helped to expand the game in the United States, where teams were now operating in New York, Boston and later Detroit. Morenz's goal-scoring exploits compared to Babe Ruth's achievement in home runs. As good as Morenz was as a goal scorer, Toronto general manager Conn Smythe was just as impressed with the centre's all-round game. Morenz knew that you needed the puck to score, so he'd work at checking to get the disk back and charge up the ice for a shot on goal. Morenz was perhaps the one player more than any other who established the Montreal Canadiens' crowd-pleasing, fire-wagon style of play.

Morenz's goal production slipped to 17 in 1928–29, but he rebounded with a career high of 40 tallies the next season. The Habs reclaimed the Cup in 1930, and Morenz led the league in scoring again in 1930–31 with 51 points (28 goals, 23 assists) in just 39 games. The Habs won the Cup for the second straight season with Morenz's winning goal against Chicago in the finals. Morenz also scored the important first goal of the game in the fifth and deciding contest played at the Montreal Forum on April 14, 1931. It was his only goal of the playoffs, essentially his last great moment as a Hab. He had a good year in 1931–32 (24 goals) but then a decline took place over the next two years (only eight

Facing page: Howie Morenz was a three-time winner of the Hart Trophy (1928, 1931, 1932) as the NHL's most valuable player. (James Rice/HHOF)

Above: Howie Morenz was a two-time first all-star team selection at centre. (Imperial Oil-Turofsky/HHOF)

Facing page: *The Montreal Canadiens were offered $60,000 by the New York Rangers and $75,000 by the Montreal Maroons for the rights to Howie Morenz but both were turned down.* [James Rice/HHOF]

goals in 1933–34). Montreal fans were starting to get to Morenz, and the Canadiens finally sent him to Chicago in what would once have been an unthinkable deal.

Never comfortable as a Black Hawk, Morenz was dealt again to the New York Rangers one year later, but he managed a combined six goals with both clubs. The Canadiens bought Morenz in a cash deal with the Rangers, and his return was much anticipated before the start of the 1936–37 season. During a game against Chicago on January 28, 1937, however, Morenz crashed into the boards as he tried to dance around Black Hawk defenceman Earl Seibert. (The Chicago blueliner felt he was unfairly blamed for causing Morenz's spill into the boards). His leg was badly broken, and his season ended with four goals and 20 points in 30 games.

While recovering in hospital, Morenz received many visitors (including opposing players) but may have had too much to drink with some of his guests. He talked about making a comeback for the next season, which may have been wishful thinking. Morenz

would never make a comeback because he suddenly died in hospital of a suspected embolism. He had been checked thoroughly just an hour before he died on March 8, 1937. To many, Morenz died of a broken heart because he knew his career as a player and more importantly as a Montreal Canadien was over. This might be a romanticized version of what happened, but Morenz's state of mind probably played a role (he was by nature a worrier) that night when he went to sleep and never awoke.

An estimated 50,000 people walked by his casket as he lay in state at the Forum, clearly a reflection of how well-liked Morenz was in the city that saw his greatest exploits on the ice. His funeral service at the arena was broadcast over CFCF radio in Montreal. On November 2, 1937, a benefit all-star game was played (the Canadiens versus NHL all-stars) in Montreal and over $26,000 was raised for the children of Howie Morenz. The Canadiens' first star player died tragically young, his legendary status in the history of the team (and hockey) assured.

MORENZ'S CANADIENS STATS:	GP	G	A	P	PIM
regular season	470	257	160	417	499
playoffs	47	21	12	33	69
STANLEY CUPS: 3					

Montreal moment:

One of Howie Morenz's greatest strengths was his competitive nature and fiery approach to the game, despite his small size. One example was the game of December 24, 1931, when the Leafs were playing against the Canadiens at the Montreal Forum. The Leafs and Canadiens had played through 60 minutes and were tied 1–1 but had to play a 10-minute overtime period. Most players thought this was a crazy way to spend Christmas Eve and wanted to get off the ice as soon as the 10-minute extra session was over. The game finally ended but referee Cooper Smeaton announced a timekeeping error and called the teams back for 10 more seconds of play with the faceoff at centre ice. Morenz was fuming and told Leaf centre Joe Primeau to let the puck sit there until the clock ran down. Primeau said nothing but really didn't like the idea, so he just slapped the puck over to the left wing. Leaf winger Harvey Jackson suddenly picked up the puck and steamed toward the Montreal net. He used a defenceman as a screen and let a shot go that hit the post behind goalie George Hainsworth and then went into the net! The time of the goal was 9:55 of overtime. Morenz was furious since he thought Primeau went along with his plan. Morenz wasn't going to take this lightly and told Primeau, "I'll remember that the next time we meet!" He made sure he got revenge a few days later in Toronto when the Habs beat the Leafs 2–0. The Montreal star scored the game's first goal in overtime on a solo effort with the Leafs short-handed!

For the record:

In December of 1950, Howie Morenz was named the greatest player for the first half of the century in a poll of sports editors and broadcasters. Morenz garnered 27 votes compared with four for runner-up Maurice Richard. Other players to be considered for the award were Eddie Shore, Cyclone Taylor, Nels Stewart, Newsy Lalonde, Aurel Joliat and Syl Apps. When in 1999 The Hockey News ranked the 50 all-time greatest hockey players, Wayne Gretzky was number one, but Morenz still came out near the top at number 15.

HERBERT "BUDDY" O'CONNOR

HERBERT O'CONNOR, born in Montreal on June 21, 1916, dreamed of playing in the Montreal Forum for the Canadiens. He didn't grow up to be a big man (5'8", 142 pounds). His younger brother couldn't pronounce "Herbert" very well so that it sounded like "Buddy." The name change stuck. Determined not to let his small size hold him back from playing a game he loved, Buddy O'Connor learned to skate after borrowing a pair of skates from a friend at the age of eight. (He eventually got a new pair one Christmas.) O'Connor made it to the Forum while playing midget hockey in the Montreal area, and although his team was badly beaten that day, he played the entire 60-minute contest!

Together with his good friend, Peter Morin, another would-be hockey player, O'Connor would go about town asking for tryouts, only to be turned down more often than not. Eventually both players got to play for the Montreal Royals in the Quebec Senior Hockey League, and O'Connor put up some good numbers to get himself noticed. The whippet-like centre led the QSHL in assists in 1936–37 with 17 with 19 contests and did so again on two other occasions. (He had a high of 38 helpers in 1939–40.) He wasn't a high goal scorer but would usually manage to score more than 10 a season, with as many as 16 in one year. O'Connor and Morin played on the same line for the Royals and were soon joined by Gerry Heffernan. The trio became known as the "Razzle-Dazzle Line." Soon the senior Royals were outdrawing the Canadiens!

The entire line was finally given a chance to play for the Canadiens to start the 1941–42 season. (The fact that many NHL players were serving in the armed forces during World War II helped to give many players a chance at the big league.) O'Connor

did reasonably well as a 25-year-old rookie, scoring nine goals and adding 16 assists in 36 games. He scored a goal in his first game with the Canadiens at the Forum, and the crowd roared its approval and cheered the underdog. O'Connor was fortunate to play as a second centre behind the great Elmer Lach, which relieved some of the pressure on him. He displayed a smooth skating style and excellent stickhandling skills that would keep him in the NHL for years. His second season as a Canadien saw him score 58 points (including 43 assists) in 50 games; 1943–44 saw his playmaking skills stay strong with 42 assists in just 44 games and marked his first season on a Stanley Cup-winning team.

O'Connor's point production declined in the next two seasons, but he did score 11 times in 1945–46 when the Habs won another Cup. He was very good in the playoffs that year with five points (three goals, two assists) in nine games. After a 30-point season in 1946–47, the Canadiens, determined to make changes, dealt O'Connor to the New York Rangers. Montreal fans weren't pleased that new manager Frank Selke, interested in giving new players a chance to wear the Canadiens' red, white and blue, dealt away a favourite. O'Connor was reportedly devastated to leave Montreal, but in the "Big Apple" he showed that he was still capable of playing in the NHL by winning the Hart (for most valuable player) and the Lady Byng (for gentlemanly play) Trophies for his performance in 1947–48 (24 goals, 60 points). O'Connor was the first player to win both awards in the same season. He played three more years for the Rangers before retiring in 1951. Elected to the Hall of Fame in 1988, he passed away in 1977.

O'CONNOR'S CANADIENS STATS:	GP	G	A	P	PIM
regular season	271	78	155	233	22
playoffs	35	10	15	25	2

STANLEY CUPS: 2

In a somewhat unpopular deal, the Montreal Canadiens traded Buddy O'Connor along with defenceman Frank Eddolls to New York in exchange for Hal Laycoe, Joe Bell and George Robertson from the Rangers. (Imperial Oil-Turofsky/HHOF)

DIDIER PITRE

DIDIER PITRE may have been one of the first hockey players to be known for his great shot. His drive was hard, accurate and would often leave the under-protected goalies of the era with bumps and bruises. Even when he missed with his drive, the sound off the boards was impressive to the fans. Pitre's shot helped him to become known as "Cannonball," and his drive, coupled with tremendous speed, made for an impressive hockey player. He would become the idol of many French-Canadian hockey fans.

Pitre was born in Valleyfield, Quebec, on September 1, 1883, and began his pro hockey career as a defenceman. He started with the Montreal Nationals of the Federal Amateur Hockey League but switched to the International Hockey League with the American Soo Indians. He played there beginning in the 1905–06 season and scored 41 times in 22 games. One of his teammates was Jack Laviolette, who would be entrusted with signing the best French-Canadian players for a new team to be called the Montreal Canadiens of the National Hockey Association. Pitre became the first player Laviolette signed for the new team, giving him $1,700 because he knew Pitre had another team willing to pay him $1,100. It was money well-spent: the two men played together on the blue line, and their great speed caused the day's sports writers to dub the team the "Flying Frenchmen." Eventually Pitre moved to forward (on right wing) to take advantage of his fast skating. No matter what position he played, Pitre could score goals, posting seasons of 10, 19, 27, 24, 30 (a career high and nearly one half of the goals the team scored all year), 24 and 21 while the Habs were in the NHA.

Cup that year, and Pitre had four goals in five playoff games. He was a star in the finals against Portland when the Habs beat the Rosebuds 3–2 in games (scoring a hat trick in the third game of the series to help Montreal to a 6–3 win). The next season saw the Montreal club lose the Cup final to the Seattle Metropolitans, but they were back in the final again in 1919. (Due to a breakout of influenza, no winner was declared in their series with Seattle.) Pitre was still productive, scoring 17, 14, 14 and 16 goals (by now the Canadiens were in the newly formed National Hockey League) but he was having difficulty controlling his weight. He was eventually relegated to a substitute role and was able to jump into the lineup during the 1923 playoffs when defencemen Sprague Cleghorn and Billy Coutu were suspended. Pitre moved back to the blue line and helped the Canadiens make a respectable showing. It was the last great moment of Pitre's career. His goal-scoring made him a target for the opposition, but he fought through the tough checking and kept driving to the net. He finished with 313 professional goals in 338 games, a truly remarkable record.

He died in 1934. His great career was recognized when he was elected to the Hockey Hall of Fame in 1962.

He also played one year with Vancouver of the PCHL, scoring 14 goals in 1913–14.

His best season in the NHA was in 1915–16 when he led the league with 39 points in 24 games. Pitre was on line with Laviolette and the great Newsy Lalonde to form a truly formidable line that could skate circles around the opposition. The Canadiens won their first Stanley

PITRE'S CANADIENS STATS:	GP	G	A	P	PIM
regular season*	127	64	34	98	84
playoffs*	9	2	4	6	16

STANLEY CUPS: 1

* for games played with the Canadiens in the NHL only

Didier Pitre had two five-goal games while with the Canadiens (one in 1911 and one in 1915) and both came against the Montreal Wanderers. (HHOF)

ALBERT "BABE" SIEBERT

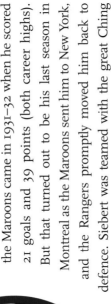

BLESSED WITH A powerful body and broad shoulders, Albert "Babe" Siebert played hockey with a great deal of heart and determination. He was certainly not afraid to use his body, and while he racked up penalty minute totals (982 penalty minutes over his entire NHL career), Siebert was a complete player whose career as a Montreal Canadien included winning the Hart Trophy as the best player in the league.

Siebert was born in Plattsville, Ontario, in 1904 and grew up on the eastern shore of Lake Huron. He was a husky, powerful youngster who enjoyed sports, first playing organized hockey at the age of 16 in Zurich, Ontario. His older brothers ridiculed him for his simple, straight-ahead style that showed no finesse. But he must have been doing something right because he was invited to play junior hockey about 100 miles from home for Kitchener of the Ontario Hockey Association. He made it to the Memorial Cup in 1923, and although his team lost to the University of Manitoba, Siebert impressed the scouts with his play. The Montreal Maroons showed an interest but told Siebert to play some senior hockey to polish his game, which he did in Niagara Falls, Ontario.

By the 1925–26 season, he was ready for the big league and was signed as a free agent by the Maroons. Siebert scored 16 times as a rookie (in 35 games) and added another two goals in the playoffs as the Maroons won the Stanley Cup. He was with the Maroons for seven seasons and spent much of his time on a line with Nels Stewart and Hooley Smith. The trio was known as the "S Line." They struck fear in the hearts of their opponents by averaging over 200 minutes in penalties for three of the years they played together. Siebert's best year with

the Maroons came in 1931–32 when he scored 21 goals and 39 points (both career highs). But that turned out to be his last season in Montreal as the Maroons sent him to New York, and the Rangers promptly moved him back to defence. Siebert was teamed with the great Ching Johnson, helping the Rangers take the Stanley Cup by knocking off the Toronto Maple Leafs in the finals in 1933.

During the early stages of the next year, Siebert was on the move again, this time to Boston. The Bruins were in dire need of a defenceman ever since Eddie Shore had received a long suspension. Siebert helped to fill in the gap. He was with the Bruins for two more years before a trade brought him back to Montreal, this time with the Canadiens. By this point Siebert was an all-star defenceman, and his acquisition helped the Habs get back into the playoffs during the 1936–37 season. He was named the most valuable player in the NHL when he scored eight goals, earning 28 points in 44 games. Siebert was teamed on the blue line with Walter Buswell, and he brought a fighting spirit to the Canadiens that had been lacking. Siebert was always willing to fight if necessary, but off the ice he was very much a gentleman and family man who took care of his ailing wife and was greatly admired by teammates and fans. He finished playing after the 1938–39 season and was going to be the next Canadiens coach the following year.

However, in the summer of 1939, Siebert drowned while trying to recover an inner tube for his young daughter. It appeared that Siebert got tired while swimming in a strong tide. A day of relaxation along the shores of Lake Huron ended in tragedy. The NHL held an all-star game to benefit his family.

Siebert was elected to the Hockey Hall of Fame in 1964.

SIEBERT'S CANADIENS STATS:	GP	G	A	P	PIM
regular season	125	25	38	63	120
playoffs	11	2	3	5	2

"Babe" Siebert was a three-time first team all-star (1936, 1937, 1938), the last two selections as a Montreal Canadien. [James Rice/HHOF]

GEORGES VEZINA

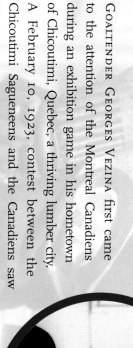

GOALTENDER GEORGES VEZINA first came to the attention of the Montreal Canadiens during an exhibition game in his hometown of Chicoutimi, Quebec, a thriving lumber city. A February 10, 1923, contest between the Chicoutimi Sagueneens and the Canadiens saw Vezina turn back shots taken by the best Montreal players like Didier Pitre, Newsy Lalonde and Jack Laviolette. While wearing a red toque in net, Vezina didn't allow the Canadiens a single goal as the Sagueneens and his brother Peter scored the game-winning goal! The Habs were very impressed with Vezina's composure and the way he used his goal stick to block shots. One year later Vezina was tending goal for the Canadiens, and he wouldn't relinquish the job until an untimely illness forced him to retire.

Used to playing hockey while wearing his boots, Vezina didn't learn to skate until his late teens (which might account for his becoming a goaltender). Eventually he tried skates and was soon recognized as the best goalie in his area. He could block shots with ease and not give up juicy rebounds. The rules of the era meant he had to be a reliable netminder, but few perfected the position the way the very calm Vezina did in this era of hockey. Montreal manager Joe Cattarinich (a former goalie himself) was very impressed with the way Vezina played and his devout Catholic lifestyle. (He was married at 20 and produced 22 children!) Vezina spoke only French and would work only on a handshake agreement. Even though he didn't speak English, he always felt well-treated and made many friends during the team's training in Grimsby, Ontario. Vezina loved to play the game, believing that sport was one way to unite people all over the world.

In his first game as a Hab on December 31, 1910, Vezina gave up an uncharacteristic five goals to Ottawa in a 5–3 loss, but he and had the best goals against average three times in his career. He took Montreal to their first two Stanley Cup championships (1916 and 1924) and was especially strong in the '16 playoffs when he only gave up three goals in five games.

On November 25, 1925, the Pittsburgh Pirates were in Montreal to play the Canadiens at the Mount Royal Arena. It was the opening game of the '25–'26 season, and some 6,000 fans were in attendance. What they didn't know was that Vezina hadn't been feeling well for some time. Vezina came out for the start of the second period but was experiencing chest pains along with a high fever. He carried on as best he could, but he eventually collapsed and was immediately sent to the hospital. He was diagnosed with an advanced case of tuberculosis: his lungs were in such bad shape that he had no chance of surviving. Vezina made one trip back to the arena to get his jersey and said a very emotional goodbye to his teammates. On March 24, 1926, Vezina passed away, but he would never be forgotten by his team or the NHL.

Soon after his death, the Canadiens donated a trophy in honour of Vezina to be awarded every year to the best goaltender in the league (based on the fewest goals allowed and later for the goalie judged to be the best). It's fitting that such an award exists to keep the name of Georges Vezina synonymous with great goaltending.

would soon come to dominate the goaltending position in the National Hockey Association (NHA). He never missed a game in his entire career with the Canadiens (playing in 328 consecutive games) and would often win more than half the games he played. He posted a career high 17-win season in 1924–25 (a year that saw the Habs play a 30-game schedule for the first time)

VEZINA'S CANADIENS STATS:

	GP	Wins	Losses	Ties	Shutouts	GA
regular season*	190	103	81	5	13	3.28
playoffs*	13	9	4	–	2	2.77

STANLEY CUPS: 2

Georges Vezina was so cool playing in net that he was known as the "Chicoutimi Cucumber." [HHOF]

Background photo: Vezina won a total of 175 games in 328 games played while wearing a Montreal Canadiens uniform. [HHOF]

THE VOICES OF MONTREAL HOCKEY: A HISTORY OF CANADIENS BROADCASTERS

by Frank Orr

A CANNONADING SHOT! A scintillating save! A Savardian spinnerama! Danny Gallivan included those descriptive gems in his distinctive play-by-play call and led the way for the voices who have told the Montreal Canadiens story on radio and television to form a high-level — and privileged — group of broadcasters.

After all, they had the opportunity to watch the National Hockey League's most successful and exciting team throughout its history. The team on the ice had more Hall of Fame-calibre players than any other over the years, but the men who called the games on radio and television matched in quality the men whose exploits they described.

Six who told the Canadiens story electronically — Danny Gallivan, Richard Garneau, Rene Lecavalier, Dick Irvin, Doug Smith and Gilles Tremblay — collected the Foster Hewitt Memorial Award, which ensures entry into the Hockey Hall of Fame. These six illustrious broadcasters are joined by at least two dozen others who have called the *bleu-blanc-rouge* games since the first radio coverage, in French, in the late 1920s.

Three of them — Gallivan, Lecavalier and Irvin — are Canadian broadcasting giants, their talent and longevity placing them on the same level as Foster Hewitt, caller of the Toronto Maple Leafs game on coast-to-coast radio and TV. Hewitt is perhaps the best known Canadian name from the 1930s to the '60s.

Gallivan was the English voice of the Montreal team from 1952 to '84. In those 32 seasons, he described 16 Stanley Cup victories. A master at spinning the action on the ice into "pictures" for radio, Gallivan developed a trademark style in his use of words. When he said that Boom-Boom Geoffrion had unloaded "a cannonading drive," listeners knew that the net's or end boards' resilience was about to be tested, or the goalie about to be bruised from the puck's speed. Just as Hewitt had made the Leafs a "national" team in the six-team NHL days, Gallivan took the Canadiens across the country with his Sunday night radio broadcasts of their games.

"He [Gallivan] was the voice of the Canadiens, with all the hucksterism that can imply," wrote Red Fisher — who has covered the Canadiens for six decades for the *Montreal Star* and *Gazette* — in his autobiography *Hockey, Heroes and Me.* "But he was also their

severest critic when individual and team performances weren't what they should be."

Lecavalier was a suave intellectual with a trim moustache who covered the games in French for more than 30 years on both radio and television. He was the first to do play-by-play of a televised hockey game in 1952. Until Lecavalier took over, the French hockey vocabulary contained many fractured English phrases because of poor translations into French. He changed that by substituting phrases in perfect French, part of his flawless use of the language. The puck became *le rondelle.* Language specialists credit Lecavalier with doing more than any educator to maintain, even upgrade, the quality of the French language in the province of Quebec. The gentlemanly Lecavalier was once called "the Jean Béliveau of broadcasting," his erudition and polished conduct earning a comparison to the great centre, universally regarded as the classiest athlete ever.

"I always thought of myself as a storyteller, and the story I was telling was what was happening on the ice when the Canadiens played hockey," Lecavalier once said.

For more than 40 years, Irvin was the hockey broadcaster who could — and did — do it all on the air. He spent two decades as colour commentator and analyst, supplying a perfect complement to Gallivan's play-by-play. But he also had a wide background as a television host, between-periods interviewer and feature reporter. He took over the game-action call when Gallivan retired in 1984 and continued to contribute features and commentary to *Hockey Night in Canada*'s playoff telecasts after his "retirement" well into the new millennium. The son of Hall of Fame player and exceptional coach Dick Irvin Sr., Irvin Jr. had roots deep in the game's history, knowledge he used to produce several excellent books on the sport, including his autobiography *Now Back To You Dick,* Gallivan's often-used words to turn the talk over to his analyst.

In the early years of hockey on radio, the Canadiens were carried only in French with J. Arthur Dupont supplying the play-by-play. His initials formed the call letters of CJAD, the high-power English radio station he owned. The crosstown rivals, the Montreal Maroons, who existed from 1924 to '36 and won the Stanley Cup twice, had English radio coverage part of the time with Charles Harwood at the mike. When the Maroons folded, the Canadiens increased their audience with Michel Normandin as French play caller for close to 20 years. Doug Smith then described the games in full-time English radio coverage, starting after World War II, often with Keith Dancy as colour analyst.

When Gallivan and Lecavalier took over the play-by-play, the "Two Solitudes" each had extraordinary coverage on radio, which blossomed onto television on a modest scale in 1952. The broadcasts were frequently simulcast in the two media.

Such superb broadcasters as Don Wittman, based in Winnipeg, and Dan Kelly did stints on Canadiens telecasts. Kelly went on to an exceptional career as the top hockey announcer in the U.S. both with the St. Louis Blues, who joined the NHL in the 1967 expansion, and on various TV networks. When *HNIC* telecast host Frank Selke Jr. joined the '67 expansion Oakland Seals as general manager, it created an opening for the young Irvin. The stylish

Garneau and Lionel Duval joined Lecavalier on the French telecasts. When asthma ended his strong playing career in 1969, winger Tremblay started a television analyst's career that led him to the Hall of Fame in 2002.

When Lecavalier limited his coverage to television, Winstone McQuade became the French radio voice, followed by Pierre Rinfret. Pierre Houde (play-by-play) and Yvon Pedneault (analyst) were *HNIC*'s mainstays, while Alain Crete handled the mike on regional telecasts on RDS, the Quebec wing of the Sports Network. For a decade, the English radio play-by-play has been called by Dino Sisto, with former players Peter Mahovlich, Steve Shutt and Murray Wilson adding their expertise.

Rene Lecavalier: a broadcasting legend in the French-speaking hockey world. (HHOF)

the powerhouse is built 1940–1960

D esperate to turn the fortunes of the Montreal Canadiens around, Senator Donat Raymond secured a new coach for the 1940–41 season in the person of Dick Irvin. Raymond had agreed to Toronto owner Conn Smythe's proposal to let his coach leave the Maple Leafs and join the Montreal club. Irvin's success as Leafs coach included many trips to the finals but only one Stanley Cup. Smythe's patience ran out, and the timing couldn't have been better for the Habs, who had to replace a disinterested Pit Lepine behind the bench.

But Raymond didn't stop there. He secured the services of Tommy Gorman as the team's general manager. A bit of an eccentric, Gorman was a knowledgeable hockey man, having managed the Ottawa Senators to a pair of Cups (in 1921 and 1923) and coached the championship clubs of the Chicago Black Hawks (1934) and the Montreal Maroons (1935).

Facing page: Canadiens stars — players and team builders — of the 1950s (from left): Ralph Backstrom, Ab McDonald, coach Toe Blake, Bernie Geoffrion and general manager Frank Selke. (Imperial Oil-Turofsky/HHOF)

Above: Defenceman Glen Harmon played in 452 career games for the Canadiens, scoring 50 goals and adding 96 assists between 1942–43 and 1950–51. He was on Cup-winning teams in 1944 and 1946. (Imperial Oil-Turofsky/HHOF)

Marcel Bonin played for the Canadiens between 1957 and 1962, scoring 68 goals and 205 points in 280 games. He was on four Cup-winning teams and recorded 22 points in 34 playoff games. [HHOF]

With not much left on the Montreal roster when the two men took over, they weren't even sure that Raymond would continue to keep the team alive. (Gorman managed to convince his boss to keep the operation going.) Since Georges Mantha was the last player to have been on a Canadiens Cup-winning club, Mantha's release six games into the '40–'41 season marked the passing of the previous era. Irvin gave the team some discipline, while Gorman made sure the Canadiens were well-connected to the Quebec amateur leagues. Like other clubs during World War II, the Habs lost a few players, but they also found good additions in the likes of Glen Harmon, Buddy O'Connor, Murph Chamberlain, Bob Fillion, Gerry Heffernan, Billy Reay, Phil Watson, Ken Mosdell and Ken Reardon. All these players contributed to the Cup wins of 1944 and/or 1946. But the biggest addition to the team was a young man who joined the club for the first time in the 1942–43 season.

Maurice Richard scored his first NHL goal at the Forum on November 8, 1942, in a 10–2 rout of the New York Rangers. Few might have predicted that the fiery but often injured Richard would be one of the all-time greats, but the man dubbed the "Rocket" soon proved he was strong enough to compete in the NHL. As he pumped in the goals, his so-called brittleness disappeared, and by the 1944–45 season he scored 50 goals in 50 games, a truly remarkable feat. He also developed a reputation for scoring big goals in the playoffs, starting with his five-goal effort versus Toronto in a March 23, 1944, semifinal playoff series at the Forum. Just like Howie Morenz years earlier, Richard came to define his hockey era and inspired extraordinary pride in the famed Canadiens sweater. He led the Habs over the Chicago Black Hawks to give Montreal its first Cup win since 1931.

Of course, Richard didn't do it alone. He had the good fortune to play the right wing on a line with Elmer Lach at centre and Toe Blake on the left wing. The trio formed the famed "Punch Line" and terrorized the NHL until a broken leg forced Blake to retire. Emile "Butch" Bouchard anchored the defence while Bill Durnan was as good a goalie as any in the league. This group of players peaked in 1946 when the Habs won their sixth Stanley Cup by defeating Chicago and Boston in the playoffs. The Canadiens clinched the Cup on Forum ice with a 6–3 win over the Bruins on April 9, 1946, in the fifth game of the finals.

Despite the Cup triumph of '46, the Canadiens believed it was time for a change in upper management. Gorman had done a good job of keeping the team afloat during a difficult period, but it was believed that the organization's future required a more reliable and steady leader. Once again, the Canadiens looked toward Toronto and found Smythe's right-hand man available to take control of the Habs. Frank Selke had done a superb job of building up a farm system that had kept the Maple Leafs on top of the NHL for many years. When he arrived in Montreal on August 1, 1946, he sought to do the same for the Canadiens. Senator Raymond meant it when he gave Selke the go-ahead to do whatever was needed to make the Habs consistent winners. Selke realized that the

"Montreal doesn't like to lose

and maybe that's why Montreal doesn't lose very often."

Frank Selke, Sr. (Montreal general manager, 1946 to 1964)

Don Marshall (#22) and Phil Goyette (#20) were key support members of the Canadien teams that won five straight Stanley Cups between 1956 and 1960. Marshall recorded 254 points (including 140 assists) in 585 games with Montreal while Goyette had 182 (including 120 assists) in 375 games as a Hab. (HB)

One of the greatest teams of all-time: the 1958-59 Montreal Canadiens. (HB)

Canadiens had to sponsor teams in all parts of Quebec as well as all over Canada. He also knew that the Cup champs of '46 had only a few good players that could continue to contribute.

It took a while for Selke's plan to bear fruit, but when the Habs made it to the finals in 1951 (a loss to Toronto), it marked the first of 10 straight years that the team would make it to the championship round. Future Hall of Fame players were added to the team: Bernie Geoffrion, Doug Harvey, Jean Béliveau, Dickie Moore, Henri Richard, Tom Johnson, Bert Olmstead and goaltender Jacques Plante. (Other Montreal netminders of this era included Gerry McNeil and Charlie Hodge.) From 1952 to 1958 the Habs usually battled the Boston Bruins and the Detroit Red Wings for the Stanley Cup. The Canadiens reclaimed the Cup in 1953 on Lach's overtime goal against the Bruins but lost to Detroit in 1954 and 1955, both times in seven games. The loss in the '55 finals was especially bitter for the Habs, since "Rocket" Richard had been harshly suspended by NHL president Clarence Campbell, forcing the Habs winger to miss the entire postseason.

Selke decided to make a painful coaching change and replaced Irvin with Blake for the 1955–56 season. By this point the Canadiens had a star-studded lineup as well as an excellent support cast with defenders like Jean-Guy Talbot, Bob Turner, Al Langlois and Dollard St. Laurent, plus forwards such as Claude Provost, Andre Pronovost, Marcel Bonin, Floyd Curry, Ab McDonald, Bill Hicke, Don Marshall and Phil Goyette. For the next five consecutive seasons, the Cup belonged exclusively to the Canadiens. Superbly coached and organized by Blake (his playoff record between '56 and '60 was an incredible 40 wins and nine losses), the Canadiens steamrolled the opposition. Their power play was virtually unstoppable — until a rule change slowed down the game when two-minute penalties were no longer served in full — and Plante provided Vezina Trophy-winning goaltending. In 1959 and 1960 the Canadiens beat the Maple Leafs both times in the finals, and it took Montreal a combined total of only nine games to win both Cups.

After winning the Cup in '60, Maurice Richard decided to retire, having spent his last few seasons battling injuries and weight problems. The Canadiens still looked formidable on paper, but the loss of Richard and the decline of others forced Selke and the Habs to emphasize recruiting once again. Just as it had in 1946, rebuilding took time but once completed the Habs dominated again, only in a much less flashy manner. Selke wouldn't be in charge when the Habs took off again in 1965, but there's no doubt his handiwork was stamped all over the team of the sixties. Another change would see the Habs sold: Senator Hartland de M. Molson and his brother Thomas bought the team and the Forum in September of 1957. The purchase ended the successful reign of Senator Raymond as head of the team and arena.

AWARDS SUMMARY 1940–1960

STANLEY CUP: 8 (1944, 1946, 1953, 1956, 1957, 1958, 1959, 1960)

VEZINA TROPHY: 10 (Bill Durnan, 1944, 1945, 1946, 1947, 1949, 1950; Jacques Plante, 1956, 1957, 1958, 1959)

NORRIS TROPHY: 6 (Doug Harvey, 1955, 1956, 1957, 1958, 1960; Tom Johnson, 1959)

ART ROSS TROPHY: 5 (Elmer Lach, 1948; Bernie Geoffrion, 1955; Jean Béliveau, 1956; Dickie Moore, 1958 and 1959)

HART TROPHY: 3 (Elmer Lach, 1945; Maurice Richard, 1947; Jean Béliveau, 1956)

CALDER TROPHY: 3 (John Quilty, 1941; Bernie Geoffrion, 1952; Ralph Backstrom, 1959)

LADY BYNG TROPHY: 1 (Toe Blake, 1946)

EMILE "BUTCH" BOUCHARD

EMILE "BUTCH" BOUCHARD didn't start skating until he was 16 and in high school. Since his father worked only in the winter and made little money, Bouchard had to rent and make little money, Bouchard had to rent skates at five cents per use. He eventually borrowed $35 from his brother and bought a complete set of hockey equipment. In just four years, Bouchard was in the National Hockey League, playing for the Montreal Canadiens, his hometown team. Awkward and gangly at first, Bouchard showed steady improvement, playing junior hockey for the Verdun Junior Maple Leafs for a few games and then joining the Montreal Junior Canadiens for the 1940–41 season. He played in 31 games (two goals, 10 points) and then the Canadiens, after signing the free agent on February 21, 1941, assigned him to the Providence Reds of the American Hockey League for 12 games.

Canadiens coach Dick Irvin wanted new players to add to his squad in 1940 and had been impressed by Bouchard when the defenceman attended the Habs training camp. Irvin suggested Bouchard needed a little more seasoning, and so Bouchard spent a bit of time in the minors. But Irvin clearly liked what he saw, especially when the brash youngster took on a veteran like Murph Chamberlain. One year later, with regular Canadiens blueliner Ken Reardon in the armed services, Irvin gave Bouchard the spot ahead of a more highly touted prospect. He was teamed with Glen Harmon and began to develop his game. He got into 44 games as a rookie and didn't score a goal until the playoffs when he scored one against Detroit. He did show a talent for making a good pass out of his own end and made up for his lack of great skating skills by playing solid positional hockey. Bouchard also gained a reputation as a player not to be messed with.

Bouchard was big (6'2", 205 pounds) and he was strong. With his chiselled body, he could easily outrun opponents along the boards, but he was never a bully. Bouchard maintained control and had to be seriously provoked to drop his gloves. (He had a record 863 penalty minutes in his career.) His best year came in 1944–45 when he scored a career high 11 goals and 23 assists. His performance earned him a berth on the NHL's first all-star team (the first of four times he was selected a league all-star) but most of the time he was a solid defender interested in keeping the puck out of the Habs net. His leadership skills were becoming more evident, and in 1948 his teammates voted him team captain. A father figure to many new players who joined the Canadiens, Bouchard would smooth over problems. His generosity extended to giving players who were short of cash some money on road trips.

Montreal won four Stanley Cups while Bouchard was on the team (1944, 1946, 1953, 1956) and he made a major contribution to three of these championships. In the 1946 finals against the Boston Bruins, the normally low-scoring Bouchard scored two goals and added one assist in five games, despite a bad knee. His last full season with Montreal was in 1954–55 when he played in 70 games. He was set to retire but newly appointed coach Toe Blake wanted the veteran around in case of injury. Bouchard got into 36 games in 1955–56 and played one game in the playoffs. The final game was the Stanley Cup-clinching game for the Habs, and Bouchard had the pleasure of accepting the trophy one last time as team captain. It was a classy move by Blake and a great way for Bouchard to end a Hall of Fame career.

Butch Bouchard's son Pierre played for the Canadiens in the 1970s, making the two the first father-son pair to play for the Habs. [Imperial Oil-Turofsky/HHOF]

Montreal defenceman Butch Bouchard helps goaltender Gerry McNeil defend against a Toronto attack. Bouchard was the first captain to carry the torch at the ceremony that closed the Montreal Forum. (HB)

BOUCHARD'S CANADIENS STATS:

	GP	G	A	P	PIM
regular season	785	49	144	193	863
playoffs	113	11	21	32	121

STANLEY CUPS: 4

FLOYD CURRY

EVEN THE GREATEST hockey teams, if they are to succeed, need players willing to tackle the unglamorous jobs. The great Montreal teams of the fifties were no exception to this rule, and right-winger Floyd Curry was the type of foot soldier who did his job effectively and without complaint. Players like Curry don't often get the recognition they deserve from the fans and media, but any of their teammates will confirm just how valuable they are to successful hockey clubs. Curry's role was to shut down the opposition's best players so that the Montreal stars like Maurice Richard, Jean Béliveau and Bernie Geoffrion were free to concentrate on scoring and keeping the Canadiens on top of the NHL.

Curry was born in Chapleau, Ontario, on August 11, 1925, and played junior hockey in Kirkland Lake, where the Canadiens spotted him. He was invited to the Montreal training camp when he was just 15 years old, but the Canadiens sent him home since it was too early for him to be in the NHL. As a player for the Oshawa Generals of the Ontario Hockey Association, he was a good goal scorer (55 goals in 72 games) in the regular season and was effective in the playoffs. In the 1944 postseason, Curry scored 11 goals in 10 games as the Oshawa club defeated the Trail Smoke Eaters for the Memorial Cup. Loaded with future NHL players like Bill Ezinicki, the Generals were coached by the legendary Charlie Conacher. Curry then spent one season playing for three different Toronto-based teams before joining the Montreal Royals of the Quebec Senior League for two seasons (scoring 45 goals in 72 games). He spent the next three seasons between Montreal and their farm team in Buffalo before finally sticking with the Canadiens to start the 1950–51 season.

The hard-working Curry stayed with the Habs for the next eight

seasons and shared in four Stanley Cup triumphs. He was never a spectacular player, scoring a career high of 20 in 1951–52, but was dependable. Coach Toe Blake noted, however, that Curry tended to play his best hockey in the playoffs. For example, during the 1952 playoffs he was tied for the lead in scoring with seven points in 11 games played (finishing tied with others such as Gordie Howe and Ted Lindsay of Detroit). In 1955, he led all post-season scores with 12 points (eight goals, four assists) even though the Red Wings took the Cup. Perhaps his most memorable moment came when he recorded a hat trick — with Queen Elizabeth in attendance at the Montreal Forum on October 29, 1951 — as the Habs beat the Rangers 6–1. Curry thought he was about to be sent to the minors when the three-goal outburst kept him in the NHL. The Queen remembered his performance even years later!

His final season in the NHL was 1957–58 when he appeared in 42 games. The Canadiens came to the conclusion that Curry's career was coming to an end. Managing director Frank Selke called the popular 33-year-old Curry into his office and asked if he wished to be traded. Curry declined, not wanting to face the Habs as an opponent. A little while later, he coached in the Canadiens system (including his old Royals club) and helped out with other duties. For instance, he tipped off the Canadiens about minor-league prospect John Ferguson, one of the best acquisitions the Montreal club ever made.

The Canadiens showed their appreciation for Curry's career by giving him a special night at the Forum, an honour bestowed to that point only on Butch Bouchard, Ken Mosdell, Elmer Lach and Rocket Richard.

CURRY'S CANADIENS STATS:	GP	G	A	P	PIM
regular season	601	105	99	204	147
playoffs	91	23	17	40	38

STANLEY CUPS: 4

After his career with the Canadiens, Floyd Curry became an executive with the team and boldly predicted the Habs would win the Stanley Cup in 1971 if they used a rookie goaltender named Ken Dryden. (HHOF)

BILL DURNAN

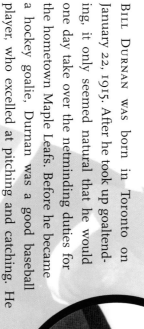

BILL DURNAN was born in Toronto on January 22, 1915. After he took up goaltending, it only seemed natural that he would one day take over the netminding duties for the hometown Maple Leafs. Before he became a hockey goalie, Durnan was a good baseball player, who excelled at pitching and catching. He also played soccer during his public school days, but then with a pair of used skates he tried to play in goal. Steve Faulkner, a supervisor of local teams, realized that Durnan's size (he would grow to 6' and 190 pounds) and his large hands would make him an ideal goaltender. Faulkner taught Durnan how to catch a puck and how to block shots. Durnan soon became known for his mobility and his ability to catch the puck with either hand. He became the first (it seems the only) goalie in NHL history to play the game ambidextrously.

As interested as the Leafs were in Durnan, they quickly lost their enthusiasm when the goalie injured a knee while wrestling with a friend and then broke a leg playing softball in 1935. Even though he had played with Sudbury- and Toronto-based teams from 1931 to 1936, it appeared that his pro aspirations died with the lack of interest by the Maple Leafs. He moved back north to take a job (earning $75 a week) and play senior hockey for the Kirkland Lake Blue Devils. He stayed in Kirkland Lake until 1940 (winning one Allan Cup championship) but was offered a job by the Montreal Royals. Durnan made a good salary with the Royals and had a job at a local plant. He stayed with the Royals until 1943 when he was offered a spot at the Montreal Canadiens training camp after regular Habs netminder Paul Bibeault went into the army. Durnan made the team at the ripe old age of 28, and a legend was born.

Durnan signed his contract with the Canadiens a few minutes before the opening of the 1943–44 season in a game against Boston. He hesitated to sign, feeling that he was too old to start playing professional hockey, but about 10 minutes before the game Durnan put his name on a contract (missing the pregame warm-up as a result) and then earning a 2–2 tie against the Bruins. Coach Dick Irvin had seen something he liked in Durnan and recommended that he be signed. The Canadiens weren't exactly sure what they were getting, but Durnan kept improving each time he played. Montreal manager Tommy Gorman commented that Durnan was as big as a horse but as nimble as a cat, always giving his team a spark. With specially made gloves to help him and in a unique style, Durnan would catch the puck with either hand. He would switch his goalie stick between hands to cover the open side of the net with either glove (depending on the angle of the shooter). An intense competitor, he wanted to stop every shot. Giving up a goal bothered him, a reaction that led to his premature retirement. His entire NHL career lasted only seven seasons, but he put up some remarkable numbers.

The Canadiens won two Stanley Cups with Durnan in goal (1944 and 1946) and he led the NHL in goaltender wins on four separate occasions, twice recording a career high 38 wins in 50-game seasons. He was a first team all-star six times and won six Vezina Trophies in an era when the award was given to the goalie that allowed the fewest goals against. In addition, he set the modern NHL record by recording four consecutive shutouts and going 309 minutes and 21 seconds between allowing goals (from February 24, 1949, when Roy Conacher of Chicago beat him, to March 9, 1949, when Gaye Stewart, also of the Black Hawks, put one past him).

As his health gave way, Durnan decided to retire while he was still on top. He had received a bad cut to his head from a skate during the season, but when he lost a playoff contest to the New York Rangers, Durnan decided that was it for him. He never went back into the net. He ran a hotel in Ottawa after his retirement and also tried his hand at coaching junior hockey. He later represented a brewery but died too soon in 1972 from a stroke. It was the same year that his longtime goaltending rival and friend, legendary Maple Leaf netminder Turk Broda, also passed away. He was elected to the Hall of Fame in 1964.

Bill Durnan was the last goaltender allowed to be a team captain. Durnan served in that role during the 1947–48 season along with Toe Blake. (Imperial Oil-Turofsky/HHOF)

Bill Durnan was once told by a referee to hurry up and get a cut stitched because he had to go back out and face a penalty shot! (Imperial Oil-Turofsky/HHOF)

DURNAN'S CANADIENS STATS:	GP	Wins	Losses	Ties	Shutouts	GA
regular season	383	208	112	82	34	2.36
playoffs	45	27	18	–	2	2.07

STANLEY CUPS: 2

BERNIE "BOOM BOOM" GEOFFRION

WHEN BERNIE GEOFFRION was a little boy he dreamed of playing at the Montreal Forum for the hometown Canadiens. He would tell his mother that he would make it big, but in fact some junior teams rejected him up until he turned 14. His first major junior squad was the Montreal Concordia Civics in 1946–47, and the next season he went on to play for the Laval Nationale, scoring 20 goals in 29 games. Never lacking for confidence, Geoffrion was on his way to stardom.

After a 52-goal season as a junior in 1949–50, Geoffrion soon found himself in the Canadiens system where he played senior hockey for a couple of years. By the 1950–51 season, the Habs were interested in some new prospects, and Geoffrion joined the team for 18 games that season, scoring eight times. (He retained his rookie status for the next season since he didn't play in 25 contests.) The 1951–52 season was Geoffrion's first full year as a Hab. The cocky rookie told an interviewer that he would win the rookie of the year award. In fact, Geoffrion did win the Calder Trophy with 30 goals and 54 points in 67 games played. Montreal coach Dick Irvin predicted that Geoffrion would eventually take over as the star of the Montreal Canadiens once Maurice Richard retired. Irvin said that Geoffrion could score goals like anyone in hockey and that his shot was the best in the NHL.

If Geoffrion was known for anything besides his gregarious personality, it was his great shot. Early in his hockey career (at the age of 12), Geoffrion noticed how the puck travelled when he took a big windup to shoot it. The sound off the boards reverberated, making a noise something like "boom-boom." Geoffrion brought this nickname and his new way of shooting to the NHL. Soon the goals followed. Usually near the 30-goal mark, he led the entire NHL in goals scored in 1954–55 when he had 38, the same year he won the scoring title with 78 points (his first of two Art Ross Trophy wins). Geoffrion soon found himself playing on the point on the Canadiens' vaunted power play alongside Doug Harvey. The Habs were so good with the man advantage that

the NHL had to change the rule about a two-minute penalty being served in its entirety. Being a member of the Canadiens wasn't always easy for Geoffrion, in spite of his great play.

His first point-scoring championship was marred by Richard's suspension for his part in a brawl in March of 1955. Geoffrion, who was chasing his teammate for the points leadership, didn't let up and eventually surpassed the sidelined Richard. Geoffrion got police protection as overzealous Richard fans threatened harm if he surpassed the legendary Canadiens star for the Art Ross Trophy. To his credit Geoffrion did his best to ensure that the Canadiens kept winning (they were battling Detroit for first place) and he legitimately took the scoring title. Years later, in 1961, he faced controversy again when the team captaincy was given to Jean Béliveau. The emotional Geoffrion was terribly upset. But again, as a true professional, Geoffrion came back to the Habs and played three more seasons, scoring a total of 67 goals.

Serious injuries were another main problem throughout Geoffrion's career. Nearly dying after one practice, he had emergency stomach surgery. (He remarkably came back for the playoffs in 1958 and even scored six goals and five assists in 11 postseason games!) He also hurt his knee in 1961. Harvey helped remove the cast on the way to Chicago for a playoff series. Forced to drop out as the result of a hit from Bobby Hull of the Black Hawks, Geoffrion showed just how much of a competitor he was and how much he loved to play and score goals.

After the 1963–64 season, which saw Geoffrion score 21 times in 55 games, the Canadiens wanted to make changes that would give some of their youngsters more ice time. Geoffrion retired and took a coaching position with the Quebec Aces of the American Hockey League on the understanding that he would one day coach the Canadiens. But the Canadiens had no intention of changing coaches as long as Toe Blake wanted to stay. Geoffrion was left out in the cold when the owner of the Aces no

On December 7, 1960, Geoffrion scored his 270th and 271st career goals to surpass his father-in-law, Canadiens legend Howie Morenz, on the all-time scoring list. (Imperial Oil-Turofsky/HHOF)

51

A tough and determined hockey player, Geoffrion took some 400 stitches in his face and suffered nine broken noses over the course of his career. [HB]

Bernie Geoffrion won the Hart Trophy for the 1960–61 season when he became the second player in NHL history to score 50 goals in one season. (HB)

longer wanted him. Bitter at his treatment, Geoffrion came out of his two-year retirement and signed on with the New York Rangers. He played in New York for two years, then became the

Rangers coach. In 1979 he found himself behind the Canadiens bench, but he lasted just 30 games (15–9–6) due to health and other issues. He was elected to the Hockey Hall of Fame in 1972.

Montreal moment:

During the 1960–61 season, Frank Mahovlich of the Toronto Maple Leafs looked like a sure bet to score 50 plus goals and break Maurice Richard's record. But Bernie Geoffrion scored 23 in his last 26 games to tie the mark of 50 goals in one season, while Mahovlich couldn't get more than 48. Geoffrion scored his 50th on the night of March 16, 1961, during a game at the Forum against Mahovlich and the Maple Leafs. With both players gunning for 50 on the same night, Geoffrion

(who had 49 going into the contest, one behind the "Big M") stole the show in the third period when he beat Leaf goalie Cesare Maniago. The goal came after Béliveau won a faceoff in the Toronto end and got the puck over to Gilles Tremblay, who relayed it to Geoffrion. The Forum went wild, and his teammates jumped on the ice to congratulate the heroic Geoffrion, who had come from such a long way back to tie one of the great records in hockey.

Geoffrion, with an "A" on his sweater, celebrates success with teammates (from left) Andre Pronovost, Jean Béliveau and Dickie Moore. [HHOF]

GEOFFRION'S CANADIENS STATS:	GP	G	A	P	PIM
regular season	766	371	388	759	636
playoffs	127	56	59	115	88

STANLEY CUPS: 6

DOUG HARVEY

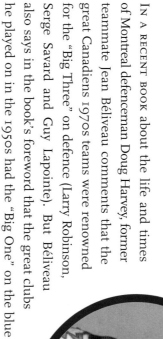

In a recent book about the life and times of Montreal defenceman Doug Harvey, former teammate Jean Béliveau comments that the great Canadiens 1970s teams were renowned for the "Big Three" on defence (Larry Robinson, Serge Savard and Guy Lapointe). But Béliveau also says in the book's foreword that the great clubs he played on in the 1950s had the "Big One" on the blue line — Harvey — and that Harvey was all they needed. No other words are necessary to explain Harvey's value to the Canadiens during a glorious era. Béliveau's prose speaks volumes about his teammates' high regard for the talented defenceman.

Harvey grew up in the Notre-Dame-de-Grace district of Montreal. His house was so close to a nearby rink that he practically kept his skates on all the time. He delivered newspapers as a boy, and one of his customers was future teammate and netminder Bill Durnan. Harvey played centre as a bantam and junior, learning valuable playmaking skills. A gifted athlete, he excelled at football and baseball. Although he served in the Royal Canadian Navy during World War II, he still played some hockey and when he got out, Harvey joined the Montreal Royals of the Quebec Senior Hockey League. After he posted 26 assists in 40 games during the 1946–47 season, the Canadiens turned the 5'11", 187-pound defenceman professional the following year. He played in 35 games for the Habs while also playing 24 games for Buffalo of the American Hockey League.

The Canadiens kept Harvey on their squad for the full season in 1948–49 on a contract that earned him $6,000 in salary plus $2,000 in bonuses. It was the beginning of a long and successful career with the Habs that would not end until the 1960–61 season. In between those seasons, Harvey won the Norris Trophy as the NHL's best defender six times. Making the first all-star team nine times with Montreal, he was a vital cog in six Stanley Cups captured by the team. Harvey's game relied on his great ability to head-man the puck to teammates breaking on a rush. His passes had just the right touch, and his view of the ice allowed him to spot the open man. Few players found getting around Harvey an easy task. He was especially careful with the puck late in the game if the Canadiens were protecting a lead. But he generally didn't like giving the puck away for no reason, and his puck handling could cause some anxious moments for his coaches. He was never a goal scorer (nine was his highest total) but he had 15 years of 20 or more assists and had seven seasons of 30 or more helpers.

Harvey's laid-back style didn't always go over well (coach Toe Blake once said Harvey played the game as if he was in a rocking chair) but he was supremely confident in his abilities, rarely letting the side down. One such occasion occurred during the 1960 playoffs against Chicago when Harvey lost the puck to Bill Hay, who promptly scored and tied the game. Harvey told his teammates that he would make amends because it was his fault. In the overtime, it was Harvey who scored the winner to give the Habs a 4–3 win. Harvey was also a prankster, who could keep his teammates loose with a quip or a practical joke. Known to be kind and generous (money didn't mean much to him) he would hang out with the boys when they tried to get away from the pressures of the game. The players voted him captain, a title he held for one season, his last one in Montreal.

Montreal management wasn't thrilled to see Harvey named captain in 1960 and moved him out as soon as the opportunity arose. The chance came when the Habs finally gave up the Cup in 1961 after five straight wins. In the late 1950s, Harvey had been key in the movement to start a players association. The establishment never looked kindly upon such players. Add in the fact that Harvey had little time for formal rules (he was always late) and that management knew of Harvey's habits off the ice, it's a wonder that he lasted in Montreal as long as he did. He was given to the New York Rangers in a deal that saw Montreal land defenceman Lou Fontinato, which allowed Montreal to avoid a contract squabble with Harvey and get new blood on the team.

Harvey had a great first year on Broadway, winning the Norris Trophy again in 1962 as player-coach for the Rangers, but he would

Doug Harvey was just 11 years old when he played for a team whose sweaters were paid for by the Montreal Canadiens. (Imperial Oil–Turofsky/HHOF)

On October 26, 1985, the Montreal Canadiens retired Harvey's jersey: number 2. [HB]

be released two years later. He then drifted between the minors and the NHL for several years but was still a top defenceman wherever he played. Coach Scotty Bowman called Harvey up to the St. Louis Blues during the 1968 playoffs. Bowman said the veteran was his best blueliner and helped his club win a seven-game series against Philadelphia.

Once playing hockey was over, Harvey tried a management role in the World Hockey Association (signing the three members of the Howe family for Houston was quite a coup for him) but mostly he drifted through a variety of jobs. His drinking problem

grew worse over time, and eventually he developed cirrhosis of the liver, a disease that would end his life in 1989. But before he died, he returned to the Canadiens as a scout. (He had a good eye for spotting prospects.) This classy move by the organization brought the once great defender happiness before he passed away.

Right: Harvey earned a career high 43 assists in 1954–55, establishing a new mark for NHL defencemen. [HB]

56

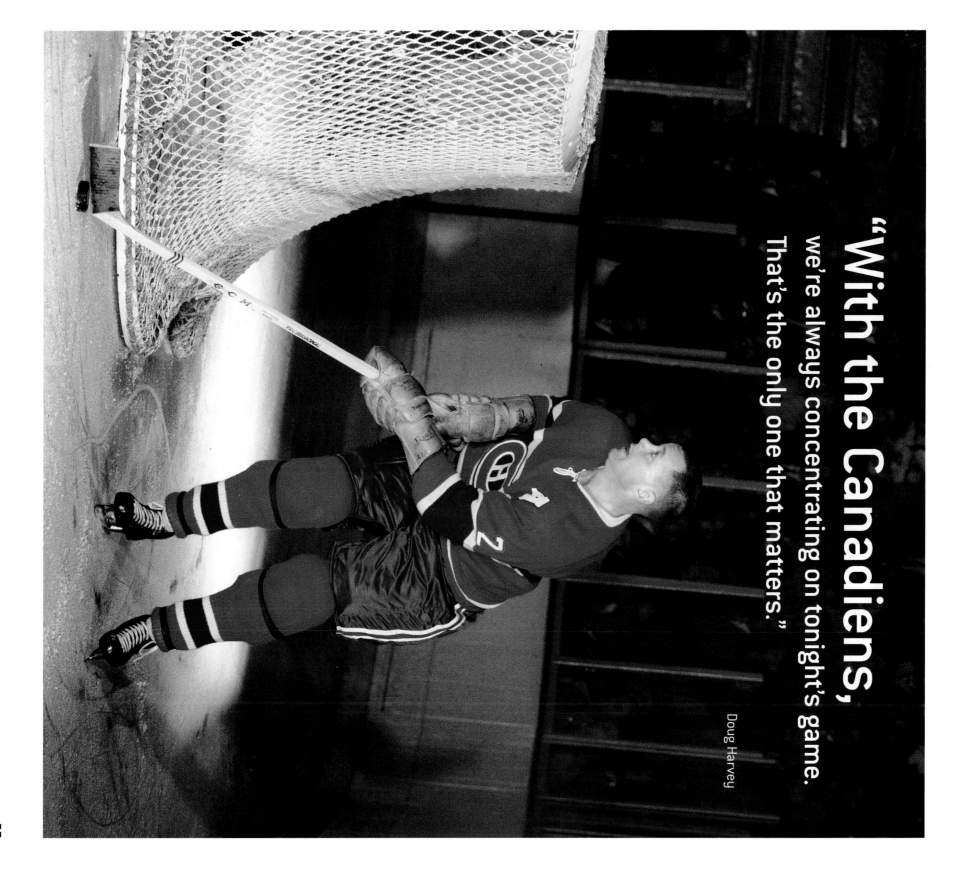

"**With the Canadiens,**
we're always concentrating on tonight's game.
That's the only one that matters."

Doug Harvey

Afraid that he might lose his job, Harvey never wanted to miss a game. (He played 1,113 career games in the NHL.) (HHOF)

HARVEY'S CANADIENS STATS:	GP	G	A	P	PIM
regular season	1005	254	335	589	469
playoffs	126	25	38	63	86
STANLEY CUPS: 9					

DICK IRVIN

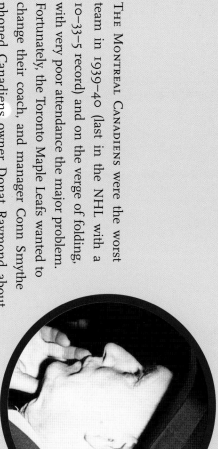

THE MONTREAL CANADIENS were the worst team in 1939–40 (last in the NHL with a 10–33–5 record) and on the verge of folding, with very poor attendance the major problem. Fortunately, the Toronto Maple Leafs wanted to change their coach, and manager Conn Smythe phoned Canadiens owner Donat Raymond about hiring their bench boss, Dick Irvin. Raymond knew a good thing when he heard one and shortly thereafter Irvin was signed on as Habs coach. For the next 15 seasons, Irvin would patrol the Canadiens bench, giving the team three Stanley Cup wins and some of the most exciting hockey Montreal has ever seen.

The first thing Irvin did was to give the Canadiens clear objectives and a winning attitude, which he brought with him from his successful tenure as the Leafs coach. An admirer of legendary Notre Dame football coach Knute Rockne, Irvin stressed conditioning, discipline and a work ethic. He knew how to challenge young players, always telling prospects at the Canadiens camp that two or three of them would stay. He would then challenge the veterans to see if they would allow young guys to take their jobs. The team needed a complete make-over, but he did keep Toe Blake and Ray Getliffe on the squad. Soon he added the likes of Maurice Richard, Bill Durnan, Elmer Lach and Butch Bouchard as the nucleus of a championship club.

One of Irvin's first encounters with Richard saw the fiery winger slam the door on his coach after he was told he wouldn't be playing. Rather than get upset, Irvin liked Richard's win-at-all-costs approach that would soon make him the most feared player in the NHL. In his first game behind the Montreal bench on

November 3, 1940, Irvin gained a tie when the Canadiens and Bruins played to a 1-1 draw. The Habs made the playoffs for Irvin's first three years. By the 1943–44 season, the Canadiens went unbeaten for 25 games and finished on top of the league (38–5–7). They went on to win the Stanley Cup that year by beating Toronto and Chicago in the playoffs.

The Canadiens won the Stanley Cup once again in 1946 by taking out the Bruins in a five-game final (three games went into overtime). Then six years passed before Montreal won the Cup again in 1953. It wasn't easy for the Habs to win the Cup in '53, and Irvin had to make a tough decision when he got goaltender Jacques Plante to take over in the net. The gutsy move worked, and the Canadiens were champions again after many frustrating years of losing in the playoffs. But the next two years saw the Habs lose the finals to the Detroit Red Wings (both in seven games). Irvin had been accused of losing control of his star player, as Richard missed the entire 1955 playoffs after attacking an official. It was the final straw for the Habs management, who replaced Irvin with Toe Blake — who had learned a great deal from watching his former mentor — as coach. Offered a position in the organization, Irvin wanted to keep coaching instead and so took a job with the Chicago Black Hawks, even though he was dying from bone cancer. Chicago offered Irvin $20,000 a year, the most he ever made as an NHL coach, starting with the 1955–56 season. He died in May of 1957.

At the funeral, Smythe told Irvin's son, Dick Jr., that his father had saved hockey in Montreal. It's a statement that's difficult to dispute.

IRVIN'S CANADIENS STATS*:	GP	W	L	T
regular season	896	431	313	152
playoffs	115	62	53	–

STANLEY CUPS: 3

* as coach

Dick Irvin and Pat Burns are the only two men in NHL history to coach both the Toronto Maple Leafs and the Montreal Canadiens. (HB)

TOM JOHNSON

Big Tom Johnson was born in the small town of Baldur, Manitoba, on February 18, 1928. He played junior hockey in his native province, joining the Winnipeg Monarchs for the 1946–47 season. He scored 10 goals in 14 games that season, marking the first time he had ever played in an indoor arena. He was an overlooked player, but Montreal manager Frank Selke liked what he saw when the youngster had a good game and signed him as a free agent on April 30, 1947. He played most of the 1947–48 season with the Montreal Royals in the Quebec Senior Hockey League and got into one game with the Habs. He then spent the next two years developing his game with the Buffalo Bisons of the American Hockey League, becoming a full-time member of the Habs in 1950–51 when he appeared in all 70 games, scoring two goals and 10 points.

Johnson had shown the Canadiens that he had the right attitude by learning how to play defence in Buffalo. He worked on his skating (he was never fast) and making good outlet passes. The Canadiens were moving out blueliners like Hal Laycoe, Glen Harmon and Ken Reardon, creating a need for some new blood on defence. As a rookie he racked up 128 penalty minutes, showing that he could mix it up and stake a reputation as an NHL blueliner. He was initially teamed on defence with Montreal captain Butch Bouchard, who had a great influence on Johnson's career. (He would later pair up with Jean-Guy Talbot.) Having fellow defenceman Doug Harvey on the team meant that Johnson wasn't expected to lead the offence, but Johnson scored 10 goals during one season. Primarily, though, he stayed back and let Harvey do most of the attacking from the blue line. In spite of his good size (6′, 180 pounds) Johnson wasn't aggressive but would throw his weight around as required. He was especially good as a penalty killer

and was deft at getting the puck out of the corners and out of danger in the Canadiens' zone. Johnson was good at breaking up opposition attacks with good positional play. Realizing that he was more valuable on the ice, he avoided foolish penalties.

When Harvey was injured during the 1958–59 season, it was Johnson's time to shine. He responded with a first team all-star selection and was named winner of the Norris Trophy as the NHL's best defenceman (an award perennially won by Harvey). He scored 10 goals and added 29 assists, while helping to keep the Canadiens on top of the NHL. The award was the crowning achievement of Selke's career, and he felt justified in saying that Johnson was the best defensive blueliner he had ever managed. Johnson was always a dependable player (rarely missing a contest) and an integral contributor to the five straight Stanley Cups the Canadiens won between 1956 and 1960.

At a practice during the 1962–63 season, Johnson was cut near the eye by the skate of teammate Bobby Rousseau. By that time Johnson's immense skills were declining, and the Forum crowd was getting to him. The next season saw Johnson picked up by the Boston Bruins for $20,000 (the waiver draft cost) and he managed to play in all 70 games, scoring four times and adding 21 assists. In some books, he was the year's comeback player. The Bruins had known that he would provide the team with leadership and show a losing team how to win. He played one more season as a Bruin before an injury forced him to retire.

Moving to Boston wasn't a bad move for Johnson, as he was eventually named coach and won a Stanley Cup in 1972. He remained with the Bruins in an executive role for many years. His efficient and excellent career was recognized by the hockey world with his election to the Hall of Fame in 1970. [HB]

Defenceman Tom Johnson was named a first team all-star in 1959 and was named to the second team in 1956.

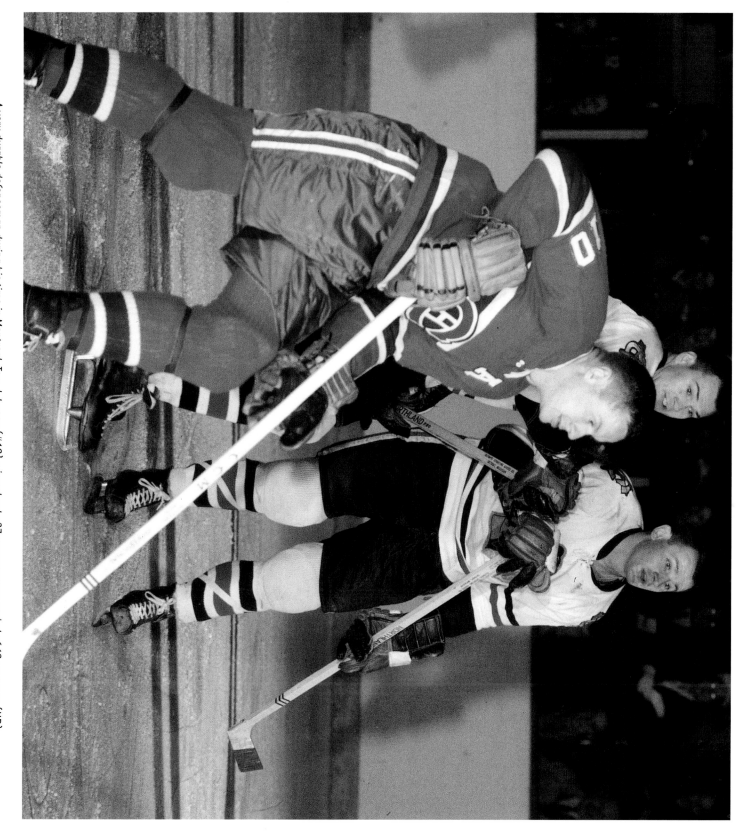

A very durable defenceman during his time in Montreal, Tom Johnson (#10) missed only 27 games over a period of 13 seasons. (HB)

JOHNSON'S CANADIENS STATS:

	GP	G	A	P	PIM
regular season	857	47	183	230	897
playoffs	111	8	15	23	109

STANLEY CUPS: 6

ELMER LACH

ELMER LACH was born in Nokomis, Saskatchewan, on January 22, 1918, and was well thought of when he played senior hockey in his home province. The 5'10", 165-pound centre showed good speed and skill around the net (60 goals in 106 games) that earned him a look by the Toronto Maple Leafs in 1937. But Leafs manager Conn Smythe dismissed Lach as too small for NHL hockey and sent him back home (along with another prospect named Doug Bentley, whose size was also deemed inadequate). The New York Rangers tried to entice Lach to their organization, but he declined their offer to return to Saskatchewan.

In 1940 the Montreal Canadiens sent injured player Paul Haynes to do some scouting in western Canada. World War II was creating openings for new players to the NHL. Haynes liked what he saw of the quick-skating centre. He invited Lach to the Canadiens training camp. Lach made the team for the 1940–41 season and scored seven goals in 43 contests, but his first few years were marred by injuries. (Injuries — to his elbow, wrist, skull, cheekbone and to his jaw on two occasions — plagued Lach throughout his career.) By 1942–43 Lach established himself as an offensive force by scoring 18 times and registering 40 assists in just 45 games. Lach didn't have a hard shot, but it was accurate, and he could make passes easily to his linemates. A strong competitive spirit drove Lach to ever greater heights and augmented his superb playmaking skills. Although known to needle the opposition on the ice, he wasn't a fighter.

Lach was teamed with Maurice Richard (who joined the team for the 1942–43 season) and Toe Blake on the other side to form the fabled "Punch Line." The threesome led the Canadiens to three Stanley Cups (1944, 1946, 1953) and each player posted excellent offensive numbers. Lach scored over 20 goals four times

(including a career high 30 in 1947–48) and recorded over 50 assists twice (including a career best 54 in 1944–45 when he took the Hart Trophy as the NHL's best player). He led the NHL in points on two occasions and became the all-time point leader in NHL history when he surpassed Bill Cowley of the Boston Bruins on February 23, 1952, with a four-point night against the Chicago Black Hawks. He scored his 200th career goal on November 8, 1952, the same night that Richard broke Nels Stewart's all-time scoring record of 324. The "Punch Line" carried the Habs to some of their greatest moments.

One such moment came in the 1953 finals against Boston in a game at the Montreal Forum. The scoreless April 16 contest went into overtime, with the Canadiens needing a goal to clinch the Stanley Cup. Montreal winger Eddie Mazur took the puck into the Bruins end early in overtime. Bruins star Milt Schmidt took the puck away but noticed Richard coming at him quickly. Schmidt's clearing attempt was scooped up by a lurking Lach, who fired the puck into the Boston net past goaltender Jim Henry for a 1–0 victory and the Cup-winning goal. Lach and Richard jumped into each other's arms to celebrate. Lach broke his nose in the collision, but it was one time the sight of blood didn't seem to bother anyone!

Montreal fans and team management showed their appreciation to Lach by holding a special night for him on March 8, 1952, when he was showered with $11,000 in gifts: a new car, a rowboat, a dining room set and a television. Lach ended his career with Montreal after the 1953–54 season — scoring just five times in 48 games — part of which he spent recovering from a broken leg, the result of a game against Chicago. Rather than try coming back, Lach decided to retire: he was making more money outside of hockey anyway. He was elected to the Hockey Hall of Fame in 1966.

Elmer Lach retired in 1954 as the NHL's all-time assist leader with 408. Gordie Howe passed the mark during the 1957–58 season. [HHOF]

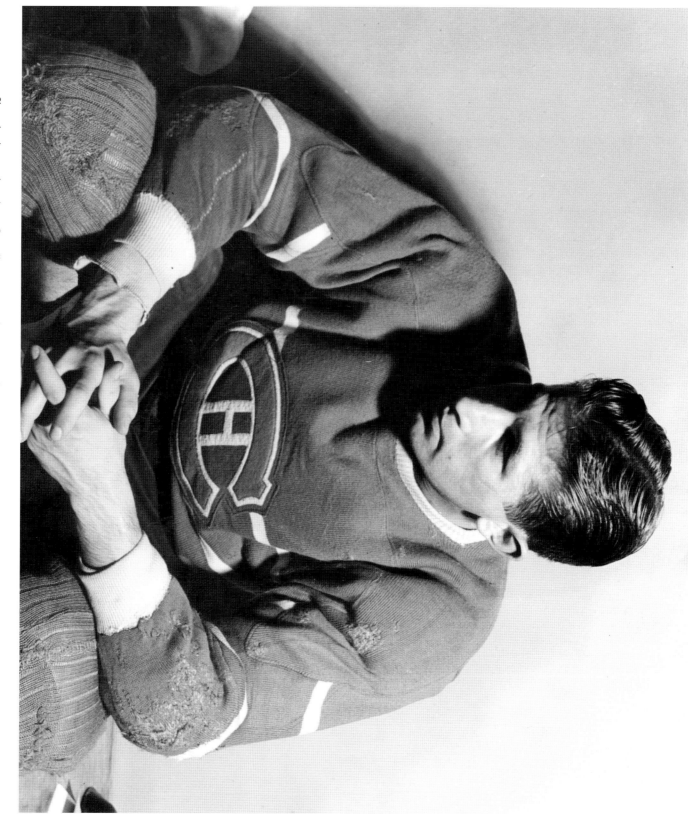

Elmer Lach was signed to a Canadiens contract by manager Tommy Gorman, who also signed up Maurice Richard, thus locking in two future Hall of Fame players. (Imperial Oil-Turofsky/HHOF)

LACH'S CANADIENS STATS:	GP	G	A	P	PIM
regular season	664	215	408	623	478
playoffs	76	19	45	64	36

STANLEY CUPS: 3

GERRY MCNEIL

A NATIVE OF Quebec City, goaltender Gerry McNeil didn't play junior hockey in his hometown, but the Montreal Canadiens still managed to unearth the netminding prospect from his minor hockey days. Defenceman Mike McMahon tipped off the Canadiens that McNeil was someone to keep an eye on. Montreal manager Tommy Gorman invited McNeil to the Canadiens training camp in 1943 at the age of 17. (With so many veterans in the armed services, the NHL looked to younger players.) McNeil couldn't beat out incumbent Bill Durnan for the regular goaltending job, but he was happy to play senior hockey in Montreal for the Royals and practise with the Canadiens. Proving to be an excellent senior goalie, McNeil was part of the team that won the Allan Cup in 1947. He played eight games for the Habs between 1947–48 and 1949–50, winning three. He then got a big break when Durnan decided he was through with hockey in the middle of the 1950 semifinals with the New York Rangers.

The Rangers beat the Canadiens in that playoff series, but McNeil's performance showed that he might be a good goalie. He played all 70 games for the Habs in 1950–51 and posted a 25–30–15 record for the third-place Canadiens. Pitted against the first-place Detroit Red Wings in the first round of the playoffs, McNeil was outstanding in leading the Habs to a major upset of the Motowners in six games. The 1951 finals between Montreal and Toronto was a classic that saw all five games go into overtime. Unfortunately for McNeil and the Canadiens, the Leafs won four of the extra-session contests, including the final game at Maple Leaf Gardens in which Bill Barilko scored the winner. It was a heart-breaking defeat, but McNeil bounced back the next season with a 34–26–10 record in 70 games. The Canadiens took out the Boston Bruins in seven games but lost to the Red Wings in four straight in the finals. The smallish (5'7", 155 pounds) McNeil played in 66 games (with a 25–23–18 record) for the Canadiens in 1952–53 when he led the NHL in shutouts with 10.

Montreal went on to win the Stanley Cup that year, but McNeil got help from future star Jacques Plante when he was faltering during the semifinal versus Chicago. McNeil got back into the nets during the finals against Boston, and he closed out the series on April 16 at the Forum with a 1–0 whitewash, his second of the series.

McNeil's last full season with Montreal was in 1953–54 when he got into 53 games, winning 29 times. The Habs knocked off the Bruins in the semifinal but lost another hard-fought final, this time with Detroit. The series was tied up at three games each when the seventh game went into overtime at the Detroit Olympia. Tony Leswick of the Red Wings was heading off the ice when he drifted a shot toward the Canadiens' net. Montreal defenceman Doug Harvey tried to grab the puck but in doing so the disk bounced off Harvey's glove and into the net past McNeil. It was a shocking end to a great series that marked the end of McNeil's career with the Canadiens (although he did return briefly during the 1956–57 season for nine games). The pressures of goaltending in the big league were getting to McNeil, and he gladly returned to the minors at about half the pay (from $12,000 to $6,000). Luckily, the Canadiens had Plante on the rise so the loss of McNeil was easier to take. McNeil passed away in 2004.

MCNEIL'S CANADIENS STATS:	GP	Wins	Losses	Ties	Shutouts	GA
regular season	276	119	105	52	28	2.36
playoffs	35	17	18	–	5	1.89

STANLEY CUPS: 2

Gerry McNeil was named as the second team all-star goalie for the 1952–53 season. In this photo he stops a shot from Toronto forward Harry Watson. (HB)

DICKIE MOORE

LEFT-WINGER Richard Winston "Dickie" Moore is a good example of the home-grown makeup of the Montreal Canadiens dynasty of the fifties. He grew up in the blue-collar area in north end Montreal called Park Extension, learning to play hockey on the outdoor rinks. As a young man with eight brothers, Moore developed a tough-as-nails approach to hockey and life. (He played with his brother Terry, who went on to play in the minor pro leagues.) If necessary he would defend any of his siblings, once climbing into the stands at a hockey game to do so. As a child he was hit by a car. Injuries to his knees and legs threatened his hockey career from an early age, but he was so stubbornly determined to play for the Canadiens that nothing got in his way. (Montreal nearly traded him away over concerns about his frequent injuries.)

Hard-working and intense were words that stuck to Moore from an early age. In junior hockey he started out playing for the Montreal Royals (in 1947) but switched to the Montreal Junior Canadiens in 1949–50. With a genius for ending up on championship clubs, he was on a Memorial Cup-winning team for both the Royals (1949) and the Junior Habs (1950). As a junior he showed an ability to score goals, and although he didn't collect an overabundance of markers, Montreal liked his feisty nature. Sam Pollock, one of Moore's junior coaches, said that Moore, at the age of 14, was one of the best prospects available! After finishing his junior career, he knew he wasn't ready for the NHL. Nonetheless, he demanded from the Canadiens a $2,000 signing bonus in addition to his $7,500 salary. He got his deal and spent the next three years between Montreal and the minors. (He was a member of the Stanley Cup-winning team in 1953.) By 1954–55 Moore was a regular for the Habs and proved to be a gritty addition to a team loaded with superstars.

Moore's goal-scoring prowess was no better in the NHL than it had been in junior, but then in 1956–57, while with the Canadiens, he scored 29 and followed that with seasons of 36, 41, 22, 35, 19 and 24. His assist totals were even better (a career best 55 in 1958–59) but it was Moore's willingness to play through injuries that really made him special. One year, with a cast on his broken wrist he played the entire season and won the NHL scoring title (one of two Art Ross Trophies he received). His 96-point season in '58–'59 broke Gordie Howe's single-season scoring record of 95. Since he had a broken wrist, he was willing to step aside to let linemate Henri Richard win the scoring race, but Richard wouldn't allow that. Moore won the race by four points. This story shows that the Canadiens on those wonderfully talented clubs of the 1950s were great team players.

After five straight Stanley Cups, Moore and the Canadiens were knocked off their perch by the Chicago Black Hawks in the 1961 playoffs. During the series' key third game, Moore was penalized in overtime, which allowed the Black Hawks to win the contest and take the series. Legendary Canadiens television broadcaster Danny Gallivan called it the best game he ever witnessed, even though it was key to ending the Habs' reign as champions. Moore stayed with Montreal until the end of the 1962–63 season (a 50-point campaign for Moore) but knee injuries forced his retirement. He came back to the NHL two years later and joined the Toronto Maple Leafs for the 1964–65 season, getting into 38 games and scoring two goals. He then left hockey again until the 1967–68 season when he joined the St. Louis Blues. He was outstanding in the playoffs, contributing 14 points (seven goals) in 18 postseason games.

Since his retirement he has been very successful in business, and his great career was recognized by his election to the Hall of Fame in 1974.

Although Dickie Moore was a feisty player, he never accumulated more than 65 penalty minutes in one season. [HB]

Dickie Moore (#12) was claimed by the Toronto Maple Leafs in the 1964 intra-league draft and played one season for them, later playing for the St. Louis Blues. In this photo he slaps one past Toronto netminder Johnny Bower. (Imperial Oil-Turofsky/HHOF)

Dickie Moore was a first team all-star left-winger on two occasions and made the second team once. Here he scores on Leaf netminder Ed Chadwick. (HHOF)

Montreal moment:

On March 25, 1954, during a playoff game at the Montreal Forum, Dickie Moore enjoyed his greatest postseason performance when he set an NHL record with six points. Moore opened the scoring at the 10-second mark and then scored once more before assisting on two Bernie Geoffrion goals. He then helped Jean Béliveau score two more goals as

one eight-point night).

the Habs destroyed the Boston Bruins 8–1. The record stood until 1969 when Phil Esposito also had a six-point night. It has been surpassed by only three players: Wayne Gretzky (who had seven points three times), Mario Lemieux (one eight-point effort) and Patrik Sundstrom (also

MOORE'S CANADIENS STATS:	GP	G	A	P	PIM
regular season	654	254	340	594	575
playoffs	112	38	56	94	101

STANLEY CUPS: 6

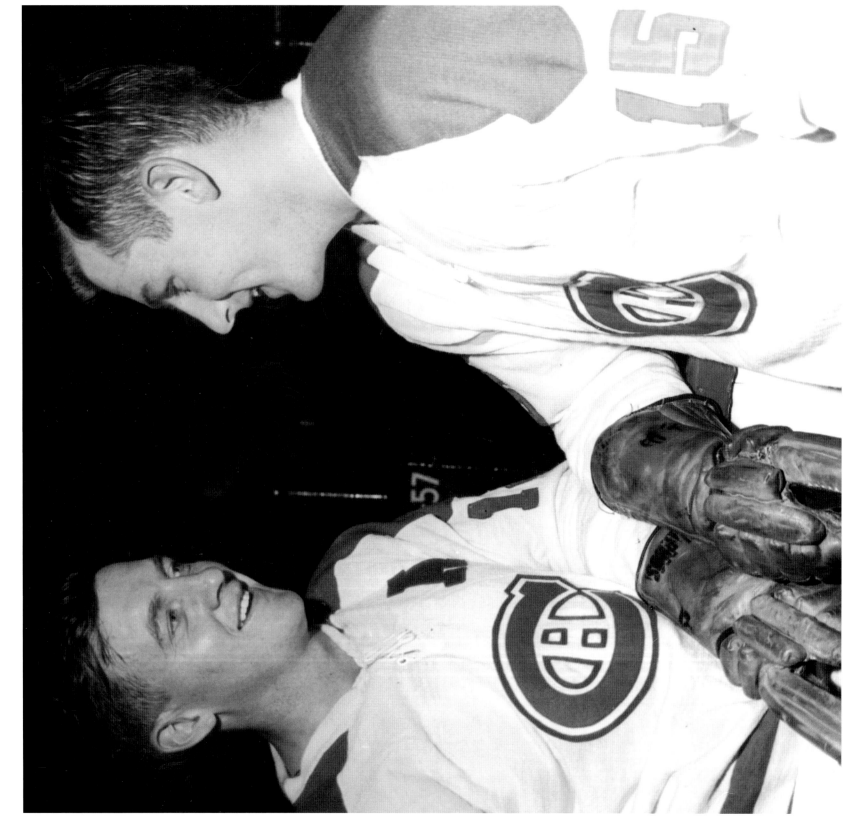

One of Dickie Moore's many injuries was a broken collarbone that caused him to miss most of the 1953–54 season. Here he discusses strategy with teammate Wayne Connolly (#15). (HHOF)

KEN MOSDELL

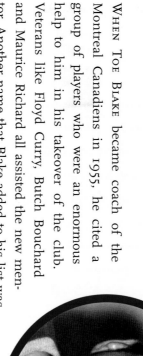

WHEN TOE BLAKE became coach of the Montreal Canadiens in 1955, he cited a group of players who were an enormous help to him in his takeover of the club. Veterans like Floyd Curry, Butch Bouchard and Maurice Richard all assisted the new mentor. Another name that Blake added to his list was speedy centre Ken Mosdell, a Montreal native. An underrated player throughout his entire NHL career, Mosdell was a very good skater and playmaker who worked very hard to be successful. His strong work ethic helped Mosdell to win four Stanley Cup championships before he retired.

Mosdell began his National Hockey League career with the Brooklyn Americans in 1941–42, scoring seven goals and earning 16 points in 42 games. (He had played junior hockey in Montreal, where pro scouts noticed him.) A member of the Royal Canadian Air Force between 1942 and 1944, he still managed to play some hockey. When he returned from duty, the Brooklyn Americans were no longer in business, and his rights were transferred to the Canadiens. He joined Montreal for the 1944–45 season when he scored 12 goals in 31 appearances. The next season, he split his time between the Habs and the Buffalo Bisons of the AHL. He was with the Canadiens for the 1946 playoffs and had four goals in nine postseason games that led to Montreal's Stanley Cup win. Mosdell became a regular with the Habs the next season, scoring five goals in 54 contests. He soon became known for his defensive play but missed most of the 1947–48 season after suffering a knee injury in a softball game. Although generally not an aggressive player (only 475 career penalty minutes), Mosdell got into a stick-swinging duel with Gus Mortson of Toronto on November 25, 1948, which saw

both players badly cut. His battle with his longtime rival led to other fights. (Canadiens Billy Reay, Hal Laycoe and Richard fought Leafs Joe Klukay, Garth Boesch and Bill Barilko.) Referee "King" Clancy handed out eight majors by the end of the game.

With Elmer Lach as the main offensive centre during Mosdell's early years with the Habs, Mosdell still managed some good scoring years. In 1953–54 he scored 22 times and repeated that the following year. (He totalled 100 points over those two seasons.) His performance didn't go unnoticed: he was a first all-star team selection in '54 and a second team selection in '55. After winning the Stanley Cup in 1956 (his third championship), Mosdell was dealt to Chicago, along with Eddie Mazur and Bud MacPherson, for $55,000 in cash. (The Canadiens held the first right of refusal on his playing rights.) Mosdell lasted only one season as a Black Hawk, playing in just 25 games and scoring two goals. Although his playing rights were returned to Montreal for '57–'58, he spent most of that season playing senior hockey with the Montreal Royals (scoring 27 goals and 42 assists in 67 games). Mosdell spent the following year in the Canadiens' minorleague system but made it to the NHL for the 1959 playoffs, filling in at centre for the injured Jean Béliveau. He played in just three games but got his name on the Cup one more time. He played one more year for the Royals (scoring 26 times in 61 games) before retiring from professional hockey.

Richard felt that his teammate was one of the most underappreciated players he ever had the pleasure of playing with, and he enjoyed Mosdell's company off the ice as well.

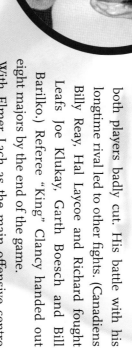

MOSDELL'S CANADIENS STATS:	GP	G	A	P	PIM
regular season	693	141	168	309	475
playoffs	80	16	13	29	48

STANLEY CUPS: 4

Ken Mosdell scored an overtime winning goal during the 1954 playoffs in the finals versus the Detroit Red Wings, but the Habs lost the Stanley Cup in seven games. (HHOF)

BERT OLMSTEAD

BERT OLMSTEAD began his National Hockey League career with Chicago in 1948–49 and had a 20-goal season with the Black Hawks in 1949–50. Olmstead played on a line with Bep Guidolin and Metro Prystai, managing 49 points. But the next season saw him play on the Milwaukee team of the IHL. Although transferred to Detroit in December of 1950, he never played a game for the Red Wings. Being shipped back to the Canadiens just a few days later was a sort of homecoming for Olmstead, who had started in the Canadiens system (in Kansas City of the United States Hockey League) after a junior career in Moose Jaw, Saskatchewan. The Habs offered him back to Chicago for centre Gus Bodnar but were turned down. It's a good thing for the Canadiens that the Black Hawks rejected the deal because Olmstead established himself in the big league as a hard worker who was excellent in the corners. He was never a high goal scorer (17 was the most he got as a Hab, in 1952–53) but he was a great playmaker and racked up assists totals like 28, 28, 37, 48, 56, 33 and 28 before he left the Canadiens. He led the NHL in assists for two straight seasons (1954–55, 1955–56) and enjoyed an eight-point night on January 9, 1954, when he had four goals and four assists in a 12–1 Montreal victory over the Black Hawks (equalling a record set by Maurice "Rocket" Richard in 1944).

Olmstead's work ethic and his tireless checking efforts made up for his lack of superior skating skills. He could be aggressive at times but wasn't a classic fighter, often starting more fights than he finished. The strapping right-winger (6'2", 183 pounds) was also not shy about chewing out a teammate, including the great Richard, for a lack of effort. He was probably the only player ever to get away with needling Richard. (It helped that Olmstead had coach Dick Irvin's

approval.) For his part, Richard didn't mind playing with Olmstead on his line, since the man known as "Dirtie Bertie" rarely played a bad game, but the Rocket wasn't fond of his teammate's verbal tirades. Even Richard, however, had to be happy when Olmstead checked Gordie Howe on the final night of the 1952–53 season to stop the big Red Wing right-winger from notching his 50th goal of the season, a record held by Richard at the time. His style of play was much liked by coach Toe Blake, who saw Olmstead as a very important playoff performer (42 points in 86 playoff games).

At the end of the 1957–58 season, Bert Olmstead was ready to retire from the Stanley Cup champion Montreal Canadiens. The hard-nosed left-winger won the Cup, his fourth with Montreal, in his last game as a Hab on April 20, 1958, but the team had made it clear he wasn't going to be protected for the June intraleague draft. He was going to try coaching, but Toronto Maple Leafs coach Billy Reay had other thoughts. As a teammate of Olmstead's in Montreal, Reay knew that the veteran could help the young team the Leafs were assembling. Selected by the Leafs, Olmstead went to Toronto to help an old friend and show a team how to win. Olmstead's decision to continue his career was one of the best things that ever happened to the Maple Leafs. (Olmstead closed his NHL career in 1962 with a Stanley Cup win in his final game with Toronto.) As Olmstead's replacement, Montreal chose another large winger named Ab McDonald. The 6'3" McDonald never matched Olmstead's contributions to the Habs, but he did stick around for three Stanley Cups with the Canadiens.

A native of Scepter, Saskatchewan, Olmstead tried his hand at coaching in the NHL with Oakland in 1967, but he lasted just one season. Olmstead was elected to the Hockey Hall of Fame in 1985.

OLMSTEAD'S CANADIENS STATS:	GP	G	A	P	PIM
regular season	508	103	280	383	609
playoffs	86	8	34	42	78
STANLEY CUPS: 4					

Bert Olmstead twice led the NHL in assists when he had 56 in 1955–56 and 48 in 1954–55. [HHOF]

JACQUES PLANTE

GETTING THROWN into the middle of a playoff series is tough for the best of goaltenders. But it's even more difficult when the goalie is a raw rookie as Jacques Plante was in 1953. Sure, Plante had played in three games for the Montreal Canadiens during the 1952–53 season (subbing for the injured Gerry McNeil) but a playoff game is different. Still, Montreal coach Dick Irvin put his job on the line and selected Plante to replace a faltering McNeil during a playoff series against Chicago. Extremely nervous before the contest played at the Chicago Stadium, Plante was assured by Maurice Richard that everything would be fine. Perhaps the soothing words of the team's best player did the trick because Plante went out and stopped the Black Hawks cold in a 3–0 shutout. The Canadiens had staved off elimination, and Plante won the next game as well to give the Habs the series win, four games to three. Plante played the first two games of the finals versus Boston before giving way to McNeil, but there was no mistaking that a goaltending legend had been born.

A native of Shawinigan Falls, Quebec, Plante was the oldest of 11 children from a very poor family. He had to help raise the family, but he also found time to play hockey. Because he had asthma, Plante had to play in goal to cut down on heavy skating. (He had tried to play defence.) One day Plante offered to go into the net as a replacement when his school coach and the team's goaltender were arguing. He never looked back. He wanted to play for the Canadiens — spurring the Toronto Maple Leafs who once had him on their list — but thought that getting to wear a Habs uniform would be difficult, since Bill Durnan and Gerry McNeil seemed firmly entrenched. He played for the Montreal Royals — with whom he starred as a junior and then as a senior — and practised with the Canadiens before playing very well for Buffalo of the American Hockey League. By 1954 Plante was ready for the NHL on a full-time basis: Durnan had retired and McNeil went to the minors. The Canadiens had a new star in goal.

Plante's goaltending was all about the science of the position. He emphasized being at the right place at the right time to make the save. A strong student of the game and self-taught, Plante was never shy about making innovative moves. For instance, he was the first goalie to step out of his crease to handle the puck (he did this at first because in his developmental years his defence was poor), the first to raise his arm to indicate an icing and, most importantly, the first netminder to regularly wear a face mask. Keenly aware of his crease and net, he could tell if a goalpost was the proper height simply by backing into it. (He did this one night in Chicago and was proven correct when he said that one post was shorter than the other!) Plante was a supremely confident goalie and wouldn't hesitate to tell his defencemen they had made a mistake. His quirky nature and style didn't always go over well, but there was no disputing Plante's results.

The years between 1956 and 1960 saw Plante win the Vezina Trophy five straight times (he won seven over his career) and his career goals against average as a Canadien stands at 2.33 during the regular season and 2.17 for the postseason. He had seven seasons of 30 or more wins with Montreal, and three of those years saw him win 40 or more games. (His highest total was 42 wins, twice in 70-game schedules.) Ironically, he won the Hart Trophy as the NHL's best player for the 1961–62 season when he didn't lead the Habs to a Stanley Cup win and didn't have Doug Harvey playing in front of him! Plante won his awards and earned his recognition with a stand-up style that changed as the situation dictated but was always conscious of the angle he was giving to the shooter.

A loner by nature, Plante's temperament didn't always endear him to his teammates and certainly not to coach Toe Blake. By the end of the 1962–63 season, Blake had grown tired of Plante's unreliability (he never knew when Plante was ready to play) and asked general manager Frank Selke to move the netminder. Plante found himself traded to the New York Rangers in a major deal, which saw the Habs land goalie Gump Worsley in exchange. Plante played two unhappy years in New York before he suddenly

Jacques Plante was a seven-time NHL all-star over the course of his career, three times on the first team and four times on the second squad. (HB)

Jacques Plante (#1) had about 200 stitches in his face by the time he got approval to wear a face mask — the first goaltender in the NHL to do so on a regular basis. (HB)

Jacques Plante's last game with the Canadiens was a playoff contest against Toronto in April of 1963, a 5–0 loss at Maple Leaf Gardens. He was traded to the New York Rangers that summer. (HHOF)

retired. He returned to the NHL to play well with St. Louis (sharing a Vezina Trophy with Glenn Hall) before going to Toronto and Boston to finish his NHL career.

After retiring, Plante was an outspoken commentator, never at

a loss for words, on television broadcasts. Later he moved to Switzerland with his second wife. He was only 57 when he passed away from stomach cancer. He was elected to the Hockey Hall of Fame in 1978.

Jacques Plante makes a save against Eric Nesterenko of the Chicago Black Hawks. [HB]

Montreal moment:

On November 1, 1959, during a game at Madison Square Garden in New York, Jacques Plante was badly cut when he took an Andy Bathgate — a player Plante had hip checked earlier in the game — backhand shot to the face. He went in for repairs and insisted to coach Toe Blake that he wouldn't return to the nets without a face mask. (He had been using one during practices and had been looking for a chance to use it in a game.) No fan of the mask, Blake didn't have a choice at that moment, since a "house" goalie, that is, an unqualified netminder,

was the only alternative. Plante got his wish and went out to defeat the Rangers 3–1 while wearing a primitive-looking mask. From that point on, the mask became part of Plante's goaltending equipment. (He kept winning with it on so Blake no longer objected.) The mask eventually became a requirement for all goalies. Plante felt the mask got more acceptance after the great Detroit goalie Terry Sawchuk wore one and still played at his usual high level.

PLANTE'S CANADIENS STATS:	GP	Wins	Losses	Ties	Shutouts	GA
regular season	556	311	134	108	58	2.33
playoffs	90	59	29	–	10	2.17

STANLEY CUPS: 6

K E N   R E A R D O N

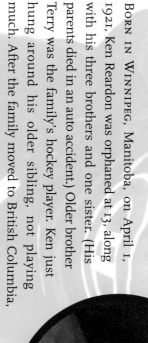

BORN IN WINNIPEG, Manitoba, on April 1, 1921, Ken Reardon was orphaned at 13, along with his three brothers and one sister. (His parents died in an auto accident.) Older brother Terry was the family's hockey player. Ken just hung around his older sibling, not playing much. After the family moved to British Columbia, where organized hockey wasn't of a high calibre, he played for the Blue River Rebels of the BCJHL in 1937–38. When Terry became a professional, Reardon got inspired to write to a junior team in Edmonton and ask for a tryout. Successful at the tryout, he went on to play defence, where he developed a physical style. His team, the Roamers, did well in the EJHL but lost the Memorial Cup to the Oshawa Generals in 1939.

Interested in Reardon at first, the New York Rangers decided against him because of his awkward skating style. The Montreal Canadiens, however, came up with a contract that the 19-year-old signed on October 26, 1940. Although he signed for $4,000 a year and a $1,000 bonus, Reardon hadn't yet made the team. The first game he played for the Canadiens (on November 3, 1940, against Boston) was his first time ever in the Montreal Forum. He played in 34 games for Montreal in 1940–41 (two goals, 10 points) and in 41 contests the next year (three goals, 15 points) before joining the Canadian army for three years. After becoming a decorated war hero, he returned to the Habs for their 1945–46 Stanley Cup win. Reardon got into 43 games, scoring five times and totalling nine points.

Reardon's game wasn't built on finesse. A fearsome, physical player, he loved to crush the opposition with thunderous bodychecks.

Not well-liked in enemy arenas, Reardon had a fiery disposition that racked up the penalty minutes (604 in 341 games played). Whatever he lacked in skill, Reardon made up in determination. Better at playing the game straight ahead rather than side to side, he was effective in driving the other team to distraction.

Reardon's best known and most bitter battle came against New York Ranger Cal Gardner. Late in a game at Madison Square Garden on March 16, 1947, Gardner cross-checked Reardon in the mouth. (Reardon might have been knocked into Gardner's stick by the Rangers' Bryan Hextall.) A wild brawl broke out when a fan tried to swing at Reardon as he went off for repairs to a badly bleeding mouth. His Montreal teammates came to his rescue, and a melee involving police and other Rangers ensued. The Canadiens blueliner vowed revenge on Gardner. The two would clash again in January of 1949 when Gardner was with the Maple Leafs. In a November 1949 contest, Reardon broke Gardner's jaw during a game played at the Montreal Forum. Hoping to end the feud, NHL president Clarence Campbell forced Reardon, while he was still on the ice, to post a $1,000 bond. The two continued to despise one other long after they retired from the NHL.

After Reardon had seven seasons in the NHL, the Canadiens told him to retire due to his bad back. He joined the Canadiens front office — assisting general manager Frank Selke — and contributed to making the Habs the best hockey team of the fifties. He was elected to the Hockey Hall of Fame in 1966.

Defenceman Ken Reardon was a five-time NHL all-star, twice on the first team (in 1946–47 and in 1949–50, his final season). [Imperial Oil-Turofsky/HHOF]

REARDON'S CANADIENS STATS:	GP	G	A	P	PIM
regular season	341	26	96	122	604
playoffs	31	2	5	7	62

STANLEY CUPS: 1

MAURICE "ROCKET" RICHARD

A MACHINIST by trade, Maurice Richard considered leaving the game when times were tough early in his hockey career. His employers, the Montreal Canadiens, mused aloud in the newspapers about his durability and contemplated trades. Coach Dick Irvin, however, saw star potential in this young player and urged the team to hold on to him. It proved to be sage advice: Richard's career was marked by extraordinary feats that few other hockey players could match.

Richard was born in Montreal on August 4, 1921, into a family that didn't have much money. As a youngster he excelled at sports (like baseball and boxing) and developed a skating style and goal-scoring ability that got him noticed. By 1939 a local coach named Arthur Therrien recommended Richard for a junior hockey team, the Verdun Maple Leafs. A role in senior hockey followed, with a team known as the Canadiens with whom he played a couple of seasons. Wartime hockey meant opportunities for young, untried athletes like Richard, who played 16 games for the NHL Canadiens in 1942–43, scoring five times. A broken leg shortened his season, but the next year he scored 32 times in 46 games and helped Montreal take the Stanley Cup for the first time since 1931 with a 12-goal playoff performance. This wouldn't be Richard's last time as the postseason's best player.

Irvin's best move to get Richard going was to place him on the "Punch Line" with Elmer Lach at centre and Toe Blake (Richard's childhood hero) on the left wing. The trio clicked right from the start. Richard had the right playmaker at centre to feed him the puck, while Blake could score well enough. Irvin's other important move was to put Richard on the right wing even though he shot left. Richard's skating style meant that he found it easier to cut to the net from the right side. This approach also gave him the long side of the net whenever he could drive to the goal. Richard could fight off a defenceman with his great strength to get his shot on goal. His determination to score drove Richard to take the puck into the offensive zone with a zeal never seen before (and not often repeated since). He lived to score. To keep a goalie off balance, he would

never show him the same move twice. Richard's desire to get goals matched his incredible sense of drama. Oozing charisma, he was a hero to Montreal fans, who carried the torch for all oppressed French Canadians.

Richard spoke little or no English in his early years with the Canadiens. His language, however, was that of all gifted goal scorers. He scored 544 career goals (retiring as the all-time leader) and in 1944–45 set the benchmark of 50 goals in one season. It's fitting that the man known as the "Rocket" was responsible for making 50 goals the magic number in hockey. He got the nickname, one of the most memorable in hockey history, from teammate Ray Getliffe who, after seeing Richard skate, said, "That kid can take off like a rocket." Richard kept delivering great numbers even after the war. (A few critics believed Richard was only a "wartime player.") While he never scored 50 again, Richard did score more than 35 goals another six times. Perhaps not the NHL's best player, he nevertheless had no equals in putting the puck into the net.

Following an afternoon of moving, Richard scored five goals and earned eight points on December 28, 1944, in a game at the Forum! He once scored five goals in one playoff game versus Toronto, even though a Maple Leaf player was assigned to check him. His habit was to shine when something was at stake. Irvin loved Richard's style of play but found it difficult to control Richard's fiery temper, which opponents could ignite with some well-chosen barbs. (When he first joined the Canadiens, Richard slammed a door in the coach's face after being told he wouldn't play in a game.)

National Hockey League president Clarence Campbell never went easy on Richard whenever the Canadiens winger landed himself in some trouble, which happened too often for a player of his stature. Campbell didn't accept Richard's claim that, more often than not, he was simply retaliating in defence. One suspension of Richard from Campbell angered Montreal fans so much that they caused the most famous riot in Canadian history. It took words from Richard himself in March of 1955 to calm an angry public. Richard's suspension for the rest of the season (and the

Facing page: Maurice Richard wore sweater number nine because his first-born child (a girl) weighed nine pounds at birth. He previously wore number 15, and the new sweater was seen as a way to give the Rocket a fresh start. (HB)

Above: Maurice Richard became the NHL's all-time goal-scoring leader when he scored his 325th marker against Chicago netminder Al Rollins (surpassing the record of Nels Stewart). (Imperial Oil-Turofsky/HHOF)

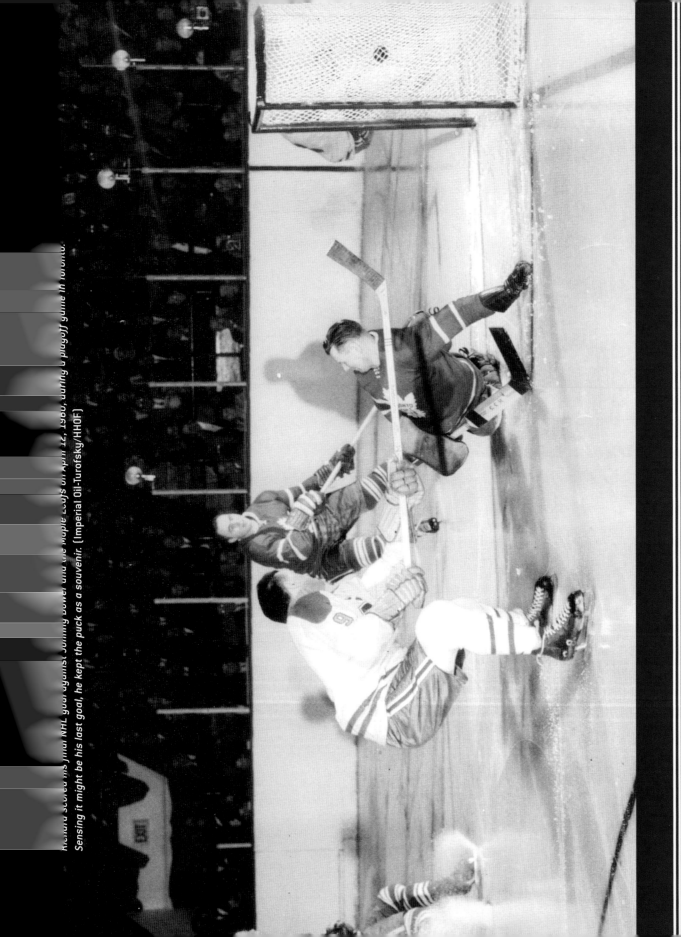

Richard scored his final NHL goal against Johnny Bower and the Maple Leafs on April 12, 1960, during a playoff game in Toronto. *Sensing it might be his last goal, he kept the puck as a souvenir.* (Imperial Oil-Turofsky/HHOF)

Montreal moment:

Maurice Richard scored many memorable goals in his outstanding career but perhaps none more so than the playoff winner he potted against Boston on April 8, 1952. Crushed by a couple of Bruins earlier in the game, he was taken to the infirmary in a wobbly state. Somehow he staggered to the bench late in the third period, refusing to miss a shift. Taking a pass from defenceman Butch Bouchard, he proceeded to weave through the entire Bruins team and sweep a shot into goalie Jim Henry's net. Bloodied and dazed from the hit he had taken, Richard still found time to shake hands with Henry after the game in one of hockey's most well-known photos. The Habs had skated away with a 3–1 win in game seven of the series. It was hard to argue with one commentator's suggestion that Richard had scored the goal in a semi-conscious fog.

For the record:

When Maurice Richard retired from the NHL in 1960, he held 17 scoring records. Many of those have since been surpassed, but Richard's record of six for most overtime winning goals in the playoffs was only recently equalled by Colorado Avalanche star Joe Sakic in 2004.

78

Always a clutch playoff goal scorer, Richard had 18 game winners in the postseason, still the fourth best all-time mark. (Imperial Oil-Turofsky/HHOF)

playoffs) cost him his best chance at the scoring title, the only major award to elude him in his great career. The Canadiens' hopes for a Stanley Cup also suffered: they would lose to Detroit in seven games. Irvin lost his job as a result of the defeat, and Blake was brought in to coach his former teammate.

Loaded with stars, including Richard's younger brother Henri, the Canadiens took off under Blake. From 1956 to 1960 the Habs dominated hockey like no other team before or since. As the years passed, Richard's role diminished (he did score 33 in 1956–57) and injuries once again took their toll. Richard also had difficulty with his weight, and by training camp in 1960 he had decided it was too difficult to get into the required shape. He scored four goals on goalie Jacques Plante during a scrimmage, and then called it a career. Richard was slated to work for the Habs as an ambassador, but his role and compensation weren't to his liking, so he left the team.

It wasn't easy for Richard when he left the game — a stint as Quebec Nordiques coach was short-lived) and he began his own business, working out of his home. In later years he attended memorabilia shows and legends games. It was clear the public never forgot him. When the Montreal Forum closed in 1996, he received a heartfelt ovation that lasted for 10 minutes. The Forum ice was filled with Canadiens legends, but the Rocket got the most genuine response. It was fitting that the man who represented French-Canadian heritage and culture was treated like nobility. Although many in attendance that night had never seen the Rocket play, his legendary status had managed to pass from one generation to the next. When Richard died in May of 2000, his funeral was broadcast live on television, an honour normally reserved for state leaders. Everyone in Canada held him in high esteem. Then again, Maurice Richard was no ordinary hockey hero.

Maurice Richard captained the Canadiens to five straight Stanley Cups from 1957 to 1960. [Imperial Oil-Turofsky/HHOF]

RICHARD'S CANADIENS STATS:	GP	G	A	P	PIM
regular season	978	544	421	965	1,285
playoffs	133	82	44	126	188
STANLEY CUPS: 8					

FRANK SELKE

WHEN FRANK SELKE SR. went to Montreal in 1946, he quietly introduced himself to all the Canadiens personnel. He let everyone know that he was in charge and had specific expectations. Selke took over the reins of the Canadiens after manager Tommy Gorman was let go, quickly going about the task of rebuilding the team and the arena. Whereas his predecessor built his teams with veteran players (who had aged by the time Selke took over), the new manager wanted to build a farm system much like he had when he worked for the Toronto Maple Leafs. Selke told the Canadiens' owner that building a hockey team simply by buying players was no longer possible. Post-war prosperity levelled the playing field in the search for new talent, so the Habs would need to develop their own players starting at the junior level. Selke also pointed out that the Canadiens had some terrific stars — like Maurice Richard and goaltender Bill Durnan — but had no reserves of NHL calibre. He asked the Habs to sponsor a junior club in every province, and he helped set up junior leagues in the Montreal area. (Senior hockey was already in good shape.) He spent a great deal of money to set up a feeder system that would pay many dividends over the years.

At the same time he ordered a complete renovation, starting with new plumbing, of the Montreal Forum. Ugly brown seats were replaced by ones with more colour, and more seating was added at higher prices. (Before Selke's arrival, about 40 percent of the Forum's seats sold for as little as 50 cents a game.) As he had done in Toronto, he worked closely with coach Dick Irvin. Although the Canadiens missed the playoffs in 1948, the team became a powerhouse by 1951

among the front office staff led to the right decision: Toe Blake replaced Irvin. Selke wasn't afraid to surround himself with competent hockey people, including Ken Reardon (his main assistant) and his eventual replacement, Sam Pollock, a shrewd assessor of talent.

Under the guidance of this management, the Canadiens won five straight Stanley Cups between 1956 and 1960, a feat yet to be matched. The Montreal system replenished the supply of quality players, and Selke wasn't afraid to replace aging stars. With the depth of the available prospects, Selke and the Habs selected the best of the group and also traded, put up for grabs and sold away players. The dynasty team of the late fifties eventually lost players to retirement, so that for a while the Habs couldn't win the Cup. Nonetheless, their future looked good because of Selke's efforts.

By the end of the 1963–64 season, the Habs owners, restless about the lack of championships, told Selke he should retire. They were also concerned about losing a sharp mind like Pollock's to another team (expansion was on the horizon). Selke could read the writing on the wall. The Canadiens won four of the next five Stanley Cups, proof that Selke had left the team in good shape. This fact helped to secure his place in hockey history. He was elected to the Hockey Hall of Fame in 1960.

and won a Stanley Cup in 1953. From 1951 up to and including 1960, the Canadiens made it to the finals. The Habs had a bevy of stars, featuring new ones like Dickie Moore, Bernie Geoffrion, Jean Béliveau, Doug Harvey and Jacques Plante. But before the Canadiens could reach their peak, a coaching change had to be made.

A difficult decision for the organization and much debate

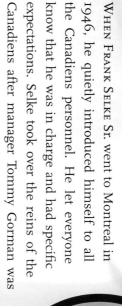

From 1951 to 1960, Frank Selke was in command of a team that made the Stanley Cup finals 10 straight seasons. In 1960–61 the Montreal payroll was estimated to be about $300,000. In this photo, Selke stands to the left of Jean Béliveau who is signing his first Canadiens contract. (Frank Prazak/HHOF; inset photo: HHOF)

SELKE'S CANADIENS STATS*:	GP	W	L	T
regular season	1,230	623	375	232
playoffs	153	89	64	–

STANLEY CUPS: 6

* as manager

THE RICHARD RIOT

by Red Fisher

OF ALL THE great stars who have worn the Canadiens jersey, Maurice "Rocket" Richard stands alone. He was the first National Hockey League player to score 50 goals in a 50-game season (in 1945), which were among his 544 goals in 978 regular-season games. More than four decades after his career ended, his 82 playoff goals still rank number seven on the all-time list. His six overtime goals still rank number one. He personified greatness under pressure.

Richard's eye-popping career numbers don't begin to describe what he meant to hockey in general and the Canadiens in particular. It has been suggested that Richard's passion for winning was the start of the French-English "thing" in Quebec. Winning at any cost was what he was all about. He meant everything to his people, on and off the ice. When he and the Canadiens won, they — his people — won. When the Canadiens lost, they lost. When the perception was that he was treated harshly by constituted authority, his people responded with anger.

That anger boiled over in what became known as "The Richard Riot" almost a half century ago on March 17, 1955. His suspension for the last three games of the regular season and the playoffs — after getting involved in a savage, stick-swinging duel with Boston defenceman Hal Laycoe — would have been, without the riot, little more than a hiccup in NHL history — as the Todd Bertuzzi attack on Colorado forward Steve Moore will certainly become. Instead, almost 50 years later, the debate still rages because there was only one "Rocket."

The Detroit Red Wings were in the city on that St. Patrick's Day, but the Canadiens would be playing without Richard. The sour odour of trouble was in the air. You could feel it as well as sense it, particularly in the area around the Montreal Forum, the hockey cathedral where Richard had scored so many of his great goals.

"Go to the Forum," I was told by my sports editor at the *Montreal Star*. "Don't worry about the game. Just hang around. Sit in the stands at the game. See what's happening. See if Richard is there. Talk to Gordie Howe. Find out what he thinks about this business."

"This business" started the previous Sunday in Boston when Laycoe struck Richard on the side of the head with his stick. Richard responded by high-sticking Laycoe on the shoulder and face. Then, when Richard's stick was taken from him, he grabbed another and struck Laycoe twice on the back. Linesman Cliff Thompson, who was trying to restrain Richard, was struck in the face.

Three days later, the day before the Canadiens-Red Wings game in Montreal, NHL president Clarence Campbell brought down the suspension that shook the hockey establishment in general and Canadiens fans in particular. It was a shot heard around the world. Richard was poised to win his first ever scoring title heading into the final three regular-season games: now it was gone. So, apparently, were the Canadiens' chances to win the Stanley Cup without Richard.

"Buy a ticket for the game, but somebody will cover it," my sports editor said. "Sit with the fans. Talk to them."

Montreal mayor Jean Drapeau had urged president Campbell not to attend the game. Instead, Campbell arrived late at his Forum aisle seat roughly a dozen rows above ice level. By that time, the Wings led, 2–0. As you'd expect, the sight of Campbell settling into his seat attracted angry cries and threats from fans. Now and then, eggs and tomatoes were thrown at the president, who sat in his seat staring straight ahead, trying hard not to pay attention to the fires of anger stoked by his presence.

At period's end, a fan walked up the steps toward Campbell, offering to shake hands with the president. When Campbell reached for his hand, he was slapped in the face. Seconds later, a tear gas bomb exploded. The thick, yellow smoke sent fans screaming toward the main lobby. People were choking, coughing and retching, their eyes streaming. Many yelled "fire." The building was ordered cleared, and with the Canadiens trailing the Red Wings, 4–1, the decision was made to forfeit the game to the visitors.

That was merely the start of what was to become a night of violence. Thousands of people, many among them thugs looking for trouble, had gathered in front of the Forum. Someone fired a bullet through one of the building's windows. Cars were overturned and set on fire.

I headed for a pay phone on the next block and called the *Star's* night city editor. "You'd better get a couple of reporters up here," I told him. "There are thousands of people in front of the Forum. They're setting cars on fire. It's getting uglier by the minute."

"Why don't you go out there and circulate in the crowd," he suggested. "Why don't you come up here and circulate in the crowd?" was my response. "The safest place right now is inside the Forum, and that's where I'm going."

There, in a stunned Detroit dressing room, the furious Red Wings general manager, Jack Adams, was telling media people that "Richard was a disgrace to hockey." Across the ice, Canadiens coach Dick Irvin Sr. was trying to douse the fire. "I've seen the Rocket fill arenas, but I've never seen him empty one," he said.

By this time, the mob outside the Forum was starting to disperse. Instead, hundreds among them started marching along St. Catherine Street, the city's busiest shopping area. Windows were shattered. Looting began. The next day's newspapers reported that 37 adults and four juveniles had been arrested. The wonder of it all was that nobody was killed on this blackest of nights.

The next day, a shaken Richard, who had attended the game, sat behind a small forest of microphones, pleading with the people to exercise calm. Since it was the Rocket asking for it, people listened — and have never forgotten.

NHL president Clarence Campbell (holding hat) mobbed by hockey fans, angry at the suspension of Maurice Richard. (Montreal Gazette)

the quiet dynasty 1961–1973

Maurice Richard's retirement marked the end of an era, arguably the greatest in the team's history. With his departure the team lost some of its heart. Other stars soon exited via trades (Plante, Harvey) or because of injuries (Olmstead, Johnson, Moore and Geoffrion).

But this transition period wasn't a disaster. Between 1961 and 1964, the Habs finished first three times, although they didn't make it to the finals. In a quiet manner the Habs added small but highly skilled players and produced the likes of Gilles Tremblay, Bobby Rousseau, Claude Larose, Red Berenson, Jimmy Roberts and the lightning fast Yvan Cournoyer. A couple of large and effective defencemen were Jacques Laperriere and Terry Harper, while skill on the blue line came from Jean-Claude Tremblay. Added to this group were hold-over veterans Ralph Backstrom, Jean Béliveau, Claude Provost, Charlie Hodge and Jean-Guy Talbot.

A kid plays for the Canadiens —

he's somebody special. He's with champions. He's on a team with a history of winning."

Sam Pollock (Montreal general manager, 1964 to 1978)

Dave Balon (#20) tries to put one past Toronto netminder Terry Sawchuk. Balon was acquired in a major trade with the New York Rangers and played in 226 games as a Hab, recording 112 points. (HB)

A couple of minor-league pickups — John Ferguson and Ted Harris — added toughness to the team while a significant trade added goalie Gump Worsley plus forwards Dave Balon and Leon Rochefort.

A 1964 semifinal loss to the Maple Leafs marked a turning point for the Canadiens who were now being firmly run by the Molson family, with David Molson as team president. It was decided that 72-year-old Frank Selke should be replaced as general manager. Sam Pollock, a man who had held a wide variety of positions in the organization, was named to the post. Pollock had been directly responsible for the development of many of the rising stars in the Canadiens organization, and he added a good veteran in left-winger Dick Duff. He wisely kept Toe Blake as coach, and by 1965 the Habs had won the Stanley Cup with a 4–0 game-seven win over Chicago. Champions again in 1966, the Canadiens beat Detroit in the finals in six games, bouncing back after losing the first two games in the Forum. The Maple Leafs pulled off a six-game upset of the Habs in the 1967 final, spoiling plans to have the Stanley Cup on display at "Man and His World" at Expo '67, held in Montreal to honour Canada's centennial. But the loss to Toronto would prove to be only a short break in the Canadiens' string of successes in the late sixties.

Just before the NHL expansion of 1967, the Canadiens wisely invited everyone (110 players, including 13 goalies) in the organization to training camp, where the team hierarchy assessed who to expose in the upcoming expansion draft. The Canadiens system at that time included the Quebec Aces, the Cleveland Barons and the Providence Reds (all of the American Hockey League), the Seattle Totems (of the Western Hockey League), the Houston Apollos (of the Central Professional Hockey League) and the Muskegon Mohawks (of the International Hockey League).

Pollock's look at all the players in the system allowed him to overhaul the Canadiens roster by adding youngsters Serge Savard,

Jacques Lemaire, Mickey Redmond, Danny Grant, Carol Vadnais and goaltenders Tony Esposito and Rogie Vachon. The Canadiens won the first Cup of the NHL's expansion era when they knocked off Western Division champs St. Louis Blues in 1968. It was the last title won by Blake, who had had enough of coaching and left the team after the last game of the finals. Claude Ruel, a loyal organization man, was named coach, although nobody seemed happy about it, including the 30-year-old Ruel, who had been groomed for Blake's job. It didn't seem to matter much, as the Canadiens once again took the Cup in 1969 with another sweep of the Blues.

The team was now playing in an extensively refurbished Montreal Forum (at a cost of about $10 million) that included over 2,400 new seats. However, the 1969–70 season was a different story, as the Habs, despite a 92-point season, missed the playoffs in the Eastern Division. A shocking 10–2 loss at Chicago clinched the Habs' fate on the last night of the season. They lost the last playoff spot to the New York Rangers on a goal differential!

The 1970–71 season wasn't going well for the team when three key moves revived it. First, Ferguson was talked out of retirement for one more year. Second, Pollock traded three players to Detroit for superstar Frank Mahovlich, who was happy to join his brother Peter (acquired earlier in another deal with the Red Wings). Lastly, a coaching change brought Al MacNeil (a one-time Hab defenceman) behind the bench. The team responded by finishing a solid third in the East, although worries about goaltending persisted. Vachon and Phil Myre weren't up to the task, so a lanky youngster named Ken Dryden (whose playing rights had been acquired from Boston years earlier) got a chance in March of '71.

Dryden came up from the minors and knocked the hockey world on its ear with a sensational performance that took the Habs all the way to the Stanley Cup. League-leading Boston peppered Dryden with all kinds of rubber, but the unheralded netminder made all the important saves required to get the Habs past the

In December of 1971, the team and arena were sold once again — this time for over $15 million — as the Molson family moved their prized assets to a syndicate headed by the Bronfman brothers (Peter and Edward). That, however, wasn't the only change of the 1971–72 season. In an unprecedented move, MacNeil was removed as coach, despite his Cup triumph. (His benching of Henri Richard in the finals wasn't forgotten.) But a capable replacement was waiting in the wings. Always in the Canadiens organization before expansion, Scotty Bowman had coached the St. Louis club to three consecutive final appearances. After he left the Blues, it was just a question of time before Pollock installed his protege behind the Canadiens bench. The change didn't work well in the '72 playoffs (when the Rangers took the Habs in six contests) but the 1972–73 season saw the Canadiens return to glory with a six-game win over the Black Hawks in the final. With Lafleur, Dryden, Lapointe and Savard in place and new drafted players like Larry Robinson, Steve Shutt and Bob Gainey acquiring experience, the team was poised for another great era of hockey.

Red Berenson (#24) skates in front of the Boston goal. Berenson was one of the first U.S. college-trained players to make it to the NHL. He was also one of the first NHL players to wear a helmet. Berenson was on the 1965 and 1966 Cup-winning Montreal teams. (HB)

Bruins in seven games. Before succumbing, a tough Minnesota team took Montreal to six games, and it took the Canadiens another seven hard-fought contests to take the Cup away from Chicago. While Dryden was the new hero, the Habs added newcomers Marc Tardif, Rejean Houle, Phil Roberto, Pierre Bouchard and Guy Lapointe, planting some of the seeds that would lead to a seventies dynasty. The only sad note in the Habs' '71 win was the retirement of Béliveau, who left the game with the dignity and grace his career deserved. The day after Béliveau officially announced his retirement, the Canadiens selected future superstar right-winger Guy Lafleur first overall at the entry draft!

AWARDS SUMMARY 1961–1973

STANLEY CUP: 6 (1965, 1966, 1968, 1969, 1971, 1973)

VEZINA TROPHY: 5 (Jacques Plante, 1962; Charlie Hodge, 1964; Gump Worsley/Charlie Hodge, 1966; Gump Worsley/Rogie Vachon, 1968; Ken Dryden, 1973)

CONN SMYTHE TROPHY: 4 (Jean Béliveau, 1965; Serge Savard, 1969; Ken Dryden, 1971; Yvan Cournoyer, 1973)

CALDER TROPHY: 3 (Bobby Rousseau, 1962; Jacques Laperriere, 1964; Ken Dryden, 1972)

HART TROPHY: 3 (Bernie Geoffrion, 1961; Jacques Plante, 1962; Jean Béliveau, 1964)

NORRIS TROPHY: 2 (Doug Harvey, 1961; Jacques Laperriere, 1966)

ART ROSS TROPHY: 1 (Bernie Geoffrion, 1961)

MASTERTON TROPHY: 1 (Claude Provost, 1968)

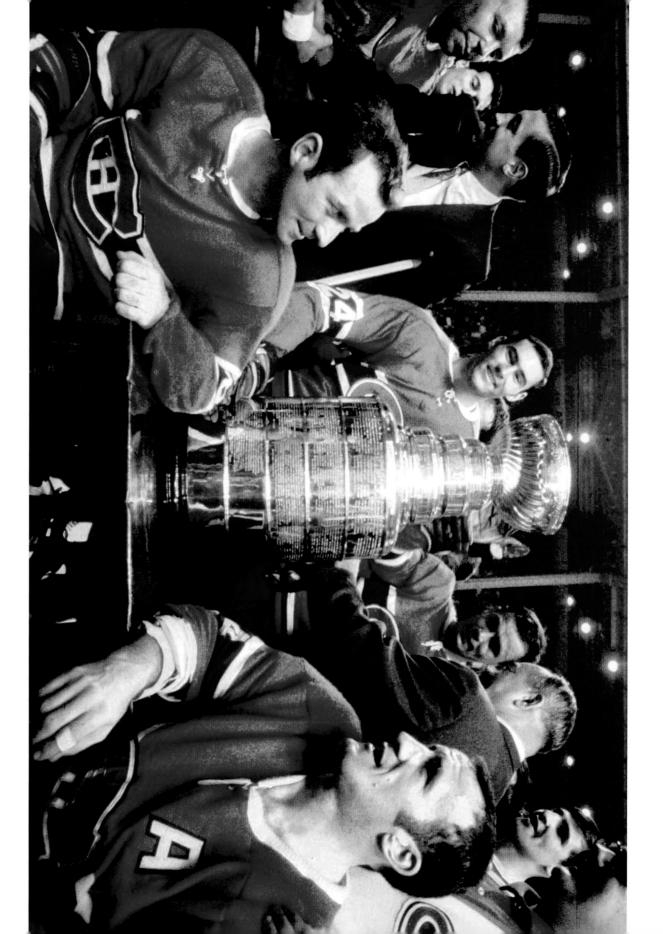

The Canadiens celebrate their 1968 Stanley Cup win over St. Louis at the Montreal Forum. Dick Duff, Mickey Redmond (#24) and Claude Provost ("A" on sweater) are at the centre of the proceedings. (Frank Prazak/HHOF)

RALPH BACKSTROM

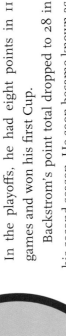

As a child growing up in Kirkland Lake, Ontario, Ralph Backstrom dreamed of playing in the NHL with the Montreal Canadiens. He always took the Montreal side of the table hockey game and wrote the names of Montreal legends like Elmer Lach, Maurice Richard and Toe Blake on the players. Backstrom was doing his part to get noticed by scoring nine goals twice in single-game performances. The youngster realized he had the potential to be an NHL player and wrote about his ambitions while in high school. The school principal quite rightly told him that his desire involved risk. Luckily for Backstrom, a family friend alerted the Canadiens to him as a prospect. With the Boston Bruins also hot on his trail, he signed a deal with the Habs. He was on his way to becoming a key support player in many Stanley Cup victories.

From the moment he joined the Montreal organization, Backstrom was tabbed as their best prospect. After a stint with the Montreal Junior Canadiens, he went on to win the Memorial Cup in 1957–58 with the Hull-Ottawa Canadiens. Considered the best junior in Canada that year, he became team captain, still playing close to 40 minutes a game. In spite of their high hopes for the speedy centre, the Canadiens had Backstrom ticketed for some time in the minors after his junior career ended. But a determined Backstrom made the team after a great camp with Montreal in September of 1958. He signed a two-year contract and got to play a bigger role than he imagined when Jean Béliveau got hurt. He stepped into the spot between Bernie Geoffrion and Ab McDonald and would win the Calder Trophy as the NHL's best rookie with 18 goals and 40 points in 64 games. Two goals against Toronto in a 2–2 tie seemed to lead Backstrom to an award-winning season.

In the playoffs, he had eight points in 11 games and won his first Cup.

Backstrom's point total dropped to 28 in his second season. He soon became known as the Canadiens' third centre (in a mainly defensive role) behind Béliveau and Henri Richard. On other teams he might have been a first-line player, but the Habs were just too deep to allow Backstrom a more significant role. Yet, the smooth-skating Backstrom still found a way to make himself valuable by often scoring around 20 goals a season (for five of his years with Montreal he scored 20 or more goals) and by trying to shut down some of the key opposing centres. He thought an eight-goal season in 1963–64 would finish him as a Hab, but Sam Pollock, his former junior coach, took over running the Canadiens and signed the talented centre to a new contract. Backstrom responded with a 25-goal season in 1964–65. A steady, dependable player throughout his tenure as a Hab, he had a knack of scoring key goals, such as an overtime winner against Boston in 1969.

The Canadiens kept Backstrom until the 1970–71 season, when he wasn't sure about playing in Montreal any further. (There was talk he was having a contract problem.) After 16 games, he was dealt to Los Angeles (fulfilling his wish, it was reported, for a warmer climate) in January of 1971. For a couple of years, he kept the Kings out of the cellar of the Western Division by scoring 57 goals before he found himself traded to Chicago in 1973. He faced the Habs as a Black Hawk in the '73 finals and had a good playoff with 11 points in 16 games. That was his last NHL action before joining the rival World Hockey Association the next season. He joined the University of Denver coaching ranks after retiring.

After his trade to Los Angeles, Ralph Backstrom scored twice for the Kings when they played the Canadiens on February 6, 1971, in a 6–3 win over Montreal. (HB)

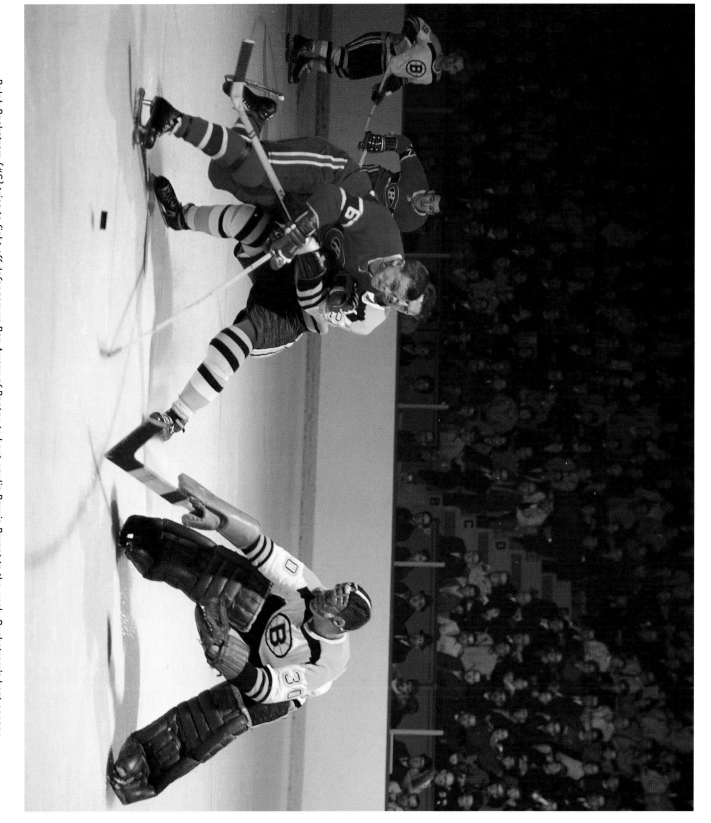

Ralph Backstrom (#6) tries to fight off defenceman Don Awery of Boston to beat goalie Bernie Parent to the puck. Backstrom's best season in Montreal came in 1961–62 when he scored 27 goals and totalled 65 points in 66 games played. (HB)

BACKSTROM'S CANADIENS STATS:	GP	G	A	P	PIM
regular season	844	215	287	502	348
playoffs	100	22	26	48	68

STANLEY CUPS: 6

JEAN BÉLIVEAU

When Jean Béliveau retired from the Montreal Canadiens in 1971 with one of the most distinguished careers in NHL history, Canadian Prime Minister Pierre Trudeau paid him homage. Trudeau called Béliveau exemplary, courageous, disciplined and honourable. He added that Béliveau possessed a lively intelligence combined with finesse and displayed magnificent team spirit. Trudeau closed his remarks by saying that Béliveau brought hockey great prestige. *Le Gros Bill*, as Béliveau was known, was not all these things and more. Perhaps no player has been as closely identified with a team as Béliveau. And no one has contributed — and continues to contribute even in retirement — more dignity and class to an organization.

Although the Canadiens took a long time to get Béliveau into uniform, it was well worth the effort. Béliveau's parents weren't interested in sports, and his father, Arthur, wanted his son to take an electrician's course so that he might work with him at Shawinigan Power. But Béliveau was a good athlete who wanted to play hockey. He played junior hockey in Victoriaville for three seasons, proving himself a good goal scorer. In 1950–51 he played for the Quebec Citadelle and scored 61 times in 46 games, making him the best junior prospect not in the NHL. He got a two-game trial with the Canadiens that year and scored his first goal. Rather than go to Montreal right away, however, Béliveau stayed in Quebec City and played senior hockey for two more seasons. He scored 123 goals and earned 102 assists in 150 games. During another three-game trial with the Canadiens, he scored five goals. With a new suit each time he scored three goals in one game — a perk he often passed on to a teammate — he was well-treated in Quebec City and found it difficult to leave. But he knew his time had come to play in the best hockey league. It was his destiny.

It wasn't easy for the Habs to sign Béliveau, but he was pleased to receive $100,000 over a five-year contract, an enormous sum for the time. Under pressure to sign the young French-Canadian star, the Canadiens knew they were getting a potential superstar.

Béliveau started slowly and got into only 44 games as a rookie due to injury, scoring just 13 goals. By his second year, the large (6'3", 205-pound) centre scored 37 and then followed that up in 1955–56 with a league-leading 47 goals and 68 points, which led to the Art Ross and Hart Trophies. The Habs won the first of five straight Cups that spring, and Béliveau continued to chalk up points and goals, scoring 45 in 1958–59. Béliveau played the game with dignity and class, but he was no shrinking violet on the ice. He was a smooth skater with a good wrist shot, excellent at finding the open teammate to receive the puck. He twice recorded over 90 points and was a five-time first team all-star.

By the start of the 1961–62 season, Béliveau was ready to become captain, a natural leadership position for him. (Maurice Richard had retired and Doug Harvey had been traded.) When teammate Bernie Geoffrion felt slighted at being overlooked (mostly because of seniority), the sensitive Béliveau offered to give him the captaincy, which Béliveau had won in an all-players vote. But Habs management would have none of it. They made a wise choice.

Béliveau had serious health concerns in the early sixties (a possible heart problem and an eye injury) but he persevered to win the Hart Trophy in 1963–64 when he had 78 points (28 goals, 50 assists) in 68 games. The next season saw the Canadiens win their first Cup under Béliveau's leadership with a seventh-game victory over the Chicago Black Hawks in 1965. Béliveau scored the opening goal of the deciding game after just 14 seconds of play. The Chicago team never recovered. The Habs took the silver mug again in 1966 and yet again in 1968 (Béliveau missed the finals that year due to injury) and 1969. When the Canadiens missed the playoffs in 1969–70, it looked like Béliveau was going to retire, but he decided to stay for one more year.

During the 1970–71 campaign, Béliveau scored his 500th career goal at the Forum in a 6–2 win over Minnesota. He finished the year with 25 goals and 76 points, and then he added eight goals

Facing page: *In 1950–51 Jean Béliveau was earning $6,000 a year playing hockey and another $3,000 working in a dairy. The native of Trois-Rivières, Quebec, also hosted a Saturday morning children's show on radio.* (HB)

Above: *No other team captain in the history of the NHL has accepted the Stanley Cup on five occasions as Jean Béliveau did in 1965, 1966, 1968, 1969 and 1971.* (HB)

"We feel that we are representing French Canada when we play hockey, and the Stanley Cup is the main objective. So that is why you see we are usually playing our best hockey in the playoff games."

Jean Béliveau

Montreal moment:

Jean Béliveau scored only one overtime winning goal in his career. It happened in the Boston Garden on April 24, 1969. The Canadiens and Bruins were tied 1–1 in the sixth game of the semifinal series with Montreal up 3–2 in games. Claude Provost stole the puck along the boards in the Boston end and whipped a quick pass over to Béliveau in the middle of the ice. Béliveau didn't have much to shoot at but noticed a small opening over goalie Gerry Cheever's shoulder. He snapped off a perfect shot, and the Habs had a 2–1 win and a trip to the finals. It was perhaps Béliveau's most memorable career goal. The Canadiens went on to easily beat the St. Louis Blues for the Stanley Cup.

Jean Béliveau and teammate Yvan Cournoyer (#12) fight for the puck with the Chicago Black Hawks. (HB)

94

and 16 assists in the playoffs to lead the Habs to another Stanley Cup win. He pulled off his sweater for the last time at the Chicago Stadium when the Habs beat the Black Hawks in another seven-game tussle. About to turn 40 years old, he went out a champion,

a very fitting end to a superb career. Upon retirement, he joined the Canadiens front office and stayed with the club until August 31, 1993, after 22 years in his management capacity.

Béliveau charges in on Toronto goalie Johnny Bower. Béliveau wore sweater number four, the same number worn by Canadiens greats Newsy Lalonde and Aurel Joliat. The team retired Béliveau's jersey on October 9, 1971. (Imperial Oil-Turofsky/HHOF)

BÉLIVEAU'S CANADIENS STATS:

	GP	G	A	P	PIM
regular season	1125	507	712	1219	1029
playoffs	162	79	97	176	211

STANLEY CUPS: 10

HECTOR "TOE" BLAKE

TOE BLAKE WAS BORN to a poor family in Victoria Mines, Ontario, on August 21, 1912, as the oldest of 11 children. His sister gave him the nickname "Toe" when she couldn't pronounce Hector, his given name. He had a tough upbringing and had much to endure as he grew up. But he found time to play junior hockey in Sudbury, Ontario, where he played on a Memorial Cup-winning team in 1932 before moving to Hamilton and playing senior hockey for the Tigers. He showed an ability to score goals. The Montreal Maroons of the NHL signed him as a free agent in February of 1935. Even though they won the Stanley Cup in Blake's only year with the team, he didn't make a great impression. But the rival Montreal Canadiens liked what they saw and completed a deal for the 5'10" 165-pound left-winger.

Since the legendary Howie Morenz was his hero, Blake was pleased to join the Canadiens. He soon showed that he was a talented player, winning the scoring title in the 1938–39 season with 24 goals and 47 points. That season his performance earned him the Hart Trophy as the NHL's most valuable player. The Toronto Maple Leafs liked Blake so much that they offered five players for his contract, but the Canadiens turned them down. By 1940 Blake was named team captain, but not until the 1944 playoffs did the team end its Stanley Cup drought by taking on Chicago in the finals and knocking off the Black Hawks in four straight games. In win their first championship since 1931. By this point, Blake was the left-winger on a line with Maurice Richard and Elmer Lach — the fabled "Punch Line." During the 1944–45 season, the trio finished 1–2–3 in scoring, with Blake finishing third based on 29 goals and 67 points in 49 games played. With Blake scoring a top mark of seven playoff goals, the Canadiens took the Cup again in 1946. He was with the Habs for two more seasons before a broken leg suffered during the 1947–48 season ended his career.

Blake wanted to stay in hockey and decided to try coaching. His first job in the Canadiens organization was with the Houston Huskies of the USHL for the 1947–48 season. He had a 13–5–2

record. He was then sent to Buffalo to coach the American Hockey League Bisons for a couple of years, but a disagreement with the local owner forced Blake to walk away in spite of a first-place finish in 1949–50. He came back to the Habs system by coaching in Valleyfield, Quebec, in the QSHL where his teams were usually around the .500 mark. When Dick Irvin was going to be replaced behind the Canadiens bench, Blake wasn't assured of the job, but a strong push from Canadiens executive Ken Reardon landed Blake the coveted position. One reason Reardon felt strongly about Blake was his belief that the new coach needed to get the most out of Richard, the best player on the team. Blake would be able to influence the Rocket: the two were former teammates, and as a youngster Richard had idolized Blake. Canadiens manager Frank Selke eventually agreed and hired Blake on June 8, 1955.

In Blake's first season behind the Canadiens bench, the team won 45 games, finished in first place and then won the Stanley Cup over the arch-rival Detroit Red Wings. Blake put his mark on the team style by promoting motion at all times. The Canadiens would go on the attack and make the most of their talented performers. For as long as he was on the team, Blake, although crusty, even profane, never singled out a player publicly for a bad performance. He would take a player aside and tell him in no uncertain terms what he was doing wrong, but he was also good at letting players do what they did best. The Hab players appreciated Blake's coaching style, taking to heart his message about wearing the famous red, white and blue sweater proudly. Blake had an interest in his players' personal lives and made sure they always travelled first class. During practices Blake was all business — as he had been as a player. He was a bad loser, however, and his anger got the better of him one night in Chicago in 1961 after his club had lost a key game in overtime. Furious at referee Dalton McArthur for calling a penalty on Dickie Moore in the third extra session, he slugged the official in the shoulder with a wild swing. That reaction cost Blake a $2,000 fine from NHL president Clarence Campbell.

Above: *Toe Blake was selected to the NHL's first all-star team on three occasions and won the Hart Trophy in 1938–39. He was elected to the Hall of Fame as a player in 1966. Here he is shown with his linemates Maurice Richard (left) and Elmer Lach (centre) — forming the famous "Punch Line."* [HHOF]

Facing page: *Nicknamed "The Old Lamplighter," Toe Blake had six 20-goal seasons as a player with the Habs.* (Graphic Artists/HHOF)

Blake's hiring worked out well for the Habs, who won five straight Cups under their new mentor and lost a grand total of nine playoff games between 1956 and 1960. They won plenty of individual awards and gained many all-star selections, but Blake never let them forget that the team came first. The Canadien teams of this era were perhaps the greatest of all time. The Habs had to remake their team after the 1960 Cup win, but by 1965 Blake had them back on top with many new players. They won

three more Cups before Blake decided he had had enough. A constant worrier, Blake announced — on the afternoon of May 11, 1968, just after the Habs won their eighth Cup under his leadership — that he was leaving. He apologized to his team for stealing the headlines. But none of the players minded: Blake deserved his accolades. He stayed in the Canadiens organization until Alzheimer's disease took his life in 1995.

CANADIENS LEGENDS

The Quiet Dynasty 1961–1973

"There is probably more pressure on a Montreal team in the playoffs than on any other club in the NHL. The Canadiens fans are more demanding. They expect us to win. We're supposed to have the best players."

Toe Blake

Toe Blake behind the bench; when Blake took over as coach of the Canadiens, he gave credit to players like Maurice Richard, Floyd Curry, Butch Bouchard and Ken Mosdell for helping make his transition smooth. [HB]

Coach Blake surrounded by his team: When the Montreal Canadiens won five straight Stanley Cups between 1956 and 1960, Blake also coached the team to 202 wins in the regular season (in 350 games played). [HB]

BLAKE'S CANADIENS STATS:

regular season (as a player)	GP	G	A	P	PIM
	569	235	292	527	282
playoffs	57	25	37	62	23

BLAKE'S CANADIENS STATS:

regular season (as a coach)	GP	W	L	T
	914	500	255	159
playoffs	119	82	37	–

STANLEY CUPS: PLAYER 2 COACH 8

YVAN COURNOYER

YVAN COURNOYER was born and raised in Drummondville, Quebec, where his father Paul, a machinist by trade, set up a hockey rink beside the family house. As a youngster Cournoyer dreamed of playing for the Canadiens, sure that one day he would be a professional hockey player (or follow in his father's footsteps). He developed a heavier steel puck and often practised his shot, even in summer when he would shoot in the garage. He played other sports but only to stay in shape for hockey. To build up his muscles Cournoyer delivered beer and to build up his powerful legs he scraped the ice. By the age of 15 he was only 5'3", and the smallest player on the Lachine Maroons, his junior club. (He didn't mind being little because he felt it made him work harder.) He was the team's only French-speaking member, but he scored 37 goals in 42 games and got noticed by Montreal scout Claude Ruel. The Canadiens' assessor of talent saw Cournoyer as a natural scorer and firmly believed he would play in the NHL.

Cournoyer played three seasons for the Montreal Junior Canadiens in the Ontario Hockey Association and scored an incredible 63 goals in his final season of 1963–64. That year he also played in five games for the Habs and scored four times! But the big team decided to keep him in junior until the next year. Coach Toe Blake liked the fact that Cournoyer would shoot the puck quickly and on net. He wasn't as enamoured, however, with the stocky (5'7", 178 pounds) right-winger's all-round game. He spent much of his first season on the bench and got out on the ice mainly for power plays, scoring seven times in 55 games. (His minor league career consisted of seven games.) He added three more markers in the playoffs that saw the Habs win the Stanley Cup. (One of his goals came in the seventh game of the finals against Chicago.) He scored 18 in 1965–66 and added five points in 10 playoff games when the Canadiens repeated as Cup champs. But by the 1966–67 season, Cournoyer was still a power-play specialist, even though he scored 25 times and added 40 points.

He upped his goal total to 28 the following year when the Habs reclaimed the Cup and had an impressive 14 points in 13 playoff games. To learn more about the game's defensive side, Cournoyer watched teammate Claude Provost ply his trade in a strong checking role. After Montreal's triumph of 1968, Blake decided to retire. Ruel took over as coach, which meant more ice time for the man known as "The Roadrunner." (Cournoyer had tremendous speed, just like the cartoon character.) He made the most of it with 43 goals and 44 assists. Using his muscular, square build to advantage, Cournoyer became known for his bursts of speed down the wing, striking terror into any backpedalling defenceman. He also became renowned for his ability to score in key situations and for playing his best in the big games. He really felt he belonged when he scored 10 times (in 20 games) during the 1971 playoffs, helping the Habs to a surprising Cup win. Named to Team Canada in 1972, he was vital in the narrow victory over the Russians. The names of Paul Henderson and Phil Esposito are most often mentioned in discussions of the fabled '72 series, but Cournoyer was easily the third best forward on the Canadian team. The Soviets had great difficulty handling his tremendous speed.

Over the next few years Cournoyer scored many goals for the Habs — posting seasons of 27, 37, 47, 40, 40, 29, 32, 25 and 24 — before he was injured and unable to play any more. His best moment may have come during the 1973 playoffs, when the explosive winger recorded 25 points (15 goals) to capture the Conn Smythe Trophy, the only individual award Cournoyer won. The Habs took the Stanley Cup once again, with Cournoyer's winning goal in the sixth game of the series, a backhanded shot over Chicago netminder Tony Esposito. He then assisted on Marc Tardif's goal, which was the insurance marker. Henri Richard, the "Pocket Rocket," accepted his last Cup as captain. The 31-year-old Cournoyer was named his successor. Cournoyer first accepted the Cup as captain in 1976 when the

Above: Yvan Cournoyer celebrates after getting one past Johnny Bower of the Maple Leafs. (HHOF)

Facing page: Yvan Cournoyer made the NHL's second all-star team on four occasions during his career (1969, 1971, 1972, 1973). (DM)

Habs took out the Philadelphia Flyers in four straight games. He repeated the honour twice more in 1977 and 1978 on powerful Canadiens teams that won four straight titles. Cournoyer wasn't around for the 1979 championship because a back injury forced the end of his illustrious career early in the '78–'79 season.

After his retirement, Cournoyer stayed in Montreal, where he ran a restaurant and served as an assistant coach on the team when Mario Tremblay was named head coach in 1995. The Hall of Fame inductee (1982) now works as a goodwill ambassador for the Canadiens.

"I enjoyed representing the team.
We were a very close-knit team. There was no French or English.
When we lost, we lost together. When we won, we won together."

Yvan Cournoyer

Above: Yvan Cournoyer's final playoff appearance came in the 1978 postseason when he had 11 points (7 goals, 4 assists) in 15 games played. (DM)

Facing page: In three seasons with the Montreal Jr. Canadiens, Yvan Cournoyer scored 115 goals in 124 games played. (HB)

COURNOYER'S CANADIENS STATS:	GP	G	A	P	PIM
regular season	968	428	435	863	255
playoffs	147	64	63	127	47

STANLEY CUPS: 10

DICK DUFF

When Dick Duff was traded from Toronto to New York during the 1963–64 season, it was a big shock to the feisty but smallish (5'9", 165 pounds) left-winger who had played his entire career with the Maple Leafs. He couldn't adjust to the hockey environment in New York, and the Rangers were disappointed with his seven goals in 43 games. Meanwhile the Montreal Canadiens wanted a little spark during the 1964–65 season and rescued Duff in a deal that saw Bill Hicke leave the Habs. At the time it didn't seem like a significant deal, but Duff soon found his bearings in Montreal, helping the Habs reclaim the Stanley Cup at the end of the '65 playoffs.

In fact, Duff had interested the Canadiens for a while. Manager Frank Selke had coveted Duff but couldn't land him. When Sam Pollock took over from Selke, he quickly moved in to scoop up the clutch goal scorer. Also a fan of Duff's, coach Toe Blake believed the smooth skater could regain his scoring touch as a Hab. (He had seen him perform well against the Canadiens in the playoffs for many years.) The coach also saw him as a good two-way player. Duff finished the '64–'65 season with nine goals in 40 games. Then in the playoffs, Duff had nine points in 13 postseason games. The Habs knocked out the defending champion Maple Leafs in the first round and then beat Chicago in a seven-game series. (Duff scored one goal in the final game, a 4–0 win over the Black Hawks.) In his first full season with Montreal, he scored 21 times and totalled 45 points. The Habs won a second straight Cup in the 1966 playoffs with a six-game win in the finals over Detroit. Duff slumped to just 12 goals in 1966–67 (mostly because a broken ankle

limited him to just 51 games) but bounced back with 25, his best mark as a Hab, the next season when Montreal reclaimed the Cup.

Duff clearly liked the Canadiens style of play with its emphasis on the attack. Appreciative of Canadiens history, he scored his 200th career goal as a Hab against Glenn Hall of Chicago. However, as Duff struggled early in the 1967–68 season, Blake told him bluntly that for him to stay on the team his game had to improve. Duff got the message loud and clear and produced a game winner and three assists in his first game after Blake issued his threat. He followed that up with a three-assist effort versus Detroit and a hat trick against the Maple Leafs. In addition to his 25 goals, Duff had 21 assists and contributed seven points in 13 postseason games. In 1968–69, his last season in Montreal, Duff scored 19 times, earning 40 points in total. In the 14 playoff games, he had 14 points, six goals and eight assists. Clearly, Blake got his point across: Duff's concentration level in the playoffs proved him still very valuable!

For the start of the 1969–70 season, Duff was still with Montreal — scoring just one goal in 17 contests — but in January of 1970 he found himself dealt to Los Angeles, where many older Canadiens players ended up late in their careers. (It's interesting to note that the Habs didn't make the playoffs in '69–'70.) With the Kings for just a short time, Duff was traded to Buffalo, where he finished his career in 1971–72. He played in 1,030 career games and finished with an impressive 283 goals and 572 points, with a total of six Cups to his credit.

Dick Duff ended his career with a total of six Stanley Cups — two with Toronto and four with Montreal. [HB]

DUFF'S CANADIENS STATS:	GP	G	A	P	PIM
regular season	305	87	85	172	166
playoffs	60	16	26	42	38

STANLEY CUPS: 4

JOHN FERGUSON

ALTHOUGH HOCKEY was his favourite sport, John Ferguson didn't learn to skate until he was 12 years old. He was actually a superior lacrosse player (a goalie) and might have played that sport professionally if it had paid nearly as much as hockey. He grew up in Vancouver, British Columbia, sticking to lacrosse as his preferred game. A growth spurt when he was 17 transformed the smallish boy into a husky 5'11" 190-pound left-winger who would one day terrorize the NHL.

As a 14-year-old stick boy for the Vancouver Canucks, a minor pro team in the Western Hockey League, Ferguson learned a lesson he never forgot. The Canucks got pushed around by the team from Edmonton, in particular by tough guy Larry Zeidel. None of the Canucks responded when Zeidel beat up Phil Maloney. Ferguson realized that that was the wrong way for teammates to act.

He moved to Melville, Saskatchewan, to play junior hockey for three years before turning professional with Fort Wayne (Indiana) in the International Hockey League. After one year in Indiana, he moved to the more established American Hockey League, joining the Cleveland Barons for three seasons. His best year saw Ferguson score 38 goals in 72 games in the 1962–63 season. His steady improvement eventually got him noticed by NHL scouts. He led the AHL in goals scored and penalty minutes. Finally, he caught up with Zeidel and beat him up!

Three NHL teams showed interest in the rugged winger, but the Montreal Canadiens offered him the best opportunity to play his physical game. Tired of having their smallish forwards get pushed around, the Habs were desperately looking for a "police-man." The Canadiens signed him for $8,750 in his first year. Coach Toe Blake told him his job was to protect the Montreal stars (like Jean Béliveau and Bernie Geoffrion) so they could play their game. Ferguson got the message loud and clear: in his first game he took on Boston roughneck Ted Green. He acquitted himself well in the scrap and then in the opening game of the 1963–64

season added two goals in a 4–4 tie! Disdainful of any opponent, anywhere, any-time, Ferguson showed the league that the days of running over the Canadiens were over. He wasn't the least bit subtle. There was little or no finesse to his game. But he was fierce and determined that his team succeed.

As a rookie Ferguson scored 18 times. He was furious that his team lost to Toronto in the '64 semifinals. He scored 17 goals the following season when the Habs took the Stanley Cup with a finals win over Chicago. It appeared the Black Hawks had regained momentum after evening the series at two games each. But then Ferguson destroyed Eric Nesterenko in a fight, and Chicago wasn't able to recover from that beating. As a result, Montreal took the Cup in seven games. (Ferguson added three goals in the playoffs.) Ferguson scored 20 goals for the first time in 1966–67 and then two years later added a career high 29. In the 1969–70 season Ferguson played only 48 games, although he managed 19 goals (including seven game winners). Nevertheless, the Habs missed the playoffs, which had the proud Canadien pondering retirement. In November of 1970 he came out of a short retirement to score 16 goals in 66 games in the '70–'71 campaign. It was an up and down year for the Habs, but a great playoff performance led to Ferguson's fifth Stanley Cup in just eight years! (In the second game of the first round, he scored two big goals in a come-from-behind 7–5 win over Boston.) It was Ferguson's last season in the NHL, and he left the game as the heavyweight champion, a title he knew he might lose if he stayed around too long.

He was a coach on Team Canada in 1972. (It was Ferguson who suggested to Bobby Clarke that he give one of the Russian players a tap with his stick. That slash ended up injuring the leg of Russian star Valeri Kharlamov.) Later he coached and managed in the NHL, most notably with the New York Rangers and the Winnipeg Jets.

John Ferguson caught the attention of the Montreal Canadiens when he accumulated 451 penalty minutes in his American Hockey League career and was named to the first all-star team in 1963. Ferguson led the NHL in penalty minutes once in his career, in 1966–67 when he had 177. (HB)

John Ferguson waits for a rebound against Roger Crozier of Detroit. Ferguson scored two very important goals in a come-from-behind victory over the Boston Bruins during the second game of the 1971 playoff series. Down 5–1 at one point, the Habs won the game 7–5, turning the series around in their favour. (HB)

Montreal moment:

When the Habs won the Stanley Cup in 1969 in a four-game sweep of the St. Louis Blues, it was John Ferguson who scored the winning goal. In the fourth game of the series, he took a pass from Ralph Backstrom at 3:03 of the third period and beat goalie Glenn Hall by giving him a shoulder shift and then putting a shot into the net. The goal gave the

Habs a 2–1 win and a road victory that clinched the championship. Ferguson had set an NHL playoff record in the '69 playoffs with a total of 80 penalty minutes, but his clutch goal proved once again that he was much more than just a tough guy.

FERGUSON'S CANADIENS STATS:	GP	G	A	P	PIM
regular season	500	145	158	303	1,214
playoffs	85	20	18	38	260

STANLEY CUPS: 5

TERRY HARPER

As a YOUNG man Terry Harper suffered third-degree burns in a fire. The damage to his arms, chest, stomach and legs required extensive skin grafting over a seven-year period. Completely immobilized for a month, he was fortunate that his legs suffered less severely than his arms and chest. Although this terrible accident weakened him considerably, Harper was determined to play hockey again. One of his doctors was quite encouraging. (Skating, it was hoped, would help to rebuild his leg muscles). His family moved to Vancouver from his hometown of Regina, Saskatchewan, but Harper went back home in 1957 to begin his career with the Regina Pats, a Montreal junior affiliate. His team — which featured future Habs like Bill Hicke and Red Berenson — made it to the Memorial Cup finals against another Montreal affiliate, the Junior Canadiens, which also featured future big-league Canadiens such as Gilles Tremblay and Ralph Backstrom. The Pats lost the junior title but by 1960 the 6'1", 200-pound Harper earned himself an invitation to the Montreal training camp.

For the next three seasons, Harper spent time in the minors (with the Montreal Royals, Hull-Ottawa Canadiens and the Quebec Aces) before being brought up to the big team for the 1963–64 season. (In '62–'63 he played in 14 games for the Habs when Tom Johnson was injured.) The Montreal organization knew it had an NHL player in Harper, switching him to forward one year to hide him from the prying eyes of other teams. When the Canadiens wanted to change their blue line corps, they added new defencemen like Harper, J. C. Tremblay, Jacques Laperriere and later Ted Harris. This collection of young blueliners joined hold-over Jean-Guy Talbot to form the nucleus of the Habs defence. Together they

shared four Stanley Cup wins between 1965 and 1969. Harper excelled in the NHL because he could play a strong defensive game. Lacking though he was in finesse, he could clear traffic in his own end. Any opposing forward who stayed in front of the Montreal net would likely get a visit from Harper. His highest point total with the Habs was 22, a mark he achieved twice in consecutive years, starting in 1969–70. Although his skating was hampered due to his accident as a youngster, he was as tough as any player in the NHL — if not a very good fighter. Perhaps under-appreciated by Montreal fans at the Forum, he was invaluable during tough games out of town.

Harper had a great season in 1969–70 when he was free of nagging injuries. He got into 75 of the Canadiens' 76 games played, recording 18 assists. The Habs missed the playoffs that year — many of the older players were moved out afterwards — but Harper stayed, notching 21 assists and one goal during the 1970–71 season and then six assists in 20 games during the '71 playoffs. His strong defensive play helped the Habs overcome the mighty Boston Bruins in the first round. Later he was instrumental in handling the explosive Chicago Black Hawks in the finals. He played one more year in Montreal, although he didn't like new coach Scotty Bowman. Harper declined a contract extension and asked for a deal. He was sent to Los Angeles and was named captain of the Kings in 1973. After a three-season stay in Los Angeles, Harper was dealt to Detroit as part of the package of players that brought Marcel Dionne to the West Coast. He would play for St. Louis and Colorado before retiring after the 1980–81 season. He played in 1,066 career games.

Terry Harper was a first team all-star in the Eastern Professional Hockey League for the 1961–62 season when he played for the Hull-Ottawa Canadiens. [HB]

Terry Harper (#19) looks to help out during an attack on net by the Maple Leafs. A 1963 brawl featuring Harper and Bob Pulford of Toronto in the penalty box at Maple Leaf Gardens led to the formation of separate "sin bins" in the NHL. (HB)

HARPER'S CANADIENS STATS:	GP	G	A	P	PIM
regular season	554	14	112	126	805
playoffs	94	4	12	16	116

STANLEY CUPS: 5

TED HARRIS

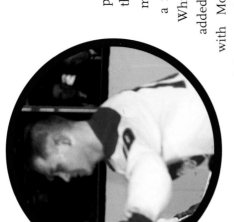

FOR THE LONGEST time defenceman Ted Harris was a minor-league player in professional hockey. He might have stayed there if the Montreal Canadiens hadn't come along. The Habs wanted to beef up the blue line for the 1964–65 season. (They had added left-winger and former minor pro John Ferguson the previous year.) Harris had just come off a great season in the American Hockey League. He had won the Eddie Shore Award as the best defenceman and was named to the first all-star team as a member of the Cleveland Barons. (He had played many years in Springfield, where a former NHL star, the demanding Shore, coached him.) The Canadiens felt they were on the verge of recapturing the Stanley Cup after a five-year drought and believed a rough and tough defender would help them immensely. They acquired Harris in June of 1963. After he played one more season in the minors (with Cleveland) his good performance got him up to Montreal the following season.

Harris was comfortable knowing that he wouldn't find himself in the limelight. Best described as a quiet soldier, he was nevertheless capable of on-ice belligerence to help a teammate in trouble or to handle large NHL forwards. He soon developed a feared reputation as one of the better fighters in the league. As a result, Harris gained confidence in his play. In one of his more celebrated fights, Harris took on heavyweight Orland Kurtenbach of the New York Rangers on the opening night of the 1966–67 season. Harris cut his opponent with a left-right combination. But he was much more than just a tough defenceman. He had learned how to carry the puck and make a good pass. (He had eight goals and 30 assists one year in Springfield). Shore had taught Harris how to play his position on the blue line and how to take the man out. One night, while he was in the minors with Springfield, Harris was put on a forward line with fellow defencemen Bill White and Bob McCord. He scored once and added two assists in a game against Buffalo. But with Montreal, Harris emphasized the game's defensive side — 25 points was his highest total as a Hab — and he did this with great consistency for as long as he was with the Canadiens. His long reach and size (6'2", 183 pounds) made him an imposing figure, and his style of play earned him respect around the league.

As a four-time winner of the AHL championship (the Calder Cup), Harris knew what it took to win. The Habs won the Stanley Cup in his first year with the team. They repeated as champs the following year, then lost the Cup to Toronto in 1967. Two more Cups followed in 1968 and 1969. Harris scored a goal in the last game of the '69 final against St. Louis, which tied the game 1–1 early in the third period. The Habs went on to sweep the series with a 2–1 win. However, the Habs missed the playoffs the next season, so changes were in the offing. With a young Serge Savard looking for a regular role on the Montreal blue line, Harris was dealt to the Minnesota North Stars, who wanted a mature defenceman — he was 34 at the time — to steady their defensive corps. He had a 30-point season for Minnesota in 1971–72 and went on to play for Detroit, St. Louis and Philadelphia before he retired. He was with the Flyers when they won their second consecutive Stanley Cup in 1975.

A native of Winnipeg, Manitoba, where he played junior hockey, Harris coached the NHL North Stars for 179 games after his retirement. The Minnesota club won only 49 of those contests.

HARRIS' CANADIENS STATS:	GP	G	A	P	PIM
regular season	407	18	95	113	576
playoffs	60	1	12	13	158
STANLEY CUPS: 4					

Ted Harris keeps a close watch on Toronto's Dave Keon. Harris was named to the NHL's second all-star team in 1968–69 when he had seven goals, 18 assists and 102 penalty minutes in 76 games played. (HB)

Facing page: *Ted Harris (#10) spent seven seasons in the minor leagues before the Montreal Canadiens gave him a chance in the NHL in 1965. He was named the best defenceman in the AHL in 1964 when he played for the Cleveland Barons.* (HB)

CHARLIE HODGE

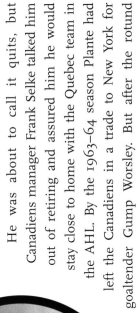

CHARLIE HODGE was born on July 28, 1933, in Lachine, Quebec. His father John soon realized that the youngster's only chance to play hockey was to be a goalie. Charlie was too small — he grew to only 5'6" and 150 pounds — to consider any other position. His father built a net in the basement of their home and took shots with tennis balls while his son played in goal. As Charlie moved up the ranks, John followed him but wouldn't live to see his son make it to the NHL. Sam Pollock recruited Charlie to the Montreal Canadiens. John would have been proud to see that Charlie persevered to become an NHL netminder.

Hodge's junior career in Montreal saw him named to numerous all-star teams and play on a Memorial Cup-winning squad in 1949–50 along with future Habs Dickie Moore and Don Marshall. Afterwards Hodge seemed destined to play out his professional hockey days in the minors, even though he was the Habs' number one replacement for injured players. It was difficult for Hodge to take the number one job away from Jacques Plante, but he respected the Canadiens netminder very much and credited Plante with giving him the confidence to use a face mask, a piece of equipment that helped him immensely in his career. Hodge played for the Habs as early as the 1953–54 season when he won seven games in 14 appearances. He got 12 starts in 1957–58 (winning eight times) and then got only three starts before the 1960–61 season, even though he was credited with a couple of Stanley Cup wins in 1959 and 1960. He played in 30 games in '60–'61 — posting a very respectable 18–8–4 record with four shutouts — but was back in the minors for the next two seasons (with the Quebec Aces of the American Hockey League). The experienced Hodge had been available to all the other NHL teams for the $20,000 draft fee, but they all passed up the opportunity, including the sad-sack Boston Bruins.

He was about to call it quits, but Canadiens manager Frank Selke talked him out of retiring and assured him he would stay close to home with the Quebec team in the AHL. By the 1963–64 season Plante had left the Canadiens in a trade to New York for goaltender Gump Worsley. But after the rotund Worsley was injured early in the season, Hodge was summoned to Montreal. This time Hodge wouldn't give up the net and played in 62 contests, winning 33 games on the way to a first-place finish for the Habs. In addition, Hodge won the Vezina Trophy by edging out Chicago's Glenn Hall by two less goals. On the last night of the season, Hodge allowed just one goal by Camille Henry of the Rangers in a 2–1 win that also clinched first place for the Habs. The Toronto Maple Leafs shattered Hodge's dream season in the playoffs, but he proved once and for all that he was an NHL goaltender. Though one of the smallest goalies of his era, Hodge was fearless and would throw his body recklessly to stop a puck.

Hodge was with the Canadiens when they won the Cup in 1965, although Worsley played in the seventh game of the finals against Chicago. That 1964–65 season, he played in 53 games, winning 26. He stayed with Montreal for another two years, but Worsley was clearly taking over. Rogie Vachon was another goaltender on the horizon. The NHL's great expansion in 1967 would give Hodge another chance to stay in the NHL. The Oakland Seals selected Hodge in the expansion draft, and he played in 58 games for the new club in the West Division during the 1967–68 campaign. He played two more seasons in Oakland. The 1970–71 season saw him play for the new Vancouver Canucks, who had selected him in another expansion draft. He won 15 of 35 appearances and posted a 3.42 goals against average for the first-year club.

Charlie Hodge recorded eight shutouts during the 1963–64 season, four of them against the Toronto Maple Leafs. (HB)

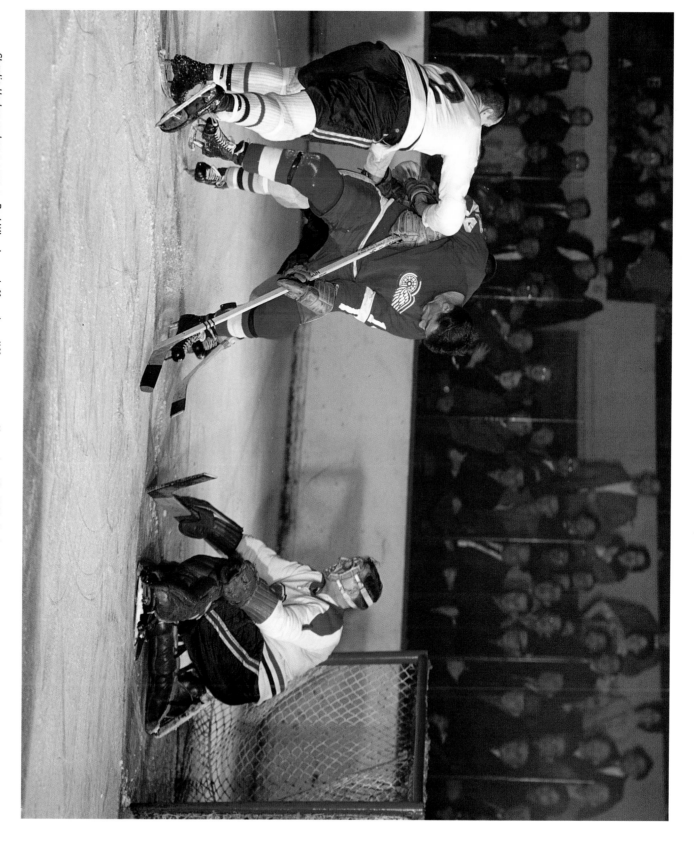

Charlie Hodge makes a save on Red Wing Larry Jeffrey. In a different game on November 10, 1963, Hodge gave up Gordie Howe's 545th career goal when the Detroit Red Wings hosted the Canadiens at the Olympia. It was a short-handed effort by the Detroit star, the third goal of a 3–0 Red Wing victory. (HB)

HODGE'S CANADIENS STATS:

	GP	Wins	Losses	Ties	Shutouts	GA
regular season	237	117	71	39	21	2.46
playoffs	16	7	7	–	0	2.39

STANLEY CUPS: 4

JACQUES LAPERRIERE

THE MONTREAL CANADIENS first spotted defenceman Jacques Laperriere as a 14-year-old playing hockey in Quebec's Rouyn-Noranda region. The Habs chief scout at the time, Lou Passador, had been alerted by another scout about the lanky (6'2", 180-pound) blueliner. Passador took a look for himself and quickly agreed that Laperriere was a top prospect. Laperriere was able to play outdoors a lot, and his skills kept improving. He was one of 10 children (six boys, four girls) and he began playing hockey at the age of six. After the Habs spotted him, he began playing for a midget team they sponsored. By the age of 16 he was playing major junior hockey for the Hull-Ottawa Canadiens. As soon as Laperriere entered the Canadiens' developmental system, he became known as another of Sam Pollock's French-Canadian prospects. The big defender's career would prove Pollock was right to guide Laperriere into the NHL.

In his final year of junior, Laperriere played for the OHA's Montreal Jr. Canadiens and set a league record for defencemen by scoring 20 goals in 48 games played. The record stood until Bobby Orr broke it years later. He also had 37 points in the 1961–62 season, which brought him closer to joining the Habs. But the Canadiens didn't wish to rush the youngster and started him out playing in the Eastern Professional Hockey League (EPHL) with Hull-Ottawa (eight goals and 19 assists in 40 games). He did, however, get into six games with the Canadiens in 1962–63 after Lou Fontinato got injured. By the start of the 1963–64 season, Laperriere was ready for the NHL and played in 65 games, scoring two goals and 28 assists to win the rookie of the year award. He got into a big brawl with Chicago's Stan Mikita, earning over 30 penalty minutes for that one scrap alone. The young defenceman knew he was being tested, but he showed great poise and an ability to control the action in his own end. He would join the attack carefully. Since it was low and hard, his shot from the point provided the Canadiens with some offence. He was also a top shot blocker, with a long reach that allowed him to poke-check opponents very effectively — just as his hero Doug Harvey had done in his great career with the Canadiens.

Laperriere was given sweater number two — which Harvey had worn — and like his idol, he was good at setting up goals for his teammates. He had eight seasons of 20 or more assists — his best total was 31 in 1969–70 — and while he was not overly aggressive, Laperriere wasn't afraid of the physical play required from an NHL defenceman. The solid blow of his bodychecks could be devastating. At times Laperriere would lose his confidence after making a bad play or two, but he learned to overcome his nervousness. He was named the best defender in the NHL in 1965–66 when he played in only 57 games but still managed to get six goals and 22 assists. He broke his leg in the 1965 semifinal against the Maple Leafs, but the Habs still managed to win the Stanley Cup. The '65 Norris Trophy win was his only one, but he also made the first all-star team on two occasions and, with a plus 78, he was the league leader in plus/minus in 1972–73. He was the backbone of the Canadiens blue line that won six Stanley Cups. In 1970–71, despite a broken wrist, Laperriere had 13 points in 20 playoff games, which helped the Habs to a surprise Cup win. In 1973 he managed to play 10 games in the postseason wearing a special helmet with a face mask to protect a broken nose, and he won his final Cup with the Canadiens.

Laperriere stayed in the NHL until the 1973–74 season when a knee injury suffered in Boston ended his career. He then tried being a head coach at the junior level but didn't like it. He found a niche, however, as a high-quality assistant coach — he didn't relish the role of head coach — with the Canadiens (winning two more Cups in that role), the Boston Bruins and the New York Islanders. Most recently, he was working behind the bench as an assistant coach with the New Jersey Devils during their 2003–04 season. Laperriere has helped to train quality NHL defencemen with invaluable work in moulding a blue line brigade. His son Daniel (also a defenceman) played in the NHL with St. Louis and Ottawa. Laperriere was elected to the Hockey Hall of Fame in 1987.

Above: When Laperriere was named rookie of the year for the 1963–64 season, he beat out teammate John Ferguson for the award. [HB]

Facing page: While playing junior hockey with the Montreal Jr. Canadiens, Jacques Laperriere would play as much as 40 minutes per game. He recorded 57 points in the 1961–62 junior season. [HB]

Laperriere battles Toronto's George Armstrong along the boards. As an assistant coach with the Canadiens, Laperriere won two Stanley Cups. The first came in 1986 with Jean Perron as head coach and the second came in 1993 with Jacques Demers as head coach. (HB)

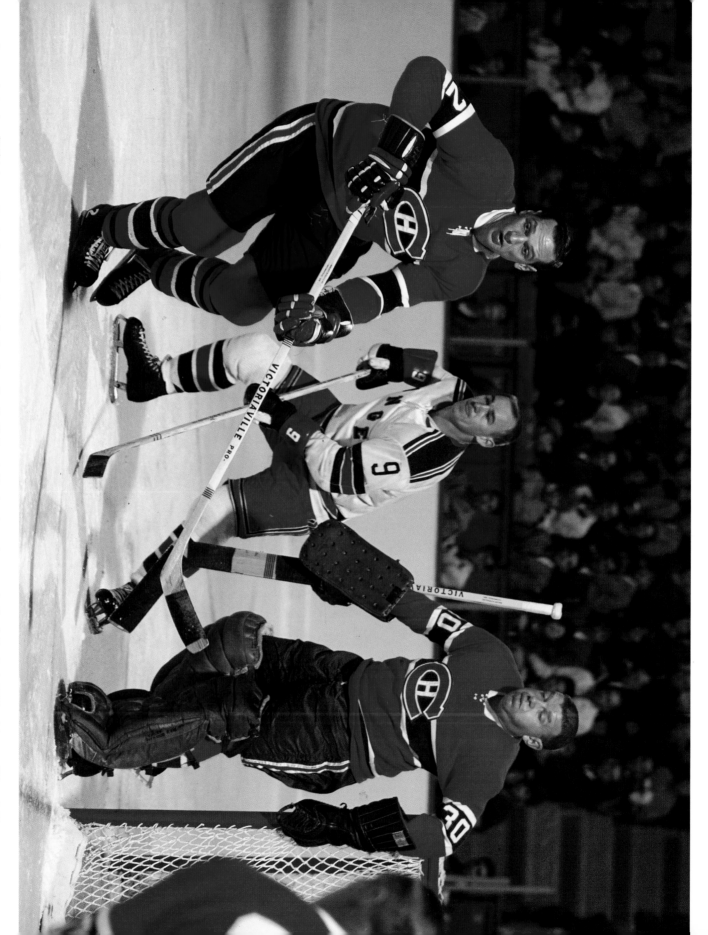

Jacques Laperriere (#2) helps goaltender Gump Worsley defend against New York's Reggie Fleming. Laperriere won the Norris Trophy in 1966, edging out Chicago's Pierre Pilote for the award. A year earlier, Pilote beat out Laperriere as the NHL's best defenceman. (HB)

LAPERRIERE'S CANADIENS STATS:

	GP	G	A	P	PIM
regular season	691	40	242	282	674
playoffs	88	9	22	31	101

STANLEY CUPS: 6

CLAUDE LAROSE

LIKE MANY YOUNG BOYS, Claude Larose dreamed of playing in the NHL with the Montreal Canadiens. The native of Hearst, Ontario, first realized his dream in 1962–63 (at the age of 20) when he got into four contests with the team. Larose started in the Montreal organization by playing for the Peterborough Petes of the Ontario Hockey Association, scoring 36 goals in 46 games in 1960–61, his best year as a junior. Larose gave credit to coaches Sam Pollock and Scotty Bowman for helping him refine his game as he went through the Montreal developmental system. Not ready to jump directly to the professional ranks, Larose apprenticed in the minors with the Hull-Ottawa Canadiens and then with the Omaha Knights of the Central Hockey League (CHL). He split 1963–64 with Montreal (21 games, one goal) and Omaha (47 games, 27 goals). Montreal coach Toe Blake heard that Larose was one of the best players in the minors. Larose got a taste of winning: Omaha took the CHL championship, helped by Larose's eight goals (to lead all players) in the playoffs.

Larose's game centred on being a grinding right-winger who could pot the occasional goal. He was not a big man (6', 180 pounds) but he was solid, not afraid to mix it up with bigger and tougher players like Vic Hadfield of New York. Blake felt Larose, willing to scrap as needed, had the size for success in the NHL. He got his first break when Bernie Geoffrion retired from the Habs in 1964. He showed a good scoring touch early on in the 1964–65 season, playing alongside centre Ralph Backstrom and left-winger John Ferguson. Being surrounded by good players helped Larose make the transition to the big club. With one third of the season still to go, he scored 21 goals but couldn't score another after that. He contributed only one assist in 13 playoff games, but the Habs still took the Stanley Cup in the '65 postseason. Larose

scored 15 goals and earned 33 points the next season but upped those totals to 19 goals and 35 assists in the 1966–67 season.

The 1967–68 season was a bad one for Larose: he split his time between Montreal (two goals in 42 games) and Houston of the CHL (six goals in 10 games). In the playoffs, however, he scored well (three goals, five assists in 13 games) to help the Habs take the Cup once again. He was likely ticketed for the minors the next season, but the Canadiens dealt him to Minnesota. Under less pressure, he scored well for the North Stars and had seasons of 25 and 24 goals, plus 215 penalty minutes. By the 1969–70 season he was captain of the Minnesota club, but suddenly the Habs wanted him back. He scored 10 times for the Canadiens in the 1970–71 season and helped the Habs pull off a major upset as they took the Cup with series wins over Boston, Minnesota and Chicago. He scored 20 goals for the Habs the next season and 11 the following year that closed with another Cup win. He broke his leg in the last contest of the '73 finals against Chicago when he slid into the goalpost near goalie Ken Dryden as he tried to check Black Hawks winger Dennis Hull. Instead of going to the hospital, he flew home with the team after the game.

Larose recovered well enough from his broken leg to score 17 goals in 39 games (on only 71 shots taken) of his last season in Montreal. (By this point, he wasn't getting along well with Habs coach Bowman.) Early in the 1974–75 season, he was dealt once again, this time to the St. Louis Blues. He was happy to go, since in Montreal he wouldn't be playing much. He enjoyed his best goal-scoring year in 1976–77 when he had 29. He played just one more year before retiring. Larose made the most of his talents and carved out a respectable NHL career.

LAROSE'S CANADIENS STATS:	GP	G	A	P	PIM
regular season	529	117	123	240	544
playoffs	82	11	16	27	118
STANLEY CUPS: 5					

The Montreal Canadiens re-acquired Claude Larose [#11] from the Minnesota North Stars in 1970 in exchange for Bobby Rousseau. Larose had his best NHL season with Minnesota in 1969–70 when he scored 25 goals and added 37 assists. (HB)

JACQUES LEMAIRE

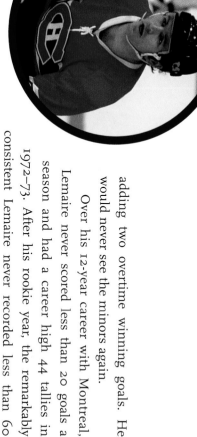

As soon as Jacques Lemaire joined the Montreal Canadiens system, he was clearly an offensive dynamo. Not a big man at 5'10" and 180 pounds, he possessed a bullet shot — developed by shooting a steel puck — and tremendous skating skills. Even as a junior — when he recorded 104 points (41 goals, 63 assists) in just 42 games with the Lachine Maroons in the Quebec Junior Hockey League — Lemaire was obviously going to fill the net. As a player with the Montreal Jr. Canadiens of the OHA, he scored 91 goals in 116 games. (Forty-one markers came in his last year of junior in 1965–66.) With no need to rush the young centre into the NHL, the Habs sent him to Houston of the CPHL for some seasoning in 1966–67.

Lemaire didn't get off to a great start with the Apollos but finished his first year with 19 goals and 49 points in 69 contests. He had many chances to score but had trouble following through. Lemaire loosened up when the coach told him to kill penalties. He was part of a new group of young players — including Serge Savard, Mickey Redmond, Garry Monahan, Danny Grant and Rogie Vachon — that the Canadiens were grooming for their big-league roster. Lemaire learned about playing left wing from the Habs' quality centres and about checking and playing the defensive side of the game. Even though he was constantly improving, he began to believe that he was going to be a minor leaguer for a long time. But an injury to Henri Richard in the 1967–68 season gave Lemaire an opportunity, which he made the most of with 22 goals and 20 assists in 69 games, playing on a line with Bobby Rousseau and Dick Duff. He lost out on the Calder Trophy to Boston's Derek Sanderson, but he made up for it in the playoffs: in the 1968 postseason, the exceptional rookie scored seven goals and 13 points in 13 playoff games, adding two overtime winning goals. He would never see the minors again.

Over his 12-year career with Montreal, Lemaire never scored less than 20 goals a season and had a career high 44 tallies in 1972–73. After his rookie year, the remarkably consistent Lemaire never recorded less than 60 points a season. Surprisingly, he never joined an NHL all-star team, never won a major award and never played on a Canadian national team. (He was overlooked for the 1972 Canada-Russia series and the first ever Canada Cup in 1976.) But Lemaire kept winning Stanley Cups (eight in total) and developed a reputation for being a clutch performer. He scored two Cup-winning goals (1971, 1977) and accumulated a total of 61 postseason goals. Not a bruising type of forward, Lemaire played in a clean manner. With speed and shot his two greatest assets, he knew he must keep moving to be most effective. The opposition had a difficult time keeping him in check.

After the Habs won the Stanley Cup in 1979, Lemaire decided he would call it a career, despite having another great playoff (11 goals and 23 points in 16 games). Fans will remember that he set up teammate Guy Lafleur for an important goal against the Boston Bruins in the semifinals. The two Canadien stars combined for one of the most memorable power-play goals in history. (Bruins coach Don Cherry was caught with too many men on the ice, and this goal allowed the Habs to tie the seventh game and win it in overtime). Lemaire had spent the last few years playing on one of the best lines in NHL history, with Lafleur and left-winger Steve Shutt. The line could have kept going, and the Canadiens might have added another Cup or two to their four straight ones between 1976 and 1979, but Lemaire's departure ended any hope of that happening. The Canadiens thought

Jacques Lemaire scored an overtime-winning goal in the Stanley Cup finals when he beat Glenn Hall of St. Louis on May 5, 1968, to give the Habs a 3–2 win. [DM]

Jacques Lemaire lets go of a howitzer past Bob Baun of the Maple Leafs. Lemaire was seen as the defensive player when he centred on a line with Steve Shutt and Guy Lafleur but still found time to contribute 61 assists and 97 points in 1977–78. (HB)

they might have a replacement in Pierre Larouche, but he was nowhere near Lemaire's calibre.

Lemaire started his coaching career in Switzerland and eventually coached the Habs for two seasons before deciding he didn't want to coach in a market that was so focused on hockey. (He was a big help to the Habs when they won the Cup in 1993.) Those who knew Lemaire weren't surprised that he would try coaching: as a player he was always questioning strategy. He coached New Jersey and helped the one-time laughingstock Devils win their first

ever Stanley Cup in 1995. In getting the Devils their first ever title, Lemaire out-duelled his former Montreal coach Scotty Bowman, who was then coaching the Detroit Red Wings. He returned to the Montreal organization one last time, but the lure of coaching got him out to Minnesota, where a new club was taking shape. Remarkably, that team made the playoffs in 2002–03, just three years into its existence.

Lemaire was elected to the Hall of Fame in 1984.

Even though he was earning around $150,000 with Montreal in 1979, Lemaire decided to give that up to begin his coaching career in Switzerland, where he would earn a reported $75,000 tax-free American dollars plus other perks. (HB)

Montreal moment:

The Montreal Canadiens had done a great job to advance to the finals in 1971, beating the Boston Bruins and the Minnesota North Stars before meeting the Chicago Black Hawks. The Habs faced trouble when Chicago jumped out to a 2–0 series lead, but the Habs evened the score, and then the teams split the next two. The seventh game was played at the Chicago Stadium. The Canadiens were down 2–0 when Jacques Lemaire wound up for a shot just as he crossed centre ice. His blast bounced past a shocked Tony Esposito in the Black Hawks net at 14:18 of the second. The Habs were on the board. Henri Richard tied the game just over four minutes later, and Chicago never recovered. Richard scored again to win the contest 3–2, but none of it would have happened had it not been for Lemaire's stunning goal.

Lemaire takes a shot on the Toronto Maple Leafs. [DM]

LEMAIRE'S CANADIENS STATS:	GP	G	A	P	PIM
regular season	853	366	469	835	217
playoffs	145	61	78	139	63

STANLEY CUPS: 8

FRANK MAHOVLICH

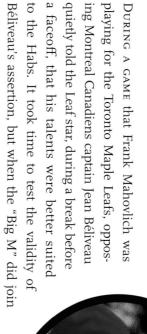

DURING A GAME that Frank Mahovlich was playing for the Toronto Maple Leafs, opposing Montreal Canadiens captain Jean Béliveau quietly told the Leaf star, during a break before a faceoff, that his talents were better suited to the Habs. It took time to test the validity of Béliveau's assertion, but when the "Big M" did join the Canadiens in 1971, it was clear that his skills would shine more in Montreal than they ever had in Toronto. From the moment he arrived in Montreal, Mahovlich felt at ease, and his numbers showed that the superstar was back on his game.

Mahovlich came to the Canadiens from the Detroit Red Wings on January 10, 1971. The Red Wings were going nowhere fast in the 1970–71 season and decided to trade one good player for some quality, quantity and youth. (Detroit received Mickey Redmond, Guy Charron and Bill Collins in return.) It was the second blockbuster deal Mahovlich had been involved in since 1968 when the Leafs dealt him to the Red Wings. Mahovlich was pleased to get out of the pressure cooker in Toronto and responded with a 49-goal season in 1968–69, his first full year in Motown. His total dipped slightly to 38 the next season, but he was still an effective player for an improving Detroit club. The next season was nothing short of a disaster for the Red Wings, and the Canadiens were pleased to sweep in and take Mahovlich, since they also needed a boost. Montreal manager Sam Pollock had always been a big fan of the large (6', 205-pound) left-winger and got Mahovlich to report right away. Happy to be greeted at the airport by Ron Caron and coach Al MacNeil, he scored a goal in his first game as a Hab, against the Minnesota North Stars. Mahovlich was also thrilled to join his younger brother Peter, who was also acquired by the Habs in a deal with Detroit.

Much to his surprise the Canadiens weren't nearly as offensive in style as Mahovlich thought, but he still had more room to manoeuvre than he ever had in Toronto. He scored 17 goals and 41 points in 38 games to finish the '70–'71 season but really caught fire in the playoffs when he established a new mark for most points (since surpassed) in the postseason with 27 (14 goals, 13

assists). It was easy to see that Mahovlich was happy in his new surroundings. He played with his brother through much of the playoffs. The dynamic duo scored many key goals and kept the Habs alive with a terrific performance in the sixth game of the finals when the Canadiens came from behind to win 4–3 and force a seventh game in Chicago, which Montreal won. Mahovlich used his great playoff performance as a springboard for the next season when he scored 43 goals and a career high 96 points. (The New York Rangers knocked the Habs off in the playoffs.)

The 1972–73 season saw the Canadiens regain the Stanley Cup. Mahovlich was superb again with 38 goals and 93 points during the regular season. He scored his 500th career goal on March 21, 1973. With the Habs clinching first place, he scored the game-winning goal on Vancouver netminder Dunc Wilson. Mahovlich had taken five shots before his goal, including a breakaway, but Wilson turned them all back. He fanned on the shot as he tried to whip in a Henri Richard pass, but the puck floated by Wilson for the milestone marker. In his 1,105th career contest, Mahovlich became the fifth player in NHL history to reach the 500-goal milestone. In the playoffs, the Habs beat Buffalo, Philadelphia and Chicago to take the championship back to Montreal. Mahovlich had 23 points in 17 games and enjoyed his sixth and final Cup win. In honour of his 500th career goal, he was given a special night in Montreal on November 28, 1973, before a game against Los Angeles. Among the gifts he received was the first set of Olympic coins issued for the 1976 Montreal Summer Games.

Mahovlich played one more season in Montreal and scored 31 goals and 80 points for the 1973–74 campaign. The Habs couldn't keep the Stanley Cup, losing to the Rangers, and Mahovlich's contract was up at the end of the season. Knowing it was going to be his last deal before retirement, Mahovlich couldn't turn down the lucrative contract presented to him by the Toronto Toros of the World Hockey Association. He played four seasons for the Toros and finished his career with 622 professional goals.

When he first joined the Montreal Canadiens, the team was on the road and had few sweaters available, so Frank Mahovlich wore number 10 for one game before he switched to his more familiar 27 [DM]

123

Frank Mahovlich scored his 50th career playoff goal the night the Canadiens won the Stanley Cup with a 6–4 victory over Chicago on May 10, 1973. [London Life-Portnoy/HHOF]

For the record:

Frank Mahovlich became the first Canadiens player to take a penalty shot during the Stanley Cup playoffs. The "Big M" was foiled on May 16, 1971, by Chicago netminder Tony Esposito during the sixth game of the finals. Mahovlich missed his chance — the shot was awarded because Esposito threw his stick — at 3:44 of the first period. However, he scored once and added two assists to help the Habs win the contest 4–3, forcing a seventh game in Chicago, which the Canadiens won 3–2 on May 18, 1971, to take the Cup.

MAHOVLICH'S CANADIENS STATS:	GP	G	A	P	PIM
regular season	263	129	181	310	145
playoffs	49	27	31	58	26

STANLEY CUPS: 2

CLAUDE PROVOST

When Toe Blake took over as coach of the Montreal Canadiens to start the 1955–56 season, he was intent on bringing in some new players. One was Montreal native Claude Provost, a sturdy right-winger who would be a part of the Canadiens for the next 15 seasons. (Other newcomers Blake inserted into the team included Andre Pronovost and Phil Goyette who were finished his junior career with Shawinigan and was likely headed to the minors to learn the pro game, but he made the Habs and played in 60 games for the club in his rookie year, scoring 13 goals and 29 points. He scored his first goal against Terry Sawchuk of the Boston Bruins with a long shot from centre ice that fooled the veteran netminder. The Habs won the Stanley Cup in '56, Provost contributing three goals and three assists. The championship was the first of five straight titles to which Provost contributed. It was certainly not a bad way to start an NHL career!

Provost was a good goal scorer as a junior, netting 45 one season, but he soon realized that his role with the Canadiens would be as a checker. The team had plenty of goal scorers but needed players for the unglamorous job of dealing with the opposition's best player and helping to kill penalties. Provost didn't consider himself a great skater, and he didn't own a rocket of a shot. He had no real finesse. Even his brother once told him he would never make the NHL. But he was good at putting a shot on goal, and he really understood the game, as any top checker must. He skated with short bursts of speed and made the safe play. While his main role was defensive, he usually scored around 16 goals a season. However, his breakthrough came in 1962–63 with 33 goals, a career high. He had an even better year in 1964–65 when he scored 27 goals and added 37 assists, which earned him a

put on line with Provost.) The lantern-jawed Provost had just

place on the first all-star team. In the '65 playoffs, Provost scored perhaps the biggest goal of the "Quiet Dynasty" when he eliminated the defending champion Toronto Maple Leafs with an overtime-winning goal to win the semifinal series. He then did a masterful job of checking Bobby Hull in the finals. The Canadiens took back the Stanley Cup and went on to win four Cups in five years.

Unlike many other players, Provost checked Hull in a clean, efficient manner, a task he undertook without complaint. Even Hull said he respected the job Provost did. In his last few years with Montreal, Provost didn't score more than 19 goals but remained valuable to the Canadiens. He had a great playoff in 1968 (10 points in 13 games) and in the 1969 semifinals versus Boston, Provost set up Jean Béliveau with a perfect pass that the big Montreal centre roofed over Gerry Cheevers' shoulder. That goal — which knocked the Bruins out of the playoffs in six games — was the only overtime winner Béliveau ever scored. In Provost's last season in Montreal, the Habs missed the playoffs (a first for Provost), which led to changes to the old guard. The Canadiens gave Provost a chance to keep playing in the NHL when they sold him to Los Angeles, but the veteran declined to go and retired instead, thus playing his entire career in Montreal.

Apart from his all-star selection and nine championship rings, Provost was rarely recognized around the NHL for his contribution. But in 1968, he was named the first winner of the Bill Masterton Trophy for his dedication to hockey. A worthy recipient of the award, he should get into the Hockey Hall of Fame, an honour that has eluded him. In 1984 he passed away suddenly at the age of 49.

A very durable performer, Claude Provost missed only 35 games over his first eight seasons in the NHL. (HB)

For the record:

Claude Provost wasn't known for his goal-scoring, but he did contribute to the Habs' attack over his many years with the team. On the night of November 9, 1957, which ended in a 4–2 Canadiens victory, Provost set an NHL record by scoring a goal just four seconds into the start of the second period. Only one other player has matched that mark — Denis Savard of Chicago in 1986 — for fastest goal from the start of a period.

Claude Provost (#14) fights for position in front of Leafs' netminder Johnny Bower during an NHL All-Star game. A one-time first team all-star (for the 1964–65 season), Provost was nicknamed "Joe" by his teammates. (HB)

PROVOST'S CANADIENS STATS:	GP	G	A	P	PIM
regular season	1005	254	335	589	469
playoffs	126	25	38	63	86
STANLEY CUPS: 9					

HENRI RICHARD

HENRI RICHARD learned to play hockey with about 25 other boys on a small lake in North Montreal. Each player would do his best to hold on to the puck for as long as possible. One of the best at doing this was young Henri.

His older brother, Maurice, was a famous hockey player whose exploits with the Canadiens were legendary. But the boys' father, Onesime, would tell anyone who would listen that Henri would also make his mark in hockey. Ever since he was a little boy, all young Henri could think about was playing in the NHL and becoming a Montreal Canadien.

Henri was just eight years old when brother Maurice scored 50 goals in 50 games. He would attend Canadiens games with his parents and cry if they wouldn't take him to the Forum. Watching the games showed Henri what the Canadiens meant to the city of Montreal and the province of Quebec. He certainly respected what his heroic sibling had done for the team. But he was determined that nothing was going to stop him from playing in the NHL too. Richard shared characteristics with Maurice: they were both fiery and intense. But Henri was actually a better all-round player, although not as good a goal scorer. Not tall or large at 5'7" and 160 pounds, the square-jawed Richard still had a solid build — not to mention a temper that could be riled severely at times. The heart of his game was great skating and an ability to control the puck. He had a terrific wrist shot and a nose for getting to the net. When he attended his first camp in 1955, he was going to prove his skill to the Montreal management to get the job he so badly wanted.

Richard was 19 years old when he went to training camp. Nobody expected him to make the club. Although successful in junior hockey with the Montreal Jr. Canadiens (89 goals and 175 points in 98 games) he was likely going to need some time in the minors. However, he simply refused to give up the puck at the camp.

and soon he was in manager Frank Selke's office negotiating a contract with Maurice's help. Convinced that his brother was ready for the pros, the Rocket helped convince Selke to keep Henri on the team. Henri got the standard amount for rookies but also $5,000 in bonus money intended to show that the Canadiens were a

class organization. Selke never regretted his decision and came to consider Henri Richard as the Canadiens' most valuable player. To Henri, the deal meant a chance to play with his brother and fulfill a lifelong dream. Richard would soon prove he was worth every dollar.

Although Richard saw himself as a playmaker rather than a scorer, he got his share of goals, starting with 19 markers as a rookie. He scored 28 two years later and then was never under the 20 mark for eight of the next nine seasons. He became known as the "Pocket Rocket." He topped the NHL in assists with 52 in 1957–58. (He usually recorded an average 35 helpers a year.) In the early years of his career, Richard played on a line with his brother and Dickie Moore, one of the NHL's best lines. The team won five straight Stanley Cups, starting with Richard's rookie year. As Maurice's career started to wind down, Richard began to step out of his brother's large shadow to become a star in his own right. (The two were 15 years apart.) Richard had never tried to compete with his older brother and wanted to take care of himself on the ice. One night in Boston, Henri took on three large Bruins, including Fern Flaman, Jack Bionda and Leo Labine. That January 1, 1958, contest featured a big brawl. Richard came off the bench to battle Flaman to a draw, get the better of Bionda and cut Labine over the eye with a punch. Bruins general manager Lynn Patrick was very impressed with that performance! Richard had carved out his own place in the NHL with this display.

Henri Richard scored his first NHL goal against the New York Rangers goaltender Gump Worsley on October 15, 1955, in a 4–1 Montreal victory. (HB)

127

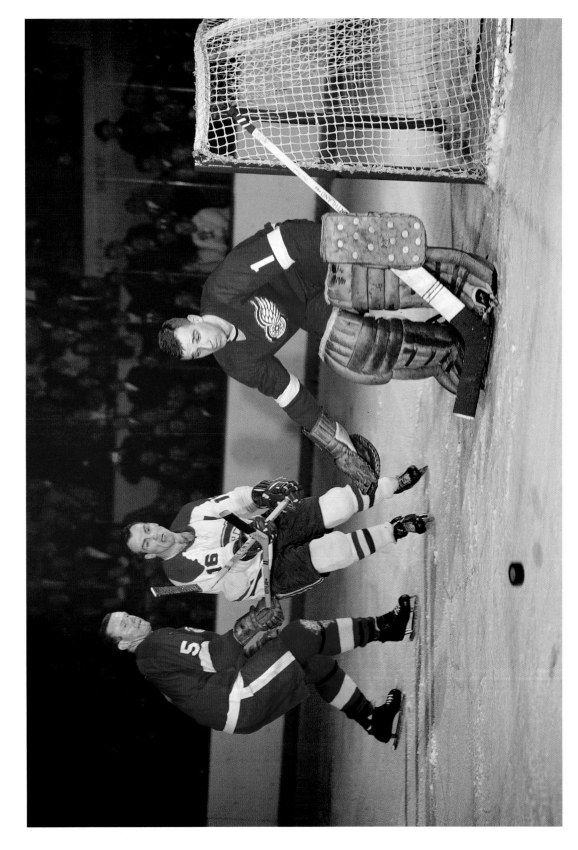

Richard is watched closely by Doug Barkley of Detroit in front of goaltender Roger Crozier. During the 1957–58 season, Richard finished second to teammate Dickie Moore in the point-scoring race (84 to 80) and was named as the first team all-star centre. (HB)

The team changed once Maurice retired. The Habs took a while to recover but when they did, Henri was front and centre with some great playoff performances. In the 1966 finals, Richard scored the Cup-winning goal in overtime — it really shouldn't have counted — by pushing the puck past Detroit goalie Roger Crozier. Richard repeated the feat in 1971 against Chicago. When Jean Béliveau retired, Richard was named captain. He accepted the Cup as captain in 1973 when the Habs knocked off the Black Hawks once again. It was his NHL record 11th and final Cup in a remarkable 20-year career.

In his last two years in Montreal, he feuded with coach Scotty Bowman. (He wasn't afraid to express an opinion that contradicted the coach.) He played in 16 games in 1974–75, his final season, recording 13 points. He was elected to the Hall of Fame in 1979.

Facing page: At the age of 37 Henri Richard signed a two-year contract that reportedly paid him $100,000 per season. (HB)

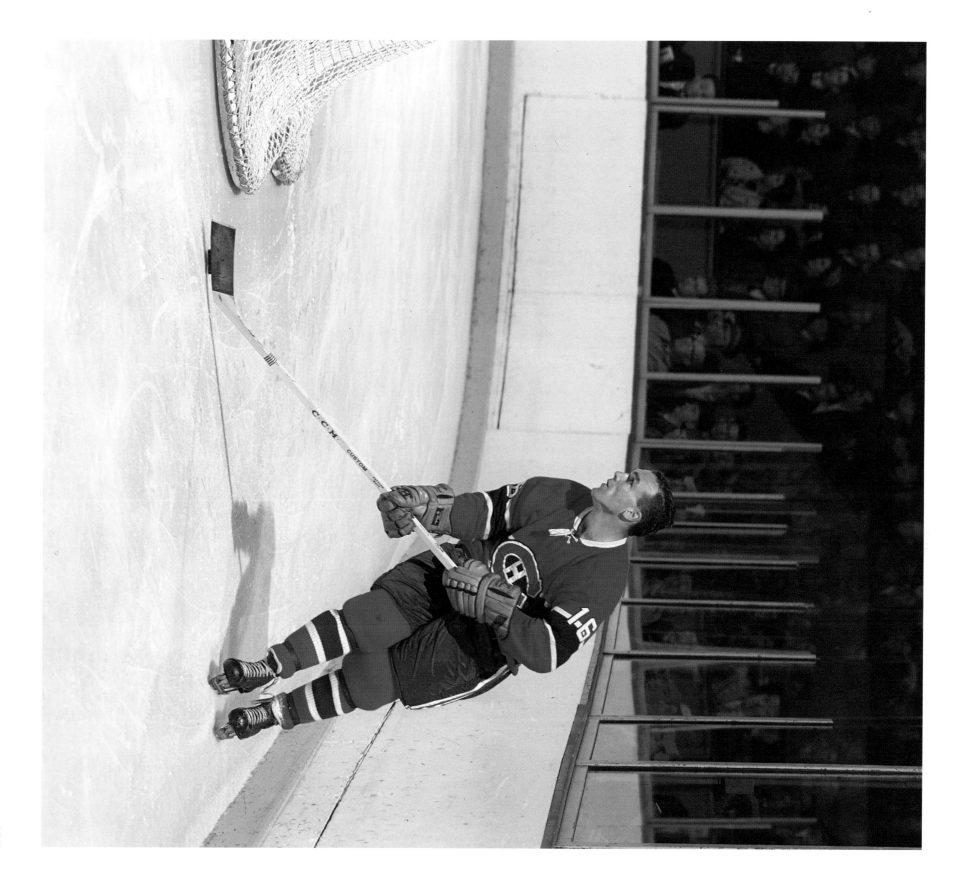

Henri Richard looks to score against Eddie Giacomin of the New York Rangers. Richard scored his 200th career goal against Eddie Johnston of the Boston Bruins on November 28, 1964. (HB)

RICHARD'S CANADIENS STATS:	GP	G	A	P	PIM
regular season	1,256	358	688	1,046	928
playoffs	180	49	80	129	181

STANLEY CUPS: 11

JIMMY ROBERTS

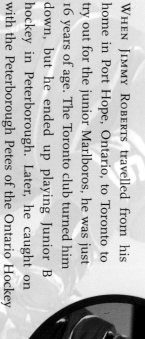

WHEN JIMMY ROBERTS travelled from his home in Port Hope, Ontario, to Toronto to try out for the junior Marlboros, he was just 16 years of age. The Toronto club turned him down, but he ended up playing junior B hockey in Peterborough. Later, he caught on with the Peterborough Petes of the Ontario Hockey Association for the 1958–59 season when he signed with the Montreal Canadiens, scoring two goals in 54 games as a defenceman. Under the tutelage of coach Scotty Bowman, Roberts and the team made the Memorial Cup finals in '59, although they lost to the Winnipeg Braves. He played another year in junior and then turned professional, first with the Montreal Royals and then with the Hull-Ottawa Canadiens of the Eastern Professional Hockey League. During the 1963–64 season, Roberts played for four professional teams — including 15 games as a Hab — and joined Omaha of the CHL for 46 games, scoring 18 times.

Roberts attended the Canadiens training camp in the fall of 1960 but was assigned to the Royals (where one of his teammates was future Hab defenceman Terry Harper). He would watch the Canadiens practise, thinking that he would never make the team. But then he caught a big break after switching to right wing. (The Habs knew they had too many prospects on the blue line and not enough up front.) While not large at 5'10" and 165 pounds, Roberts was robust in his play and became known as a top checker and penalty killer. He had good speed (a great quality for a defensive forward) and was willing to give up offence to play a sound defensive game. He hustled all the time to keep his job — even after he made the NHL in 1964–65 full-time — and

drove the opposition to distraction with his hitting. One such occasion came against Toronto on February 10, 1965, when the two teams engaged in a donnybrook. Roberts was the first off the bench, joining the fray because the Leafs had an extra man due to a delayed penalty against the Canadiens. Coach Toe Blake may have sent Roberts out to even the sides, but it was Roberts who was fined $125.

The plucky Montreal winger stayed with the team for the next three seasons — taking home the Stanley Cup twice, in 1965 and 1966 — but then went to the St. Louis Blues in the expansion draft of 1967. He joined other ex-Habs on the Blues squad, including Jean-Guy Talbot, Jacques Plante, Red Berenson, Doug Harvey, Dickie Moore and Bowman. Roberts played four full seasons for St. Louis (where he became popular), scoring respectably (59 goals in 320 games) before the Habs reacquired him in a deal during the 1971–72 season. (He rejoined Bowman, who was then coaching the Habs.) For the next five years, Roberts was a useful utility player for the Canadiens, winning three more Stanley Cups and scoring 14 times in 1973–74. His defensive skills and his ability to drop back and play on the blue line kept him in the NHL for almost his entire career. In his later years with Montreal, he showed players like Bob Gainey and Doug Jarvis how to excel in a primary checking role.

In 1977–78 Roberts went back to St. Louis for his final NHL season before becoming an assistant NHL coach for several teams. He was also a head coach in the American Hockey League as well as in the NHL with Buffalo, Hartford and St. Louis.

ROBERTS' CANADIENS STATS:	GP	G	A	P	PIM
regular season	611	63	100	163	299
playoffs	101	11	7	18	90

STANLEY CUPS: 5

Jimmy Roberts had his highest point total with Montreal during the 1972–73 season when he had 14 goals and 18 assists in 72 games played. (HB)

BOBBY ROUSSEAU

WHEN BOBBY ROUSSEAU was 12 years old he was presented with a trophy for excellence in baseball by Montreal hockey star Bernie Geoffrion. That meeting inspired the young man and cemented his desire to play for the Canadiens one day. As a native of Montreal and one of 12 children, he was under considerable pressure to succeed. (His brothers were good hockey players but not talented enough to make the NHL.) The strain got to Rousseau at times — he developed an ulcer at the age of 20 — but he persevered. Reading Norman Vincent Peale's *The Power of Positive Thinking* helped him overcome his insecurities.

Rousseau first came to prominence as a junior with the Hull-Ottawa Canadiens during the 1955–56 season when he scored 53 times in 44 games. He won a Memorial Cup with the team in 1958, contributing 17 points in 13 playoff games. He looked like a sure bet for a professional career in Montreal. Before he turned pro, the Habs lent him to the Canadian Olympic team for the 1960 Winter Games. (He had five goals and four assists in seven games, although Canada didn't win the gold medal.) He then joined the Hull-Ottawa club for the 1960–61 season, scoring 34 goals in 38 games, and also played 15 games for the Canadiens, scoring one goal against Jack McCartan of the New York Rangers, a goalie he faced at the Olympics. The next season saw Rousseau join the Habs for good. He won the Calder Trophy as the NHL's best rookie with a 21-goal and 24-assist performance, beating out Cliff Pennington of the Bruins with 144 out of 180 votes. Over the next two seasons, he had 19 and 25 goals, establishing himself as a good goal scorer.

At 5'10" and 178 pounds, the Canadiens' newest star wasn't very big, but he was quick and elusive. He decided that he wasn't going to be a physical player but used his superior skating skills to get off his hard shot. Awarded a penalty shot at one time, he stepped over the blue line and ripped a shot past startled Bruins goalie Bruce Gamble. He was hard to catch once he got going, and his speed helped to make the right-winger — he had been a natural centre — a top penalty killer. The Canadiens used players like Rousseau to rebuild their team so that by 1965 they won their first Stanley Cup. In the seventh game of the 1965 finals against Chicago, Rousseau had three assists in securing a 4–0 Montreal victory. (He had 13 points in 13 playoff games.) The 1965–66 season saw Rousseau score 30 goals for the Habs and lead the NHL with 48 assists. Rousseau added four postseason goals to help the Canadiens win their second straight Cup.

Rousseau won two more Cups with Montreal, hitting the 30-goal mark for a second time in 1968–69. The following year saw him score his 200th career goal as a Canadien. But the Habs, missing the playoffs in 1969–70, had new blood on the horizon in players like Rejean Houle and Phil Roberto. To make room for these new players, they dealt Rousseau to the Minnesota North Stars for former Canadien Claude Larose. Worried about potential language problems in Minnesota, Rousseau didn't adapt well to his new surroundings, scoring only four times in 63 games. The next season saw him go to the New York Rangers in a deal for Bob Nevin. He improved in Manhattan with 21 goals in 1971–72. He also helped to anchor the Ranger power play from the point. The New York club made it to the finals in 1972 but lost to Boston and Bobby Orr.

Above: Bobby Rousseau scored an overtime-winning goal on May 9, during the 1968 Stanley Cup finals versus St. Louis to give the Canadiens a 4–3 win and 3–0 lead in the series (which they would sweep). (HB)

Facing page: Bobby Rousseau (#15) makes a strong effort to get past Bobby Hull during the NHL All-Star game. The Montreal Canadiens had to fight off overtures made by the Detroit Red Wings to obtain Rousseau's services. (HB)

Montreal moment:

On February 1, 1964, Bobby Rousseau scored five goals in one game. He scored the goals against Detroit Red Wings goalie Roger Crozier in a game at the Montreal Forum. He scored once in the first period by putting in a rebound. He added two more in the second, getting one on a screen shot and flipping another over Crozier after taking a pass from Henri Richard. His two third-period goals included a long slapshot and a conversion of a Gilles Tremblay set-up in front of the goal. The Canadiens won the game 9–3. It was the only five-goal game by an NHL player in the sixties.

ROUSSEAU'S CANADIENS STATS:	GP	G	A	P	PIM
regular season	643	200	322	522	317
playoffs	78	16	29	45	54

STANLEY CUPS: 4

SERGE SAVARD

THE MONTREAL Canadiens first noticed Serge Savard while he was playing in a school game at the age of 15. A scout by the name of Renault — the same man who first noticed Jacques Laperriere — brought Savard to the Habs' attention. While intent on finishing school, the gangly youngster was put on the Canadiens' list. A great hockey fan, Savard's father was extremely pleased with this turn of events. Savard thought the Canadiens might be displeased when at first he couldn't make the hometown Junior Canadiens. He went back to play Junior B hockey and showed steady improvement. He started out as a forward, but his size (6'3", 210 pounds) meant that he was better suited to defence. As he progressed, Savard was named captain of the Junior Canadiens club. Although he hurt his knee in his final year of junior, Savard played plenty under coach Scotty Bowman, who at the time was handling the Junior Canadiens. After three seasons with the baby Habs, Savard was ready for pro hockey in the 1966–67 season.

The Canadiens sent Savard to Houston of the CPHL and, with seven goals and 25 assists in 68 games, he was named rookie of the year. The Habs lost the 1967 finals to Toronto and wanted new players. Savard played in 67 games as an NHL rookie and scored twice while totalling 15 points. He added two more goals in the playoffs — scoring the only goal in Montreal's 1–0 victory over the St. Louis Blues in the second game of the finals — and early in his career got a taste of winning when the Habs won the Stanley Cup in 1968. In 1968–69 Savard had eight goals and 23 assists. With 10 points in 14 playoff games in the '69 postseason, he became the first defenceman to win the coveted Conn Smythe Trophy for best player in the playoffs. Savard's game was built around his great ability to handle the puck and use his size effectively. (Always a clean player, he rarely lost his temper.) He was a good skater and didn't mind lugging the puck. Never one to panic in his game, he was very smooth defensively.

The 1969–70 season was the start of difficult times for the Habs' rising star. After crashing into a goalpost, he broke his leg badly and required extensive surgery. Then after finally recovering, he re-broke the leg at the Forum late in January of 1971 when Bob Baun of Toronto caught him with a hip check. While there was concern

over his long-term health, Savard eventually returned to form with his mobility intact. He played in only 23 games in 1971–72 but was still selected in September of 1972 for Team Canada to battle the Russians in an eight-game series. The Canadians didn't lose a game that Savard played in and eked out a 4–3–1 series win. Without Savard's steady performance on the blue line, Canada probably wouldn't have had any reason to celebrate. Then returning to the Habs lineup, he helped to regain the Cup in 1973.

Although Savard had a superb year in 1974–75 with 20 goals and 60 points (both career highs) Montreal missed the finals for two years. Savard's proudest moment came in the 1976 finals when the Habs ended the ugly reign of the Philadelphia Flyers. The Canadiens wiped out the "Broad Street Bullies" in four straight games. The articulate Savard stated what many hockey fans believed: the Flyer style of play was bad for hockey. Savard and the Habs were steady between 1976 and 1979, when he and fellow blueliners Larry Robinson and Guy Lapointe became known as the "Big Three." Under Bowman's direction, the three star defenders saw lots of ice time, especially in the playoffs.

Savard was named captain of the team in 1979 and received one Cup in that role. He scored a key goal in the finals against the New York Rangers: a clutch overtime winner in the fourth game of the series. He played two more years with Montreal. Incredibly, Montreal fans at the Forum booed him in his last year with the team (1980–81). He had slowed down a little but deserved better from Montreal patrons. Savard was all set to retire, but his former teammate John Ferguson talked him into playing for the Winnipeg Jets for two seasons. (He had a very respectable 20 points in his last year.) By 1983 the Habs needed new people in their front office and named Savard as managing director.

Under his leadership, the Canadiens won two more Stanley Cups (1986 and 1993). But then the Habs, in one of their greatest errors, dismissed him in 1995. With no one as qualified to lead the team as the savvy, business-like Savard, the Canadiens are only now starting to recover from his departure. Savard was elected to the Hall of Fame in 1986.

134

Above: Montreal Broadcaster Danny Gallivan described Serge Savard's patented move as the "Savardian Spinarama," a pirouette spin used to escape checkers, a deke that Savard learned from his hero Doug Harvey. (HB)

Facing page: Serge Savard made the NHL's second all-star team in 1978–79 when he had 33 points in 80 games played. (DM)

SAVARD'S CANADIENS STATS:	GP	G	A	P	PIM
regular season	917	100	312	412	537
playoffs	123	19	49	68	84

STANLEY CUPS: 8

JEAN-GUY TALBOT

DEFENCEMAN JEAN-GUY Talbot secured a three-game trial with the Montreal Canadiens in the 1954–55 season (recording one assist) and made enough of an impression to be invited back the next season. Talbot's first big break came when defenceman Bud MacPherson was sent to the minors. He then became a regular when rearguard Butch Bouchard — who could see that Talbot was ready to take his job — retired after being injured for most of the 1955–56 season. He played in 66 games as rookie (the same year Henri Richard broke in), scoring one goal and adding 13 assists for a team that would win the Stanley Cup in the spring of '56. Talbot learned a great deal by watching Doug Harvey work his magic from the blue line. Coach Toe Blake assigned Harvey and Tom Johnson to tutor the young defenceman both on and off the ice.

Talbot wasn't an offensive blueliner with the Habs — never scoring more than eight goals in a season — but he was a good puck handler. He could make a tape-to-tape pass as well as any NHL defenceman and had plenty of good forwards to get the puck to, although he liked to carry the puck and often displayed a burst of speed when doing so. With Montreal's great firepower up front, Talbot was content to play back most of the time. (Sometimes he would get moved up to play left wing because he could handle the puck well.) At first, Talbot had difficulty with positioning, but goaltender Jacques Plante corrected that by suggesting Talbot skate backwards a little closer to the boards when opposing forwards were leading a rush up the ice. Talbot was a physical and rugged player (5'11" and 170 pounds) but not overly so, since he recorded over 100 penalty minutes only once. (He recorded 143 penalty minutes in the 1960–61 season.) At times he displayed some temper — in junior hockey he whacked Scotty Bowman in the head with his stick for 42

stitches — but he generally controlled himself on the ice.

Like many other players in the history of the Canadiens, Talbot joined the team at just the right time, taking part in five straight Cup wins between 1956 and 1960. When that dynasty ended, Talbot and a few others — such as Jean Béliveau, Ralph Backstrom, Claude Provost and Richard — stayed as the team rebuilt itself between 1961 and 1964. Talbot was the lone hold-over defenceman from the previous era and advised young blueliners like J. C. Tremblay, Jacques Laperriere, Terry Harper and Ted Harris. His experience was invaluable to the newcomers learning how to play in the NHL. When Harvey left the team in 1961, it was Talbot who picked up the offence slack to produce his best season ever in 1961–62 with five goals and 42 assists. His performance earned him a place on the first all-star team alongside his former mentor, Harvey, who was now with the New York Rangers. Talbot's solid play helped build a defence that would lead the Habs to two more Cups in 1965 and 1966. His final season in Montreal was in 1966–67 when he played 68 games and recorded eight points.

During the 1967–68 season, he was claimed by the Minnesota North Stars in the expansion draft but played only four games before being sent to Detroit and then to St. Louis. Bowman, who obviously held no grudges, was coaching the Blues when they claimed Talbot on waivers after the Red Wings released him. It was a good move for Talbot, who extended his career for another four years, making it to the Stanley Cup finals another three times. He played 57 games for the Buffalo Sabres in 1970–71, their first year in the NHL, to bring his career total to 1,056 games played.

After his career was over, Talbot coached the St. Louis Blues and the Rangers for a combined total of 200 games.

TALBOT'S CANADIENS STATS:	GP	G	A	P	PIM
regular season	791	36	209	245	884
playoffs	105	3	16	19	112

STANLEY CUPS: 7

GILLES TREMBLAY

GILLES TREMBLAY was born in a little town near Quebec City — Montmorency, Quebec — and was first spotted at the Montreal Forum while playing a game in one of the Montreal-area junior leagues. During this contest he scored all three goals in a 3-0 victory. Watching in the stands was Canadiens scout Sam Pollock, who asked the 16-year-old if he wanted to play for his junior team in Hull-Ottawa. Tremblay accepted the offer and joined Pollock's squad for three seasons. He was a part of the Memorial Cup-winning club in 1958. The smooth-skating left-winger didn't score many goals, but he was learning to play in the Canadiens system under Pollock's watchful eye.

When Tremblay's junior career was over, Pollock didn't want him exposed to the older players in the American Hockey League, so he placed him with the Hull-Ottawa Canadiens of the EPHL for the 1959-60 season. It was a good move, as Tremblay scored 32 times in 67 games and totalled 83 points. He was ready for the NHL. The Boston Bruins offered the Canadiens winger Jean-Guy Gendron, a one-time 24-goal scorer, and $25,000 in cash in a proposed trade. The Habs wisely turned them down. (Gendron later became a Canadien in another trade involving Andre Pronovost.) Pollock knew that Montreal wingers like Dickie Moore and Marcel Bonin would eventually need to be replaced. Pollock knew whom he wanted to keep and considered Tremblay the top prospect in the Habs system. (At the beginning, he may have been the only one in Habs management to believe so much in Tremblay's abilities.) Tremblay split the 1960-61 season between Montreal and Hull-Ottawa and played his first NHL game at the Forum on November 12, 1960, in a game against Detroit. He started on a line with Bernie Geoffrion and Jean Béliveau, assigned the job of checking none other than Gordie Howe of the Red Wings! Facing a trip back to the minors, Tremblay scored twice against Chicago to keep his big-league stint going. He finished with seven goals in 45 games. Late in March he also assisted on Geoffrion's 50th goal

of the season in a game against Toronto.

Tremblay made a reported $7,000 in his first year. His second year called for $7,500, but he still had to beat out Fred Hilts, who had been acquired in a deal with Chicago for defenceman Bob Turner. Tremblay won the job at the 1961 training camp and scored a remarkable 32 goals in '61-'62, justifying Pollock's faith in the sturdy (5'10", 170-pound) winger. Montreal manager Frank Selke said he wouldn't trade Tremblay for Toronto superstar Frank Mahovlich! Coach Toe Blake considered Tremblay a top two-way player, with excellent speed and skating ability. Playing a clean game, he was a top penalty killer and, with his speed, good on the backcheck. He started scoring when he learned to relax, leaving the worry to the opposition. Tremblay used a low and hard wrist shot to great advantage. He went on to postseasons of 25, 22, 27 and 23 goals while with the Habs and would have scored more if serious injuries hadn't hampered him later in his career.

A member of three Stanley Cup teams, Tremblay played his entire NHL career with Montreal. (A broken leg in 1964-65 limited his season to just 26 games and no playoff action, so that he missed being part of a fourth Stanley Cup team.) His best playoff with Montreal came in 1966 when he had nine points (four goals) in 10 games. He also got credit for helping to shut down Howe in the finals. Tremblay's final season, 1968-69, saw him once again miss much of the year and the playoffs. But he still managed a respectable 10 goals and 25 points in 44 games. His final game that year, and his last as a Hab, came against the Los Angeles Kings. He scored one goal and added three assists.

Injuries and asthma forced Tremblay to retire, but he stayed in hockey as a colour analyst for the French television broadcasts of Canadiens games on *Le Soirée du Hockey*. His excellent work in this field was recognized in 2002 with the Foster Hewitt Memorial Award and his induction to the Hockey Hall of Fame in the broadcasters section.

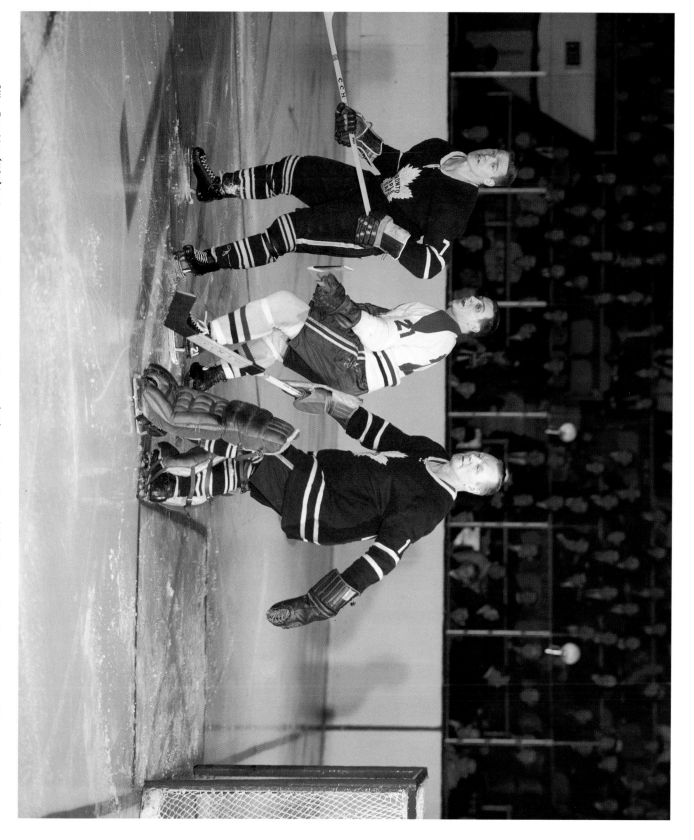

Gilles Tremblay (#21) looks to get in the action between Tim Horton (#7) and Johnny Bower (#1) of Toronto. When Tremblay scored 32 goals in 1961–62, the Canadiens gave him a $3,500 bonus. (HB)

G. TREMBLAY'S CANADIENS STATS:

	GP	G	A	P	PIM
regular season	509	168	162	330	161
playoffs	48	9	14	23	4

STANLEY CUPS: 3

J. C. TREMBLAY

A NATIVE OF Bagotville, Quebec, and the eldest of eight children, Jean-Claude Tremblay wasn't regarded as much of a hockey prospect because his skating wasn't strong. Starting out as a forward, he switched to defence, which gave him new purpose and more ice time. He played junior hockey with the Hull-Ottawa Canadiens and won a Memorial Cup with the team in 1958. (Future Habs like Bobby Rousseau and Ralph Backstrom were his teammates.) After his junior career ended, he stayed with the Hull-Ottawa club and worked on his passing and shooting skills. He made the first all-star team in 1959–60 with a great season that saw him score 25 goals and 31 assists. (He also played in 11 games for the Habs.) He split the next season again between the two leagues. But the great Doug Harvey was soon to leave, and the Montreal blue line had a large hole to fill.

Tremblay became a full-time Canadien in 1961–62. He played in all 70 games, scoring three goals and adding 17 assists. Coach Toe Blake made Tremblay a right defenceman due to his problems with certain turns. That seemed to help Tremblay's defensive game. Tremblay was never a physical player — never recording more than 24 penalty minutes in one season — and tended to use his stick to check the opposition. Montreal fans didn't always appreciate his style of play, but he was effective. He was a flawless puck handler and could produce points from the blue line. Tremblay had a knack for flipping the puck at the opposition net from centre ice. Such shots would drive goalies crazy as the puck took funny bounces. The pressure of replacing a legend like Harvey was hard on Tremblay, but he shone more as he gained experience. His assist totals started climbing, and by the 1970–71 season he hit a career high of 52 helpers. Tremblay tended to step up his play when fellow blueliner Jacques Laperriere was injured. This was especially true in the 1965 playoffs when the Habs regained the Stanley Cup for the first time since 1960.

The smooth-skating Tremblay had nine assists in the '65 playoffs to lead all players in that category and helped the Habs get by the Maple Leafs and Black Hawks in two hard-fought series. He was even better in the 1966 playoffs — in the finals against Detroit in particular — scoring two goals and adding nine assists in 10 playoff games. Tremblay felt he deserved the Conn Smythe Trophy for his stellar performance, but the voters gave the award to Red Wing netminder Roger Crozier, the first time the trophy went to a player on the losing team. The Canadiens rearguard felt that was another example of a lack of recognition for Tremblay's play. He was, however, given a special day in his hometown of Bagotville.

In 1967–68 Tremblay finished second to Bobby Orr in the voting for the Norris Trophy as the NHL's best defenceman. He did, however, set a team record for Montreal blueliners with 63 points (breaking Harvey's old mark) in 1970–71, a season that finally saw Tremblay get selected to the first all-star team. He helped the Canadiens break in new defencemen like Pierre Bouchard and Guy Lapointe. After a 51-assist season in 1971–72, the Quebec Nordiques of the World Hockey Association came up with a great offer that Tremblay couldn't ignore. (He was the first player they signed.) Accepting the offer meant that Tremblay couldn't play in the 1972 Canada-Russia series, which was a big disappointment for him. He did, however, play in the 1974 series between the WHA stars and the Soviets, recording five points in eight games. Tremblay was one of the best players in the freewheeling new league — he recorded 75 assists in 1972–73 and 77 in 1975–76 — and stayed in Quebec City until the Nordiques joined the NHL in 1979. The Nordiques retired his sweater in appreciation for his efforts with the team. He played one more year of hockey in Europe before retiring. He then became a scout for the Canadiens in Europe before his passing in 1994.

As a youngster J. C. Tremblay (#3) idolized Montreal Canadiens legends Maurice Richard, Jean Béliveau and Doug Harvey. (HB)

J. C. Tremblay looks to lead a rush up the ice. Tremblay scored the Stanley cup-winning goal in 1968 when he knocked in a pass from Ralph Backstrom from 30 feet out to give the Habs a 3–2 win over the St. Louis Blues in a game at the Montreal Forum. (HB)

J. C. TREMBLAY'S CANADIENS STATS:

	GP	G	A	P	PIM
regular season	794	57	306	363	204
playoffs	108	14	51	65	58

STANLEY CUPS: 5

ROGIE VACHON

ONE OF EIGHT children, Rogie Vachon grew up on a farm north of Rouyn-Noranda, Quebec. He began playing junior hockey in the Montreal area when he was about 16 years old. He showed some talent as a young goaltender. Although recommended to the Canadiens by Gilles Laperriere, whose brother Jacques was a Hab, there was no regular position for Vachon on the Montreal Junior Canadiens, so in 1963–64 he played for the Montreal NDG Monarchs. He split the next season between the Junior B squad in Thetford Mines and the Junior Canadiens. The 1965–66 season saw him win 25 of 39 appearances in Thetford. Montreal turned Vachon professional that same year, and he got into 10 games for the Quebec Aces of the American Hockey League.

To start the 1966–67 season, the small netminder (5'7", 170 pounds) found himself in Houston playing for the Canadiens' farm club in the Central Hockey League. (The Canadiens didn't invite him to their main training camp.) Going to Houston was an odd experience for Vachon, who wasn't used to the warm climate and the large quantity of swimming pools. He took over the main duties in goal from Gerry Desjardins and soon attracted notice. In 34 games for the Apollos, Vachon went 17–12–5. With a great sense of timing, Vachon made 50 saves the night Montreal manager Sam Pollock was in the stands to scout the youngster. Vachon quickly went up the Canadiens' depth chart. Pollock saw a goaltender who could move well on his skates and had quick hands, especially his catching glove. He had a flair for making saves, throwing his body around and relying mostly on his reflexes. Vachon was also a cool customer. Nothing seemed to bother him.

Before he knew it, Vachon was in the NHL playing for the Habs in the '66–'67 season. His first game was against the Detroit Red Wings, and the first shot on him came from the legendary Gordie Howe. Vachon later claimed that he didn't realize it was Howe he stopped. Named the first star of the game for making 41 saves, the virtual unknown was suddenly in the spotlight. That season he played in 19 games for the Canadiens and posted an impressive 11–3–4 record with a 2.54 goals against average and one shutout. The Habs swept the

New York Rangers in four straight to start the '67 playoffs. But Gump Worsley replaced Vachon, who ran out of steam in the finals against Toronto. Although Vachon's Cinderella story didn't have a happy finish, he had established himself as an NHL goaltender — despite Maple Leafs coach Punch Imlach's claim that he was nothing more than a Junior B goalie!

The 1967–68 season saw Vachon play in 39 games and win 23 times while sharing the netminding duties with Worsley. (They also shared the Vezina Trophy that year.) The Habs regained the Stanley Cup in 1968, but Vachon played in only two playoff games that year. The 1969 playoffs were a different story as Vachon played in eight games, winning seven, and was outstanding in the Habs' ouster of the rising Boston Bruins in the semifinals. The 1969–70 season saw Vachon win a career high (later surpassed) 31 games, but the defending Cup champs couldn't make the playoffs. The unflappable goalie played in 47 games for the Habs in 1970–71, winning 23, but the team faltered late in the year. Unhappy with the goaltending, the management summoned a youngster named Ken Dryden from the farm system. He was in net the rest of the way to a surprising Stanley Cup win for the Habs.

Vachon could see that Dryden was the Canadiens' goalie of the future and asked for a trade early in the next season. Even though Detroit was interested in him, Vachon wanted to go to Toronto, but the Maple Leafs weren't interested. A deal with the Los Angeles Kings began the second phase of Vachon's career. He was with the Kings for seven seasons. But the highlight of his career came with the 1976 Canada Cup and recognition as the best player on Team Canada. He had something to prove to Montreal manager Sam Pollock, who said that Vachon wasn't in the same class as Bernie Parent and Dryden.

As one of the first free agent players on the open market, Vachon signed with Detroit in 1978, but that deal didn't work out well. After two seasons as a Red Wing, he was dealt to Boston, where he played for two more years, bringing his career wins to 355.

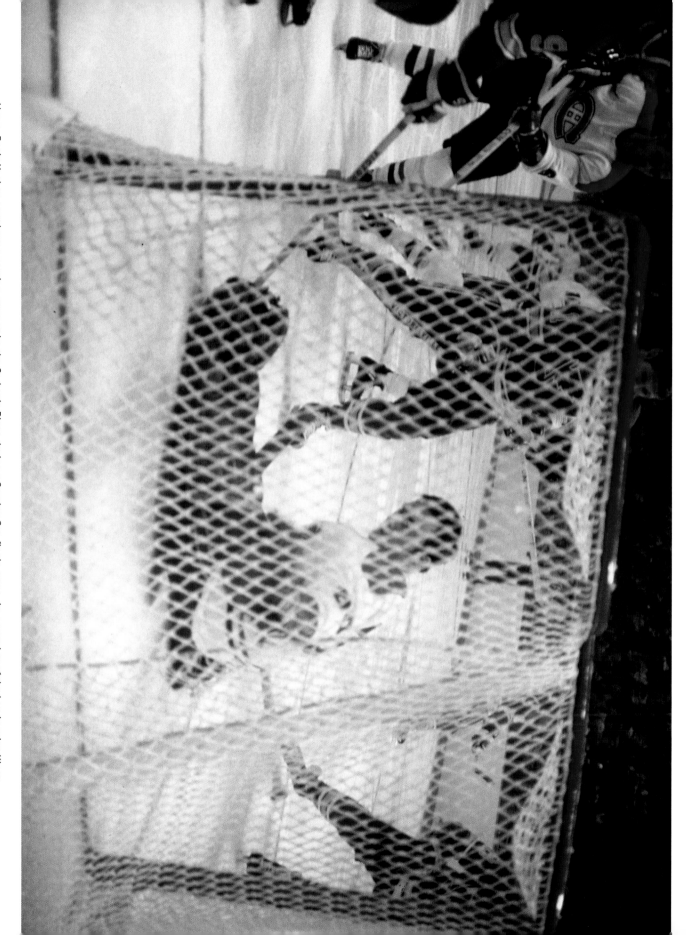

Above: Rogie Vachon smothers a scoring attempt by the St. Louis Blues during a Stanley Cup finals game. As a member of the Los Angeles Kings, Vachon was named to the NHL's second all-star team in 1975 and 1977. (HHOF)

Facing page: Rogie Vachon was traded to the Los Angeles Kings on November 4, 1971, in exchange for Dale Hoganson, Noel Price, Doug Robinson and Denis DeJordy. (HB)

VACHON'S CANADIENS STATS:

	GP	Wins	Losses	Ties	Shutouts	GA
regular season	206	110	56	31	13	2.65
playoffs	19	14	5	-	1	1.94

STANLEY CUPS: 3

LORNE "GUMP" WORSLEY

LORNE "GUMP" WORSLEY was sitting outside his Montreal home on June 4, 1963, when a friend dropped by and asked if he had heard the news. When Worsley said he hadn't, his friend told him what he had heard on the Montreal radio: Worsley had been traded to the Montreal Canadiens. Worsley was surprised. Just the day before, New York Rangers management told him that, as a fixture in the Big Apple, he wasn't going to be moved. Worsley had joked with Rangers general manager Muzz Patrick that if he had to move, he would appreciate going to the Canadiens so that he could play in his hometown. The next day, at the NHL summer meetings held in Montreal, Worsley got his wish but never got a direct phone call from the Rangers telling him he was gone! It turned out to be a great move for the Habs and the rotund Worsley.

Worsley was born on May 14, 1929, in Montreal and grew up in the tough working-class district of Point St. Charles. As a youngster he looked like a cartoon character named Andy Gump and so his friends tagged him with one of the most memorable nicknames in hockey history. A coach told Worsley early on that he was too small — he would grow up to be 5'7" — to play any position but goalie. After playing junior hockey in Verdun, he turned professional in the Ranger organization and played in various minor-league towns until the 1951–52 season when he played in 50 games for the New York club and won the rookie of the year award. He went back to the minors for one more season before becoming the Rangers' regular netminder for the next nine years. The Rangers had a poor club during most of Worsley's time on Broadway — although he did have seven seasons of 20 or more wins. At the end of his stay in New York, the easygoing goalie was constantly feuding with coach Phil Watson. A change of scenery was clearly in order. Worsley thought getting away from the Rangers was like getting out of jail.

The Habs had grown weary of goaltender Jacques Plante and were hopeful that Worsley would bring some stability to the position. But the 34-year-old netminder had a terrible start to the 1963–64 season (including a hamstring injury) and ended up playing in the minors again with the exception of eight games in Montreal. He was replaced by Charlie Hodge (who won the Vezina Trophy) and was left unprotected by the Habs in the summer of 1964. The Maple Leafs were all set to select Worsley but then took Terry Sawchuk when he became available from the Red Wings. Worsley started the next season in the minors again with the Quebec Aces, but as Hodge faltered Worsley came back to play in 19 games in '64–'65 and got into eight playoff games, winning five. One of his victories came in game seven of the finals against Chicago, a contest he wasn't expecting to play. He had been nursing an injury to a thigh muscle and didn't think he would even dress for the deciding contest. But coach Toe Blake had confidence in the veteran, and the Habs responded by jumping out to a 4–0 lead. Worsley made a good save on Camille Henry early in the game and gave the Black Hawks nothing the rest of the way. Worsley had reported back to Montreal in good condition, having quit drinking and dropped his weight from 188 to 177. His impressive performance in the postseason earned him a $5,000 increase on his salary of $30,000 to start the next season.

The 1965–66 season — when Worsley won 29 of 51 appearances — saw him share the Vezina Trophy with Hodge. In the playoffs Worsley shone again with eight wins in 10 starts to help lead the Habs to their second straight Cup. He thought he was a worthy candidate for the Conn Smythe Trophy (allowing only 20 goals in total) but the voters chose Roger Crozier, the goaltender of the Detroit Red Wings whom the Canadiens beat in six games! In the following season injuries limited his games to 18, but he did make it back for the Cup finals against Toronto. He came back to play in 40 games in 1967–68, winning 19 and sharing another Vezina, this time with Rogie Vachon. He then added 11 victories in the playoffs. Worsley played in all the finals games against St. Louis, believing again that he would get the Conn Smythe. It went instead to Glenn Hall of the Blues, a team the Canadiens had just swept!

Chico Maki (#16) of Chicago puts the puck past Gump Worsley (#30) in the Canadiens net. The last goal Gump Worsley gave up in the NHL was to Dave Schultz of Philadelphia on April 2, 1974, a player who was born the year Worsley started playing professional hockey! (HB)

Facing page: When Gump Worsley was sent to the minors after he joined the Canadiens organization, he did so without complaint and even played a game against Jacques Plante, the goalie Montreal had traded to acquire Worsley. (HB)

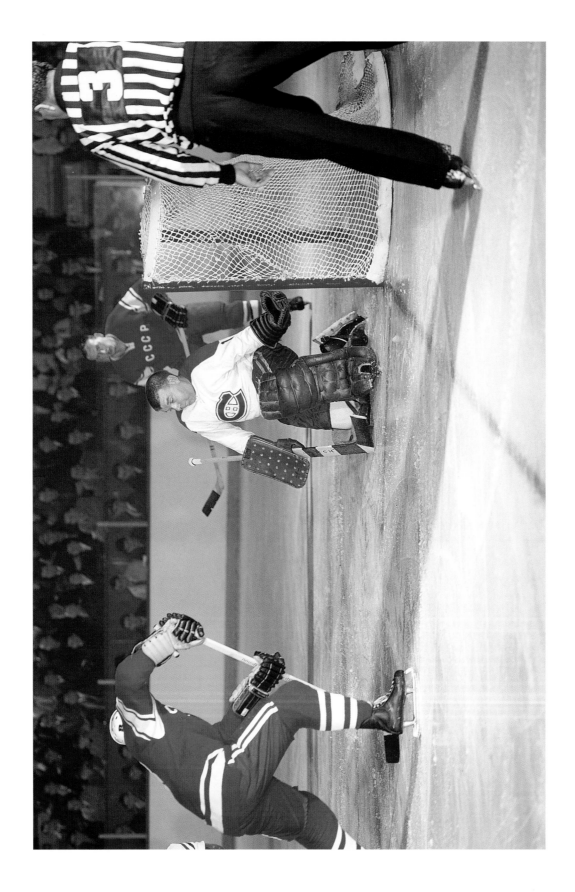

Above: *Worsley squares off against the offensive attack of the visiting Soviet squad.* (HB)

Facing page: *Gump Worsley was one of the last goaltenders in the NHL to play without a mask. He finally donned a mask in his last season, playing for the Minnesota North Stars.* (HB)

Another Cup win in 1969 was the last hurrah for Worsley in a Habs uniform. He soon found himself detesting coach Claude Ruel and had to get away from the team for a while. (Ruel had different ideas about how hard players should practise.) Told to report to the minors, Worsley refused to go. It seemed his career was over, but the Minnesota North Stars talked him into playing for them. The Stars gave the Canadiens some cash — one report suggested $40,000 — and Worsley signed a deal for $38,000. He didn't win many games for the North Stars but did record 16 victories out of 34 contests in 1971–72. He played three more seasons in Minnesota before a leg injury forced him to retire after the 1973–74 season when he was 45 years old.

Worsley endured a great deal in his career, including a pinched nerve in his spine, two torn tendons in one arm and a severe head injury from a Bobby Hull blast. (He didn't wear a mask until his final NHL season.) His marvellous career was recognized with his selection to the Hockey Hall of Fame in 1980.

WORSLEY'S CANADIENS STATS:	GP	Wins	Losses	Ties	Shutouts	GA
regular season	172	92	44	25	16	2.42
playoffs	39	29	7	–	4	1.92

STANLEY CUPS: 4

SCOTTY BOWMAN: ONE-OF-A-KIND COACH

by Red Fisher

IT WAS JUNE 11, 1979, and Scotty Bowman was saying his goodbye to the Montreal Canadiens in two languages. After five Stanley Cups, including the last four in a row, in only eight seasons behind the Canadiens bench, his message was that he was leaving because he could no longer accept certain things linked with the organization. A head coach-GM job in Buffalo awaited him.

"Listen, there was no room for [Canadiens general manager] Irving Grundman and me on the same team," Scotty said at his press conference. "It was a power struggle that I could have won over the years if we'd started from the same point, but he had the lead. It was better for them and for me that I go."

Canadiens GM Sam Pollock had hired Scotty for the 1971–72 season, even though Al MacNeil had led the team to its 16th Stanley Cup the previous season — after upsetting the heavily favoured Boston Bruins in the first round. The reason: Canadiens icon Henri Richard had been benched by MacNeil for most of Game 5 in the Cup final against Chicago. After the game, Richard exploded: "He's the worst coach I've ever played for."

The next day, GM Pollock was asked if Richard would be punished for his outburst. "Henri will probably score a big goal before this series is over." Pollock, as usual, was right. Richard scored the tying and winning goals in Game 7 after Chicago had taken a 2–0 lead.

What Pollock didn't mention was that he had already made up his mind a choice would have to be made between Richard and Stanley Cup-winning coach MacNeil. His eye for talent rarely failed him, and nowhere was this more evident than in his hiring of Bowman.

I knew Scotty long before Pollock hired him to coach the best team in hockey. I knew him casually when he coached junior hockey teams for several seasons, got to know him a little better when he scouted for the Canadiens, and a lot better when he joined the St. Louis Blues as an assistant coach in time for the NHL's expansion to 12 teams from six in 1967–68. Eighteen games into the season, and with the Blues in last place in their division, he became the team's head coach and led them to the Stanley Cup final for the next three seasons.

Strange guy. He could be friendly one moment, downright nasty the next. At times, it was for real, but often it was for show. Successful coaches are almost always good showmen, and Bowman was among the best. Most coaches are character actors, but only a few are actors with character.

Bowman: winner of 419 of 634 regular-season Canadiens games — all the while playing jut-jawed mind games with his players, opposing coaches, their players and on-ice officials.

Bowman: now and then warm and curious, at other times mean and vindictive. It wasn't personal — it was business. All of it was dedicated to getting the best out of his players.

Bowman: always looking for ways to win on the way to becoming the winningest coach in NHL history with a career record of 1,244–584–313, calling the shots for three decades. Always looking for an edge. The telephone was an extension of his right arm, talking to people who could tell him something about the team the Canadiens would face next.

Pollock and Bowman were a great team. Pollock, the shrewdest GM of his time, got Bowman the players, Scotty developed them into a dynasty from 1976 through '79 — posting a remarkable 229–46–45 regular-season record during those miracle years.

Pollock's decision to hire Bowman was a marriage made in hockey heaven, yet it was another Pollock decision which prompted Scotty to leave the Canadiens only a few weeks after he had led the team to a fourth consecutive Cup.

Coaching the Canadiens was the only job Bowman had ever wanted, until Pollock announced he was leaving hockey after the 1977–78 season. The corporate world beckoned, and Pollock knew a good thing when he spotted it.

From the start, it was obvious that there were only two candidates in the race for Pollock's GM chair: Bowman and Grundman, who had been president of the Montreal Forum. It was also evident that Pollock's successor would need his endorsement. It would be essential. Pollock, in effect, would name his own successor.

He picked Grundman.

Why?

Scotty Bowman coached the Canadiens for eight remarkable seasons during the 1970s, accumulating five Stanley Cup victories along the way. (Graphic Artists/HHOF)

Jacques Courtois, a distinguished Montreal lawyer, was the Canadiens president at the time. We were head table neighbours at a dinner honouring Pollock shortly before he left the post he had held for 14 seasons, during which his teams had won the Stanley Cup nine times.

"Who replaces Sam?" Courtois was asked. "Bowman?"

"Not a chance," he said.

"Why not?"

"Scotty is the best coach in hockey," said Courtois, with a shrug, "but he gets excited too easily. We wouldn't want to walk in one morning and find out he'd traded Guy Lafleur and Larry Robinson the night before. We don't like surprises."

Bowman was devastated by Grundman's appointment. He felt that Pollock, the man who hired him, had now betrayed him. Still, he soldiered on for another season — but when the Buffalo Sabres offered him the job of coach and general manager, there he was on 6/11 saying:

"It had reached the point where I couldn't tolerate any further deterioration of my personal situation. It was a question of hockey philosophy," said Bowman. "I was convinced I had the competence to be general manager, and I couldn't tolerate the way Grundman directed the club.

"He said he had a lot of respect for me as coach and I had some for him as a businessman, but I have no respect for him as a hockey man and I couldn't continue in this way," said Bowman.

So he walked — after leading his team to the Stanley Cup four years in a row. And everyone who knew him wasn't surprised because — even while Bowman always has been the amalgam of many things — he was, and is, among coaches, one of a kind.

149

the second great dynasty 1974–1984

fter their 1973 Stanley Cup win, the Montreal Canadiens slumped for a couple of seasons.

It all started with a contract dispute with goalie Ken Dryden. Unable to resolve it before the 1973–74 season, Dryden completed his law studies in Toronto, so the Canadiens put Wayne Thomas and Michel Larocque in net. The New York Rangers ousted the defending champions in six games, and the Habs quickly moved to bring Dryden back into the fold. The stoic netminder was in goal for the 1974–75 season — which saw the Habs tied for first overall at 113 points — but it ended with a playoff loss to the surging Buffalo Sabres. The Philadelphia Flyers won both Cups in '74 and '75. It was clear that the Canadiens would have to arm themselves to battle the ferocious Flyers.

Facing page: *Bob Gainey holds up the Stanley Cup after the Canadiens defeated the New York Rangers in 1979 to win their fourth straight title. (Bruce Bennett/BBS)*

Above: *Goaltender Ken Dryden won six Stanley Cups during his illustrious career with the Canadiens. (London Life-Portnoy/HHOF)*

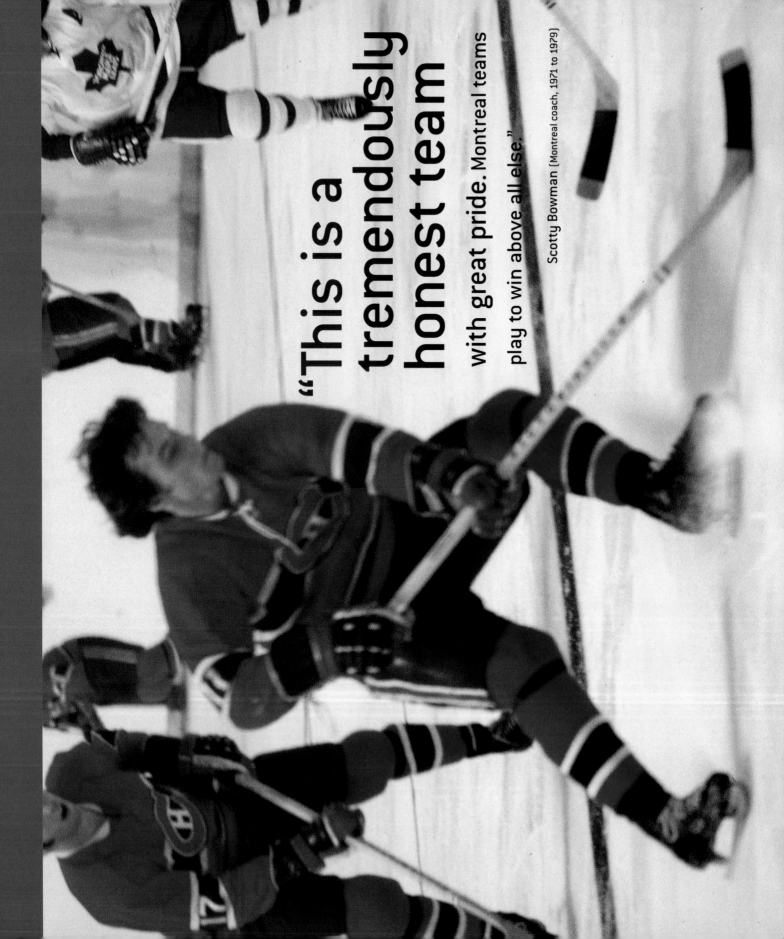

"This is a **tremendously honest team** with great pride. Montreal teams play to win above all else."

Scotty Bowman (Montreal coach, 1971 to 1979)

Marc Tardif (#11), the second player chosen in the 1969 entry draft, played in 245 career games with Montreal. He recorded 157 points and was on two Cup-winning teams in 1971 and 1973. (DM)

The Canadiens used the entry draft to rebuild their team in the seventies, and by the 1975–76 season they were ready to challenge for the Cup once again. Shrewd moves by Sam Pollock paid incredible dividends. Between 1971 and 1977 he stockpiled draft choices (many of them premium picks) and added high-quality players Guy Lafleur, Larry Robinson, Steve Shutt, Bob Gainey, Mario Tremblay, Doug Risebrough, Pierre Mondou, Bill Nyrop, Brian Engblom, Rod Langway and Mark Napier. Good support players taken at various points in the draft process included Rick Chartraw, Gilles Lupien, Murray Wilson, Cam Connor, Pat Hughes and Larocque, who all played on Cup-winning teams between 1976 and 1979. Arguably no team to date had used the draft as successfully to add new players.

These new players meshed well with the hold-overs from the '73 squad to create a league powerhouse. Two unheralded pickups also added a great deal to the team. Pollock stole centre Doug Jarvis from Toronto, and the Canadiens drafted large left-winger Yvon Lambert away from Detroit. Later on Pollock moved Peter Mahovlich to Pittsburgh for slick-scoring centre Pierre Larouche. The Habs had an embarrassment of riches, but it took a contest against Philadelphia, before the 1975–76 season, to prove the Habs weren't going to be pushed around by the brawling Flyers. When the two squads met in the '76 finals, the Habs took the Cup in four straight games. The Canadiens now had a team that was skilled, swift and tough — determined to win every game! They could score goals and shut down the opposition equally well. Between the 1975–76 and 1978–79 seasons the Canadiens won an incredible 229 regular-season games while losing just 46! Coach Scotty Bowman was relentless in keeping his team focused and ready to play, while Pollock kept his fiery coach calm whenever Bowman demanded in a fit of temper that players get moved. In short, it was a perfect combination that took the Habs to four straight Cups, making them the envy of the hockey world.

In August of 1978 things started to change, however, when the team was sold back to the Molson family from the Bronfmans. Pollock decided this was a good time to leave and pursue other business opportunities. Bowman didn't get promoted to the general manager's chair, making the 1978–79 campaign his last in Montreal. (He signed with Buffalo for the 1979–80 season.) Irving Grundman, a front-office administrator, was given the job, winning a Cup in his first season (although it was clearly Pollock's team). Dryden retired for good, as did Jacques Lemaire. Injuries forced Yvan Cournoyer to leave the game. All at once the Habs lost five key people who had made enormous contributions over the years.

Former Canadiens star Bernie Geoffrion was brought in to coach the team for the 1979–80 season, but he couldn't discipline his troops and got frustrated. On December 12, 1979, the Canadiens made a coaching change, bringing back Claude Ruel. But while the team did reasonably well the rest of the way — totalling 47 wins in 80 games — the Minnesota North Stars eliminated the Habs in seven games. The next three years saw the Canadiens win 45, 46 and 42 games during the season, but they were dismissed with shocking ease in the playoffs each time. Former NHL forward Bob Berry was named head coach in June of 1981, but he wasn't popular with the team. Guy Lafleur showed less interest in the team, and Grundman was vilified for trading away future Hall of Fame defenceman Rod Langway, a move he was forced to make. While it's true that Langway thrived in Washington, Grundman got no credit for adding the two quality players Rick Green and Ryan Walter.

Sensing a strong need for change, ownership installed Ronald Corey as president of the team. Corey's career in broadcasting and journalism, followed by executive positions at Molson, made him a good choice. He also had a hockey background as a junior prospect,

Defenceman Rod Langway was with the Canadiens between 1978 and 1982 before demanding a trade to an American-based team. In 286 games with Montreal, Langway recorded 127 points, including 101 assists. The future Hall of Famer was on the Cup-winning team of 1979. (London Life-Portnoy/HHOF)

but his poor skating abilities ended any hopes of a pro career. One of Corey's roles at Molson was head of marketing, which was in tune with the times as the Habs faced a new rival owned by another brewery. After years in the World Hockey Association, the Quebec Nordiques joined the NHL in 1979, soon becoming the Canadiens' most intense rival. While the sixties saw a great rivalry with Toronto and the seventies produced the Bruins as the arch-enemy, the eighties featured an intense battle with the Quebec rivals. Even veterans like Larry Robinson acknowledged that he had never seen anything like a game between the Canadiens and the Nordiques. The newspapers devoted many detailed pages to "La Guerre Civile." In 1982 the Nordiques won the first playoff series between the two clubs, but the Habs pulled off a six-game upset in 1984, which featured one of the wildest brawls in playoff history.

Corey's first major move — on April 28, 1983 — was to hire former Canadiens star Serge Savard as the team's new general manager. The 1983–84 season was a disaster for the Canadiens who won only 35 games, but they revived in the postseason to get close to the Stanley Cup final. One reason for the turnaround was that Lemaire replaced Berry as head coach. (He had started the season as an assistant coach along with Jacques Laperriere.) Lemaire said that the Canadiens would now concentrate on defence and reduce their "fire-wagon" style of attack. In the first few seasons at the helm of the Canadiens, Savard made many interesting choices. Both Corey and Savard had the ability to restore the team to its former glory.

Centre Pierre Larouche, acquired in a deal with Pittsburgh, scored 50 goals for the Habs in 1979–80. He won Cups with the Habs in 1978 and 1979, and played in 236 games for the team, scoring a total of 110 goals and 236 points. (DM)

Centre Pierre Mondou, selected 15th overall by Montreal in 1975, played in 548 career games, all with the Habs. His career totals include 194 goals and 262 assists and three Stanley Cups (1977, 1978 and 1979). (DM)

Defenceman Brian Engblom (#3) was with Montreal from 1976 to 1982 and played in 318 career games for the club, recording 101 points. He was on three Cup-winning teams (1977, 1978 and 1979) before he was dealt to Washington Capitals. (DM)

Above: Ken Dryden led the NHL in goaltender wins four times and had 30 or more wins seven times in his career. (London Life-Portnoy/HHOF)

Facing page: Ken Dryden's first game as a professional was on December 12, 1970, as a member of the Montreal Voyageurs of the AHL.
He recorded a 4–0 win over the Quebec Aces. (London Life-Portnoy/HHOF)

KEN DRYDEN

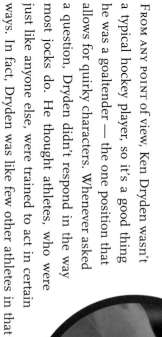

FROM ANY POINT OF VIEW, Ken Dryden wasn't a typical hockey player, so it's a good thing he was a goaltender — the one position that allows for quirky characters. Whenever asked a question, Dryden didn't respond in the way most jocks do. He thought athletes, who were just like anyone else, were trained to act in certain ways. In fact, Dryden was like few other athletes in that he wanted to play competitive sports but also complete his education. Combining a law degree and an NHL career seemed natural to Dryden, who felt he needed both for a balanced life. Although he saw himself as ordinary, his achievements on and off the ice leave Dryden with few peers.

Born in Hamilton, Ontario, Dryden grew up in the Toronto suburb of Islington, playing ball hockey in his driveway with his older brother Dave (also a goaltender) and their friends. His father thought that playing organized hockey against older boys would be good for his son's development. By the age of 15 Dryden was the top goalie in the Junior B circuit, but he decided not to play major junior because he wanted to finish high school at home. He gave up a chance to play for the Peterborough Petes but agreed to accept an honorary athletic scholarship to Cornell University in the United States. The small amount of scholarship money he received meant that he had to work as a waiter and dishwasher during the school year and on a construction crew during the summer. Nevertheless, his record at Cornell is truly remarkable. He lost only four of 83 games played and sported a 1.60 goals against average over his university career between 1966 and 1969! Dryden believed that his decision to go to Cornell guaranteed that he would never play in the NHL. (Few players came out of the American college system in that era.)

In the days before the universal draft, the Boston Bruins drafted Dryden 13th overall in 1964. But Boston traded his rights away that same year to the Montreal Canadiens for a pair of prospects, Guy Allen and Paul Reid, neither of whom played a single NHL game. None of this seemed especially relevant to Dryden, who decided to take an offer from the Canadian National Team

based in Winnipeg, where he could attend the University of Manitoba and continue to study law. The national team program folded after one year, and the Habs offered Dryden a spot on the American Hockey League Montreal Voyageurs, allowing him to complete his studies at McGill University. He played in 33 games for the Voyageurs, winning 16 times. Late in the 1970–71 season, he got a call to join the Canadiens. He got six starts and won them all, earning himself the task of facing the NHL's best goalies. Tall and lanky at 6'4" and 205 pounds, Dryden covered more of the net than most other goalies. Boston sniper Phil Esposito commented that Dryden's great reach made him feel that he was shooting at a giraffe. In spite of his large frame, Dryden was agile and extremely competitive. Good at not giving up a goal at the wrong time, he kept his teammates in a game until they got going. As the Canadiens became a dynasty, Dryden wasn't expected to be spectacular but to make key stops. He had to stay alert even when not facing many shots. To manage this, he would lean on his stick, look at the out-of-town scoreboard and keep an eye on everything going on around him.

The 1971 playoffs saw the Habs win the Cup with victories over Boston, Minnesota and Chicago. Dryden took away the Conn Smythe Trophy as the best player in the postseason. The next year saw Dryden win 39 games and capture the Calder Trophy as the league's best rookie, although the Habs lost to the New York Rangers in the 1972 playoffs. A member of Team Canada in 1972, he was in net for the final game versus the Soviet Union, which the Canadians needed to win to capture the series. Montreal regained the Cup in 1973, but Dryden shocked the hockey world: he retired rather than play under his old contract of $80,000 per

During that series against the Bruins, Dryden showed the skills that, for the next nine years, would make him one of the NHL's best goalies. Tall and lanky at 6'4" and 205 pounds, Dryden covered more of the net than most other goalies. Boston sniper Phil Esposito commented that Dryden's great reach made him feel that he was shooting at a giraffe. In spite of his large frame, Dryden was agile and extremely competitive. Good at not giving up a goal at the wrong time, he kept his teammates in a game until they got going. As the Canadiens became a dynasty, Dryden wasn't expected to be spectacular but to make key stops. He had to stay alert even when not facing many shots. To manage this, he would lean on his stick, look at the out-of-town scoreboard and keep an eye on everything going on around him.

Nothing much was expected of Dryden and the Canadiens, but they pulled off an upset in seven games. Dryden was clearly the star of the series.

Montreal moment:

On March 20, 1971, the Buffalo Sabres played the Canadiens in Montreal. Rogie Vachon started the game in the Canadiens goal while the Sabres started Dave Dryden in net. Buffalo coach Punch Imlach wanted to see Dave go up against his brother Ken, but it seemed Habs mentor Al MacNeil had no flair for the dramatic. Imlach pulled Dryden from the game and inserted Joe Daley, but then Vachon got injured and Ken Dryden entered the game. Imlach quickly sent Dave back out. The two brothers now faced each other. Montreal won the game 5–2. In a unique moment in hockey history, the brothers shook hands at centre ice.

For the record:

Ken Dryden became the third goalie in NHL history to post consecutive 40-win seasons when he won 42 in 1975–76 and 41 in 1976–77. He joined the exclusive company of Terry Sawchuk and Bernie Parent. Only Martin Brodeur has since become another member of this elite group.

Ken Dryden was a six-time NHL all-star, five times on the first team. (HHOF)

Ken Dryden won three major trophies in his career, the Conn Smythe, the Calder and (on five occasions) the Vezina Trophy. After retiring from the front office of the Toronto Maple Leafs, Dryden was elected an MP in June 2004, representing a Toronto area riding. (London Life-Portnoy/HHOF)

year. He said that there were at least six NHL goalies earning more and that pride, not just money, was the issue. The Canadiens didn't give in. Dryden articled at a Toronto law firm, but one year later he was back in the fold, earning a reported $200,000 per season. From then on, the Habs became the best team in the NHL, winning four straight Cups between 1976 and 1979. They would have been hard pressed to win so many if Dryden hadn't been there.

Dryden was only 31 years old when he retired to pursue other interests. The Habs were never the same again — at least not until goaltender Patrick Roy came along. Dryden took on a variety of roles in his post-hockey career — author, youth commissioner and hockey commentator among them — but his biggest challenge came in 1997 when he was named president of the Toronto Maple Leafs. He was elected to the Hockey Hall of Fame in 1983.

DRYDEN'S CANADIENS STATS:	GP	Wins	Losses	Ties	Shutouts	GA
regular season	397	258	57	74	46	2.24
playoffs	112	80	32	—	10	2.40

STANLEY CUPS: 6

BOB GAINEY

TO SAY THAT IN 1973 right-winger Bob Gainey was an unheralded first-round draft choice (eighth overall) would be a major understatement. In a high-scoring era, he had scored only 22 goals in his last year of junior with the Peterborough Petes. But the Canadiens weren't bothered by that. They alone seemed to know that he would be a special player. Gainey was initially surprised and even disappointed at being chosen by Montreal because he knew the organization was well-stocked with good prospects and seasoned pros. Opportunities for rookies were limited, and he thought he would be in Halifax with the farm club for the entire 1973–74 season.

After Rejean Houle and Marc Tardif jumped to the rival World Hockey Association, however, coach Scotty Bowman needed able replacements. Late in his first training camp, it looked like Gainey belonged on the big team. He earned high marks when he went after Boston tough guy Terry O'Reilly who tried to rough up captain Henri Richard. But to start the season Gainey went to Halifax with the Voyageurs. His minor-league career lasted all of six games, and he returned to the big team for 66 games — three goals, seven assists — and never looked back. It was obvious early on that Gainey would never challenge for the scoring title — he never recorded more than 47 points in one year — but it was just as clear that his great skating skills, size (6'2", 200 pounds) and strength would make him an invaluable checker. In a quiet, efficient manner, Gainey soon specialized in shutting down the opposition snipers — like Mike Bossy of the New York Islanders and Lanny McDonald of the Toronto Maple Leafs.

Gainey also contributed an infectious work ethic. He excelled at the mundane duties that make a top checker, and his small-town values — he was born in Peterborough, Ontario — made certain that playing for a glamorous team like the Canadiens would never get to his head. In addition to his checking skills, Gainey displayed a sense of anticipation that often got him in the right position to score goals.

He didn't score many — he did get 20 or more four times — but his goals were often timely, crushing any hope of an opposition rally. Being paired with another great on-ice thinker, centre Doug Jarvis, helped Gainey immensely. The two became top penalty killers who could score a key goal if needed. For example, during the last game of the 1977 semifinal against the Islanders, Gainey scored a goal at the 14-second mark to force the New York club back down on its heels. He added another marker in a 2–1 win that clinched the series. In the previous game at the Forum, the Islanders won in overtime and were set to take the Habs back to Montreal for a seventh game. Gainey was having none of that.

The Canadiens weren't the only ones to notice Gainey's hard work. In 1976 he was chosen to play for Team Canada in the inaugural Canada Cup tournament and scored two goals in five games played. During the 1979 playoffs, he was named the winner of the Conn Smythe Trophy when the Habs knocked off the New York Rangers in the finals. With 16 points in 16 games, Gainey had a superb postseason that year. In recognition of the importance of players with Gainey's skills, the NHL created the Frank J. Selke Trophy in 1978 to be awarded to the forward who excels at defence. The winner of the Selke Trophy for the first four years was none other than Gainey. (In 1982 he was the runner-up to Steve Kasper.) He was also on the Canada Cup team of 1981. His inspired play on December 31, 1979, during a Montreal 4–2 win over the Soviet army team, led Russian coach Victor Tikhanov to call Gainey "technically the best player in the world."

By 1981 Gainey became captain of the Canadiens, a role he held until he retired in 1989. He led the team to a pair of 100-point seasons (1987–88 and 1988–89) and to a Cup win in 1986. After the Habs lost the '89 finals to Calgary, he left the NHL to coach in Europe. He returned to North America after one season to coach the Minnesota North Stars. The North Stars made it to the finals in 1991

Bob Gainey scored his first NHL goal on October 27, 1973, in Montreal during a 4–2 win over the Minnesota North Stars. He was assisted by Frank Mahovlich and Henri Richard. (London Life-Portnoy/HHOF)

Bob Gainey is one of five players to play in 1,000 or more games with the Canadiens. The others are Henri Richard, Larry Robinson, Jean Béliveau and Claude Provost. (London Life-Portnoy/HHOF)

Bob Gainey recorded one career hat trick when he scored three times against the Winnipeg Jets on February 27, 1988, in a 6–0 win. (Paul Bereswill/HHOF)

For the record:

The Montreal Canadiens team of 1976–77 still holds the record for most points in one season (132) and for fewest losses (eight) in a 70-game minimum season. The Habs finished with a 60–8–12 record. Their only losses in the season were to Boston (three), Buffalo (two), Toronto (one), the New York Rangers (one) and the St. Louis Blues (one).

GAINEY'S CANADIENS STATS:	GP	G	A	P	PIM
regular season	1,160	239	262	501	585
playoffs	182	25	48	73	151

STANLEY CUPS: 5

Bob Gainey digs hard to escape Ian Turnbull (#2) of the Leafs during the 1978–79 season. Gainey was awarded the Conn Smythe Trophy for his performance in the 1979 Stanley Cup Finals. (DM)

only to lose to the Pittsburgh Penguins. Gainey soon realized he was best suited to be a general manager and hired Ken Hitchcock to coach his team. In 1999, with the team in Dallas, Gainey was once again a Stanley Cup champion. After acting in a consulting role with the Dallas club for a short while, Gainey again took on an active management position when he returned to Montreal in

June of 2003 to become the Canadiens' general manager.

Gainey had to overcome a tragedy — his wife Kathy died at a young age — to raise his family. In a typical uncomplaining fashion, Gainey successfully dealt with the problems faced by many parents. A model for doing things right, he became a worthy choice for the Hockey Hall of Fame in 1992.

REJEAN HOULE

REJEAN HOULE was the first player ever selected in the new entry draft system that the NHL implemented in 1969. Expansion in 1967 meant that all NHL teams would have "universal" access to new talent. The old system that allowed a team to sign players in their early teens was gone. But Montreal manager Sam Pollock got the league to give the Canadiens one last crack at the best available prospects in Quebec. Houle and Marc Tardif (selected second overall) represented the last two choices of a bygone era.

A native of Rouyn, Quebec, Houle's father was a miner who took his son to weekend games. The youngster played under a street light in a friend's backyard and at his high school, and followed the Habs on television every Saturday night. His favourite player was Bernie Geoffrion, but young Reggie had little confidence that he would be an NHL player one day. Good enough to be spotted by scouts, however, he left home at the age of 16 to play junior hockey in Montreal. It was easy to see why the Canadiens became interested in the 5'11" left-winger after he won the Red Tilson Trophy as the best player in the Ontario Hockey Association. As captain of the Montreal Jr. Canadiens, Houle had racked up 108 points, including a league best 53 goals in the 54 games of the 1968–69 season. He played in nine games for the Canadiens in 1969–70 but spent most of the year in Nova Scotia playing for the Habs farm team and scoring 25 points in 27 games. He was deemed ready for the big team but not in the scoring role he had played in junior.

Houle played in 66 games for the Habs in 1970–71 — scoring 10 times and totalling 10 points — but he really shone in the Stanley Cup finals when assigned to check the great Bobby Hull of Chicago. He did a good job on the Black Hawks superstar and chipped in seven points in 20 playoff games that led the Canadiens to a surprising champi-

onship win. He earned $15,000 a year in his rookie season and $19,000 more in bonuses because of the Cup win! Houle's role was cast, and he settled in with the Habs as a good role player. He won another Cup with the team in 1973. Then the World Hockey Association offered him a contract he couldn't refuse. This offer put Houle, who was always worried about financial security, in a much better salary category. He scored many goals for the Quebec Nordiques — 118 markers in 214 games — and learned he still had offensive skills.

Even though he was a WHA star, he missed being a Montreal Canadien and returned to the club three years later. He felt he had become a more mature player capable of playing any forward position. Sam Pollock and Scotty Bowman recognized Houle's versatility when they took him back. Never big at just 165 pounds, Houle was a good skater and top penalty killer. A determined forechecker, he understood the game very well. Continuing to be seen primarily as a defensive player, Houle went along with that perception since it got him ice time. But Houle proved he had indeed become a better all-round player by potting 22 goals in 1976–77 and netting 30 in 1977–78. His goal total slipped to 17 the following year, but the Habs nevertheless took their third straight Cup.

In 1981–82 Houle scored 27 times but then left the NHL after just one more season. He went to work for Molson Breweries in a public relations role. His loyalty was rewarded in 1995 when Ronald Corey named him Canadiens general manager to replace Serge Savard. With no previous hockey management experience, he faced a crisis early in his tenure when he was forced to trade superstar goaltender Patrick Roy. His on-the-job learning came to an end in November of 2000. He is now an ambassador for the Canadiens.

HOULE'S CANADIENS STATS:	GP	G	A	P	PIM
regular season	635	161	247	408	395
playoffs	90	14	34	48	66
STANLEY CUPS: 5					

Rejean Houle led the Montreal Jr. Canadiens to the Memorial Cup in 1969 on a team that featured Gilbert Perreault, Richard Martin, Marc Tardif and Jocelyn Guevremont. The Canadiens beat the Regina Pats in four straight games to take the Cup. [Paul Bereswill/HHOF]

DOUG JARVIS

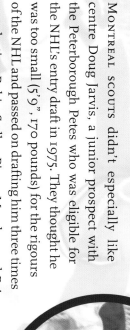

MONTREAL scouts didn't especially like centre Doug Jarvis, a junior prospect with the Peterborough Petes who was eligible for the NHL's entry draft in 1975. They thought he was too small (5'9", 170 pounds) for the rigours of the NHL and passed on drafting him three times — selecting Robin Sadler, Pierre Mondou and Brian Engblom instead. Finally the Toronto Maple Leafs took Jarvis 24th overall. But Montreal coach Scotty Bowman pestered general manager Sam Pollock to acquire Jarvis. An opportunity developed when the Leafs expressed interest in Canadiens goaltender Wayne Thomas. While dealing with the Leafs, Pollock learned of their interest in minor-league prospect Greg Hubick. Pollock proposed to give the Leafs the rights to Thomas for draft choices and to take a prospect (Jarvis) for Hubick. The master dealer Pollock had struck again! Hubick played one uneventful season for the Leafs while Jarvis anchored Montreal's top checking units for four straight Stanley Cups.

Bowman had been tipped off about Jarvis, a native of Brantford, Ontario, by his junior coach Roger Neilson. Bowman was intrigued by Neilson's insistence that Jarvis was hockey's best faceoff man. At first Bowman thought Neilson meant that Jarvis was tops at winning draws in junior hockey, but the brainy Petes coach insisted that he was the best, period. In 1974–75 Jarvis scored 45 goals and 33 points in 64 games for the Peterborough club, but not many people expected him to score at the NHL level. Jarvis was considering the World Hockey Association where he thought he would get more playing time than with the Canadiens. But Pollock convinced him to attend the Montreal training camp, luring him with possible job openings. At the end of camp Pollock was going to send the youngster to Halifax for some seasoning, but an injury to centre Jacques Lemaire gave Jarvis a reprieve.

He would make the most of his opportunity. True to his billing, Jarvis was indeed a top faceoff man and was soon paired with speedy left-winger Bob Gainey to form one of the top checking duos in the game's history. Veteran Jim Roberts was also helpful on the right side. The trio became efficient at shutting down the opposition's best line. A consistent worker, Jarvis was good at positioning himself. His intensity helped to make him a top checker and penalty killer. His faceoff ability allowed the Canadiens to control the puck in their end and to lead the NHL in fewest goals allowed year after year. While not a top goal scorer, Jarvis achieved double digits every year he was with Montreal, except in his rookie year when he scored only five. As a Hab he scored 16 times twice and 20 in 1981–1982, his final season with the Canadiens. He also produced between 30 and 40 points a year. Above all, Jarvis became known for his durability. Despite his smallish size, he didn't miss a single regular-season game in six straight seasons with Montreal.

Sometimes overlooked as a member of the powerful Canadiens teams between 1975 and 1979, Jarvis was well-respected by the opposition, who understood his true value. When the Habs were forced to trade defenceman Rod Langway to Washington, the Capitals asked for Jarvis as part of the blockbuster package that included Craig Laughlin and Engblom. (Montreal received Rick Green and Ryan Walter in exchange.) Jarvis lasted only two and a half years in Washington before he was dealt to Hartford during the 1985–86 season. After two years as a Whaler, he was sent to the minors with 964 consecutive games played in the NHL, still a regular-season record. He never returned to the NHL. He retired after the 1987–88 campaign and turned to coaching. Jarvis was an assistant coach of the Dallas Stars when they won the Stanley Cup in 1999.

JARVIS' CANADIENS STATS:	GP	G	A	P	PIM
regular season	560	91	154	245	151
playoffs	72	11	20	31	26

STANLEY CUPS: 4

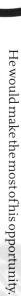

During his NHL career Doug Jarvis won two major awards, the Selke Trophy in 1984 and the Bill Masterton Trophy in 1987. (Mecca/HHOF)

GUY LAFLEUR

THE MONTH OF June 1971 was an eventful one for the Montreal Canadiens. On June 9, the great Jean Béliveau officially announced his retirement, and on the very next day, the Habs had the first choice in the entry draft, even though they had just taken the Stanley Cup! At selection time, Montreal general manager Sam Pollock decided to have some fun and called a time out, even though everybody in the room at the Queen Elizabeth Hotel knew who he was going to select. After the laughter died down, Pollock announced the Canadiens were taking right-winger Guy Lafleur, secured earlier in a trade with the California Seals. That choice fulfilled what seemed inevitable for the native of Thurso, Quebec.

Lafleur was a scoring machine in junior, who took his club, the Quebec Remparts, to the Memorial Cup in 1971. In his last two junior hockey seasons, the swift-skating Lafleur scored an incredible 233 goals in 118 games. The talk of Canada, he was clearly the hottest prospect out of junior since Bobby Orr joined the NHL in 1967. At first it looked like Lafleur was destined to be on the West Coast for either the Seals or the Los Angeles Kings. Pollock's trade secured California's first pick — they had only 45 points in the season — and Ralph Backstrom went to the Kings to help them finish higher in the standings, which they did with 62 points in the NHL's West Division. Detroit and Vancouver were also candidates to select first overall, but they ended up with 55 and 56 points respectively in the East Division. Lafleur wasn't about to go to California and might have waited to sign with the WHA's Quebec Nordiques for the 1972–73 season.

Lafleur's first few years with the Habs weren't easy. He had trouble adjusting to the big city, and the goals were harder to come by in the professional league. He did score 29 times and totalled 64 points, quite good for a rookie, but more was expected from him. Lafleur scored 28 the next year to help Montreal win the

Stanley Cup, which seemed to keep everyone happy for the moment. But a 21-goal performance in his third year raised suspicions that Lafleur was just an ordinary player. Then something magical happened early in his fourth season when he shed his helmet and coach Scotty Bowman used him in more situations, including penalty-killing duties. Once the pressure was off, the goals started coming in bunches. The 1974–75 season saw Lafleur score 53 times. He began to establish himself as the game's best player. Before injuries slowed him down, he followed that up with seasons of 56, 56, 60, 52 and 50 goals. During those years he was the game's most dominating forward, virtually unstoppable as the Habs took four more Cups.

Lafleur's game was built around his tremendous skating ability and his great sense of anticipation. He lived and breathed the game, and it showed in his play. His great shot was like a howitzer, and many a goalie whiffed while trying to stop his hard drive. Like many great players, Lafleur was all instinct on the ice, knowing exactly what to do when opportunities arose. He was a difficult player at practices: the Canadiens could never work on their power play with him because he would never follow orders. Engrained in the minds of hockey fans was Lafleur's long blond hair blowing in the breeze. Not big at 6' and 180 pounds, Lafleur was all skill and flair, like many of the great French-Canadian players of the past who had worked in Montreal. Charismatic both on and off the ice, he was regarded as the perfect player to accept the symbolic torch passed down to him from Béliveau. The former great Canadiens captain offered Lafleur sweater number four, which had been his junior number, but the youngster wisely declined in anticipation that one day kids would want to wear his sweater number (10).

In a few years, however, it all came tumbling down for Lafleur. After scoring 27 goals in two straight seasons, he added 30 goals

Guy Lafleur won three major trophies during his career with the Montreal Canadiens. He won the Hart twice, the Art Ross three times and the Conn Smythe once. (London Life-Portnoy/HHOF)

I was always a proud player

and I played for a proud team. When I hear guys say that team spirit is not important, and that you can win without it, I don't think so."

Guy Lafleur

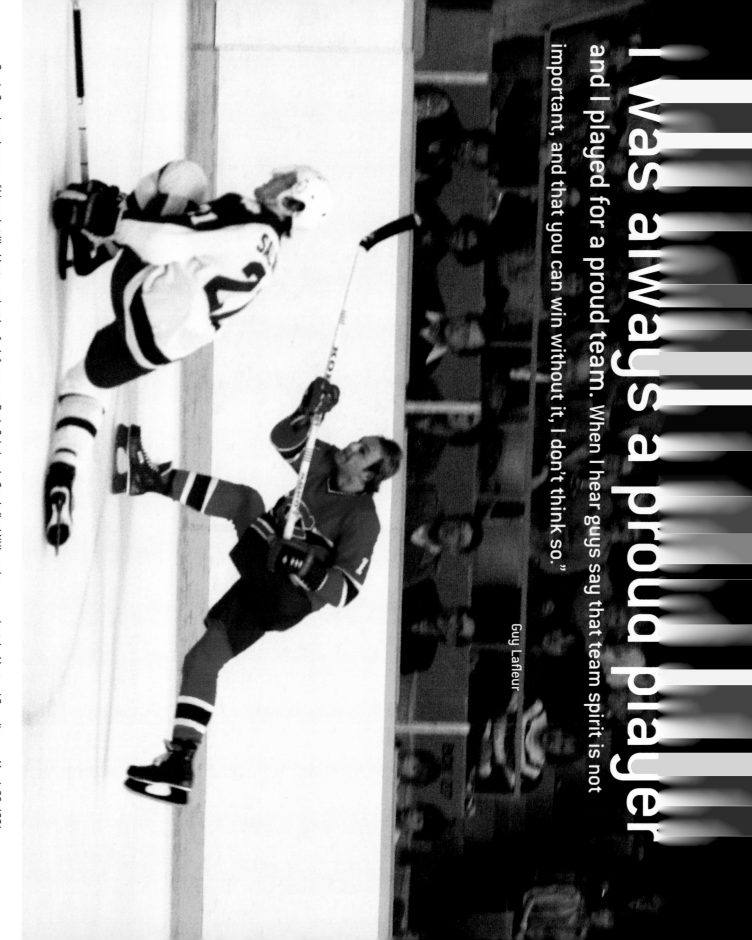

Guy Lafleur launches one of his rocket-like blasts against Leafs defenceman Borje Salming. Lafleur's final NHL goal came against the Montreal Canadiens on March 30, 1991, when he was a member of the Quebec Nordiques. He beat Patrick Roy for his 560th career marker. The Montreal Forum crowd gave him a six-minute standing ovation. (DM)

in 1983–84, but he was hardly the dominating player he had been. His office habits raised concerns at a time when the team had lost many players from their championship years. The Habs were losing many more games than ever. A new approach under coach Jacques Lemaire stressed defence and threw out the old fire-wagon style of play. In 1984–85, frustrated by his lack of playing time, Lafleur scored just two times in 19 games. Although he tried to resolve his differences with Lemaire, Lafleur abruptly decided to end his career. The Canadiens weren't about to trade their former

superstar, so Lafleur took a front-office position. In reality, Lafleur wasn't ready to retire. He eventually left the Canadiens organization, feeling that he had no significant duties and insufficient pay.

Three years later Lafleur was back in the NHL with the New York Rangers for one year and with the sad-sack Quebec Nordiques for two. In his final year, 1990–91, he had 12 goals in 59 games. It's never easy for a superstar like Lafleur to find a comfortable role in retirement, but eventually he found his way back to the Canadiens (where he belongs) as an ambassador.

167

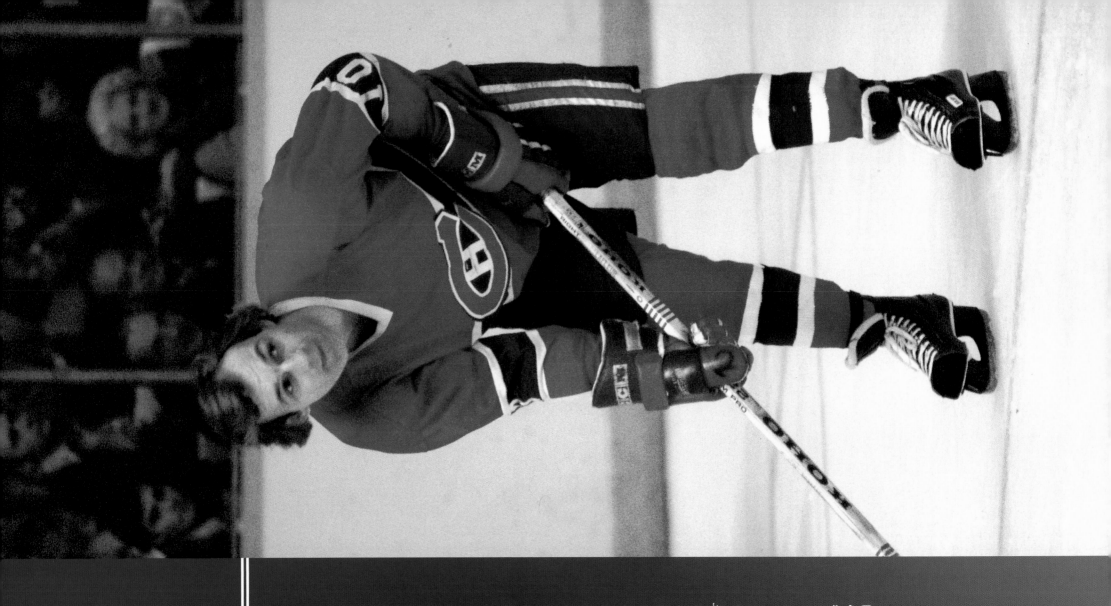

Montreal moment:

It looked like the Canadiens' hope for a fourth straight Stanley Cup was going to be stopped by the Boston Bruins during the seventh game of the 1979 semifinal played at the Forum. The Habs were trailing 4–3 late in the contest when suddenly the Bruins were called for too many men on the ice. The power play was going to be Montreal's last gasp. Jacques Lemaire carried the puck along the boards over the Boston blue line and dropped a pass back to a trailing Guy Lafleur. Without any hesitation Lafleur hammered a perfect shot into the far side of the net past goaltender Gilles Gilbert. The Bruins netminder had no chance on that rocket of a shot, and the Canadiens won the game in overtime to oust the Bruins. The Habs went on to best the New York Rangers in five games to take the Cup for a fourth consecutive time. But it wouldn't have happened if Lafleur hadn't taken his well-placed shot to kill the Bruins.

Known as "The Flower," Guy Lafleur was the NHL's first team all-star right-winger six consecutive years from 1975 to 1980. [DM]

Guy Lafleur (shown here early in his career when he still wore a helmet) scored his first NHL goal in Los Angeles during a Montreal 3–1 victory over the Kings on October 27, 1971. (DM)

LAFLEUR'S CANADIENS STATS:	GP	G	A	P	PIM
regular season	1961	518	728	1,246	381
playoffs	124	57	76	133	67

STANLEY CUPS: 5

YVON LAMBERT

RAISED ON A FARM near Drummondville, Quebec, Yvon Lambert had to do the chores because his father worked in town. As a result, young Yvon had little time for hockey, except for the occasional game on television. He began skating at 15 when he got a pair of skates for Christmas. Playing junior hockey for the Drummondville Rangers, he scored 50 goals and 101 points in 51 games in the 1969–70 season. The Detroit Red Wings' scouts selected him 40th overall in 1970 to play the 1970–71 season for Port Huron (23 goals, 41 points) of the International Hockey League. For some reason, however, Lambert was available in the reverse draft of 1971. The Montreal Canadiens liked what they saw of the rangy (6'2", 200-pound) left-winger and took him away from the Red Wings organization.

The Canadiens knew Lambert needed more seasoning and sent him to Nova Scotia of the American Hockey League for the entire 1971–72 campaign. He didn't consider himself a top prospect when he played for the Voyageurs but proved that he could score (70 goals over two seasons) and that he was willing to drop the gloves if he had to. He was the last to be cut at the Habs' 1972 training camp. But in 1972–73 he led the entire AHL in goals with 52 and in points with 104. He produced those numbers on a line with Tony Featherstone and Morris Stefaniw. (That line tore up the AHL with a combined 129 goals and 308 points.) He got into the Montreal lineup for one game of the '72–'73 season, playing one shift at centre (Peter Mahovlich needed a rest) between Guy Lafleur and Marc Tardif. He nearly scored a goal but never got back on the ice again!

Lambert's impressive AHL numbers earned him a spot in Montreal. He got into 60 games with the Habs in 1973–74, scoring six goals and

totalling 16 points. He then proved he was a bona fide NHL player with consecutive 32-goal seasons. He scored his first two NHL goals on November 17, 1973, when the Habs knocked off the Buffalo Sabres 8–5. Lambert settled in as a consistent 20-plus goal scorer and did much of the corner work required on a great hockey team. He spent much of his time in the corners or in front of the net, especially on the power play, taking a beating while getting the job done. Although not stylish, he was effective in spite of his lack of skating skills. Not overly aggressive — 74 was his highest penalty minute total — he was smart about using his large size to gain the advantage over his opponents. Lambert fit perfectly on a line with Mario Tremblay and Doug Risebrough, a second unit the envy of most teams.

Lambert had a knack for scoring timely goals. He is best remembered for his overtime winner against the Boston Bruins in the seventh game of the 1979 semifinal series when the Habs nearly lost their chance for a fourth straight Stanley Cup. He also scored a goal against the Soviet Red Army team on December 31, 1975, in what has became a legendary contest in the minds of hockey fans who witnessed the 3–3 draw at the Forum. After being on four Cup-winning teams in Montreal, Lambert was again available on waivers. The Buffalo Sabres — now coached by former Montreal mentor Scotty Bowman, who had always been tough on Lambert — claimed his rights for the 1981–82 season for $2,500. He had one very good season in Buffalo (25 goals, 39 assists). Then his career came full circle as he played with the Sabres' farm club in Rochester (of the AHL) for two seasons, before retiring at the end of the 1983–84 season. He coached the Verdun Junior Canadiens for the 1984–85 season.

LAMBERT'S CANADIENS STATS:	GP	G	A	P	PIM
regular season	606	181	234	415	302
playoffs	86	24	22	46	65

STANLEY CUPS: 4

Yvon Lambert had six seasons of 20 or more goals during his career with the Canadiens, including 22 in his last year (1980–81) with the team. (Mecca/HHOF)

GUY LAPOINTE

As Guy Lapointe was growing up in Montreal, he often thought about becoming a policeman like his brother. His father Gerard was a fireman, used to life as a public servant, but he wanted his son to continue playing hockey. An offer to turn professional by the Montreal Canadiens persuaded Lapointe to give hockey a chance as a career. The Canadiens turned out to be grateful that Lapointe's father was a hockey fan. Otherwise, they might have missed out on a Hall of Fame defenceman who helped anchor the team's blue line for six Stanley Cups!

Lapointe was one of the last players to sign with the Habs before the arrival of the universal draft. There is little doubt Lapointe would have been a high draft choice had all NHL teams been given the chance to select the solid 5'11", 200-pound blueliner. After playing two years of junior hockey in Verdun, Lapointe joined the Montreal Jr. Canadiens for the 1967–68 season, earning 38 points in 51 games. The next season saw the francophone Lapointe turn professional with the Houston Apollos of the Central Hockey League. He got into his first NHL game with Montreal. The 1969–70 season, when Lapointe had eight goals and 30 points for the Nova Scotia Voyageurs, saw him named to the American Hockey League's first all-star team. Defenceman Serge Savard's leg injury opened up a position for Lapointe in 1970–71. He quickly showed he belonged with a surprising 15 goals and 44 points. (In the minors he hadn't shown any great ability to score.) He was especially strong in the playoffs when the Habs knocked off Boston, Minnesota and Chicago to win the Cup. Lapointe was suddenly a well-known NHL defenceman.

Lapointe only got better. Like many Habs of that era he credited coach Claude Ruel with developing him as a defenceman. He played a strong two-way game, a sort of a cross between teammates

Larry Robinson and Savard. (The trio became known as the "Big Three.") He had a terrific shot from the point, hard, accurate and deadly on the power play. While not overly physical — he could get tough if riled — Lapointe was superb at lugging the puck out of the Montreal end. Few defencemen in the league could match his offensive prowess. He scored over 20 goals three times in consecutive years during his career with Montreal. A superb skater with superior passing skills, he wouldn't hesitate to hurl his body in front of an opposition blast. As a testament to his all-round play, Lapointe was selected to play for Team Canada in 1972 and 1976 and for the NHL team of the 1979 Challenge Cup. During the '72 Summit Series, Lapointe and Savard were in the lineup for all the Canadian victories.

Lapointe liked to keep his teammates loose with jokes and a carefree approach. But on the ice he was all business, unafraid to let his teammates know when their efforts should improve. He knew it was special to play for the Montreal Canadiens, and he didn't want his teammates to lose sight of that fact. Unfortunately, a serious eye injury hampered Lapointe, who realized that the team was developing new blueliners. He felt it was time to move on. During the 1981–82 season, he was dealt to the St. Louis Blues for a second-round draft choice that turned out to be Sergio Momesso. After one year with the Blues, Lapointe signed as a free agent for the 1983–84 season with the Boston Bruins, who hoped the star blueliner would replace Brad Park. As a Bruin Lapointe recorded 18 points in 54 contests.

Since retiring, Lapointe has held coaching and scouting positions. In 2002 he became the director of amateur scouting for the Minnesota Wild. He was elected to the Hall of Fame in 1993.

Guy Lapointe won a Stanley Cup as a rookie in 1970–71 while filling in for the injured Serge Savard. (London Life-Portnoy/HHOF)

Above: Guy Lapointe was named to the NHL's second all-star team for three consecutive years (1975, 1976, 1977). (Mecca/HHOF)

Facing page: Lapointe is harassed by the tenacious Bobby Clarke of the Philadelphia Flyers. Lapointe scored a career-high 28 goals in 1974-75. (Frank Prazak/HHOF)

LAPOINTE'S CANADIENS STATS:	GP	G	A	P	PIM
regular season	777	166	406	572	812
playoffs	112	25	43	68	121

STANLEY CUPS: 5

Guy Lapointe had 35 or more assists in a season seven times during his career with the Canadiens. (Mecca/HHOF)

P E T E R   M A H O V L I C H

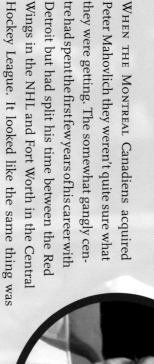

WHEN THE MONTREAL Canadiens acquired Peter Mahovlich they weren't quite sure what they were getting. The somewhat gangly centre had spent the first few years of his career with Detroit but had split his time between the Red Wings in the NHL and Fort Worth in the Central Hockey League. It looked like the same thing was going to happen to Mahovlich in Montreal. He split the 1969–70 season, playing 36 games for the Canadiens (nine goals, eight assists) and 31 games for the Nova Scotia Voyageurs. His stint in the American Hockey League led to 21 goals and 40 points. But it was Canadiens left-winger John Ferguson who did the most good. Ferguson told Mahovlich that to ensure NHL employment he should use his large size (6'5", 210 pounds) to run over the opposition. Mahovlich heeded the advice. In 1970–71 he stayed with the big team for the entire year, scoring 35 goals and 61 points with 181 penalty minutes. Mahovlich went from lackadaisical to aggressive, showing the confidence he needed to play in the NHL.

For the longest time, it looked like Mahovlich would join his brother Frank, a superstar on the Toronto Maple Leafs. Younger by nine years, Peter idolized Frank. The Leafs were set to select Peter in the 1963 draft, the first ever held, but Detroit scout Jimmy Skinner had his eye on him, and the Red Wings selected Mahovlich second overall. The Red Wings had high hopes for the youngster: Mahovlich was big and as a junior with the Hamilton Red Wings he was a point-per-game player. Scoring well in the minors, however, wasn't enough, and the Red Wings ran out of patience with the awkward pivot and dealt him to Montreal in June of 1969. It was the best thing that could happen to Mahovlich. He would make the most of his opportunity. The trade eventually reunited the Mahovlich brothers — they had been together briefly with the

Red Wings — when the Habs acquired Frank in a January 1971 deal with Detroit. Both Peter and Frank were outstanding in the 1971 playoffs and helped the Canadiens win back the Stanley Cup. Peter scored 10 goals, added six assists and sipped champagne from the Cup for the first time. Mahovlich scored 35 times in 1971–72 and was selected to play for Canada in the 1972 Summit Series against the Russians. Quite effective in the seven games he played, he scored one of the most memorable goals in the series, a short-handed one and as impressive an individual effort as anyone will ever see. Upon returning to the NHL regular season, Mahovlich's goal total dropped to 21, but the Habs regained the Cup with another finals win over the Chicago Black Hawks. By this point Mahovlich was a solid member of the Canadiens, posting 36-, 35- and 34-goal seasons over the next three years.

Naturally, it helped Mahovlich to be centring a line with Guy Lafleur and Steve Shutt, two future Hall of Famers. He enjoyed his best year in 1974–75 when he had 117 points. He followed that up with 105 points in 1975–76 when the Canadiens won another Cup. In 1976–77, although the team won another Cup, his goals started to decline (only 15). By early the next season, Mahovlich had fallen out of favour with Habs fans and management. He was dealt to Pittsburgh for centre Pierre Larouche. He scored 25 times in 57 games for the Penguins to finish the year with a total of 28, but it was his last good year in the NHL.

Pittsburgh sent him back to Detroit where the Red Wings signed him to a lucrative contract to start the 1979–80 season. He produced 66 points in 80 games, but the Red Wings weren't a playoff club. Out of hockey between 1982 and 1985, he came out of retirement to play for the Toledo Goaldiggers of the International Hockey League, totalling 14 points in 23 games.

MAHOVLICH'S CANADIENS STATS:	GP	G	A	P	PIM
regular season	581	223	346	569	695
playoffs	86	30	41	71	134

STANLEY CUPS: 4

The Canadiens acquired Peter Mahovlich along with Bart Crashley from the Detroit Red Wings for Garry Monahan and Doug Piper on June 6, 1969. (Frank Prazak/HHOF)

SAM POLLOCK

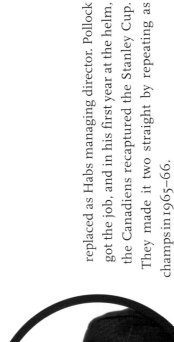

SAM POLLOCK was all of 21 years of age when Frank Selke Sr. hired him to work for the Montreal Canadiens. Given a desk in the Forum hallway when he first started, Pollock didn't mind working his way up from the bottom. The Canadiens wanted to hire him because of his work in minor hockey in the Montreal area. His main task was to groom future prospects for the Canadiens' big-league team. He got the coaching job with Montreal's top junior club, which he held between 1947 and 1952, and quickly proved himself by winning a Memorial Cup in 1950. Pollock was on his way to making a name for himself in the hockey world.

Pollock was born on December 15, 1925, in Montreal. He grew up wanting to be a baseball player. He also played hockey, although he showed no real talent for the game. Good at organizing sports teams — even though he had a regular job with a railway agency in Montreal — Pollock had a great mind for business and focused on dealing effectively with people. He brought players along slowly until they were ready, a difficult process at the best of times. Intense and driven to succeed, Pollock wasn't afraid to show his displeasure as a coach in the next season. Pollock imposed strict codes on his athletes — always expecting a shirt and tie — and was interested to learn how youngsters reacted to his discipline. By the 1959–60 season Pollock was named general manager of the Hull-Ottawa Canadiens of the newly formed EPHL, which brought him one step closer to managing the Habs.

In addition to winning games as a coach, Pollock forged a reputation for developing players who allowed the Habs to make a transition after winning five Stanley Cups in a row. Players like Bobby Rousseau, Ralph Backstrom, Jacques Laperriere, Yvan Cournoyer, Claude Larose, Gilles Tremblay, J. C. Tremblay, Terry Harper and Jim Roberts were all considered "Sam's boys." Pollock worked at replacing aging players with younger ones who could take their place. By the 1962–63 season Pollock said the Habs owned 75 professional players and had the rights to over 200 amateur prospects. By the end of the 1963–64 season, Canadiens upper management felt that it was time for Selke to be

replaced as Habs managing director. Pollock got the job, and in his first year at the helm, the Canadiens recaptured the Stanley Cup. They made it two straight by repeating as champs in 1965–66.

As general manager of the team, Pollock emphasized that no one season was more important than the long-term health of the organization. For example, he stuck with coach Scotty Bowman, even though the Habs had gone through a couple of down years, and it paid off later with four straight Cups. He was adept at handling difficult situations, and although he didn't have to make many blockbuster deals, he could still pull one off when necessary — such as the acquisition of Dick Duff in 1964 and Frank Mahovlich in 1971. Pollock wasn't afraid to take back players he had disagreed with — like Ken Dryden and Rejean Houle — if it meant the team was better off. The first hockey manager to recognize the value of draft picks, he traded older players who could still contribute for high selections from teams hungry to win in the short term. In the early seventies he stockpiled many draft choices that kept Montreal well-fortified for years. Sometimes he was able to turn one draft choice into more by trading down slightly if he knew he could still get what he wanted. His managerial style and clever deals took the Canadiens to a remarkable nine Cups in the 14 seasons he was in charge!

Never one to smile much — hence the nickname "Sad Sam" — or to relish the tag of genius given to him by hockey observers, Pollock sensed it was time to move on when the team was sold in 1978. Molson Breweries repurchased the team, and Pollock decided to resign, since he had a guaranteed contract (and was a stockholder) with the previous company owned by the Bronfman family of Montreal. Although he missed out on the Habs championship of 1979, it was still clearly his team. His departure ensured that Bowman would leave, which would set the Canadiens organization back for years until Serge Savard took over.

There has never been a general manager as successful as Pollock. His influence over many people who worked for the Canadiens persists: plenty of them have achieved great success in many different organizations. Pollock was elected to the Hockey Hall of Fame in 1978.

"People build teams in certain ways. I've always traded for futures — not pasts."

Sam Pollock

Sam Pollock did not think of himself a "hockey genius" but considering his record as Habs general manager it's a moniker that suited him perfectly. (Frank Prazak/HHOF)

POLLOCK'S CANADIENS STATS*:	GP	W	L	T
regular season	1,068	644	248	176
playoffs	162	116	46	—

STANLEY CUPS: 9

* as general manager

DOUG RISEBROUGH

DOUG RISEBROUGH wasn't expected to make the Canadiens lineup right out of junior, so it was no surprise when the feisty centre was sent to the Nova Scotia Voyageurs of the American Hockey League to start the 1974–75 season. In seven games, Risebrough scored five times and added four assists. At the same time, the big Montreal team needed to shake things up after a rough start to the season. Risebrough got the call to go up to the NHL. He made the most of his opportunity and stayed in Montreal for the rest of the '74–'75 campaign, posting a respectable 47 points (15 goals, 32 assists) in 64 games. Risebrough would never be in the minors again.

With the seventh overall selection, the Canadiens chose the 5'11" 180-pound Risebrough in the 1974 entry draft. The Montreal scouts liked the way Risebrough played. He scored well with the Guelph Biltmores and the Kitchener Rangers during his junior career, which caught the attention of the Montreal bird dogs. He became an invaluable member of the Habs during their Stanley Cup run in the seventies. The line he centred with Mario Tremblay and Yvon Lambert scored many key goals and often set the tempo for the Habs.

When Montreal won the Stanley Cup in 1976, the 1975–76 season began with the Philadelphia Flyers as defending champions. The Habs knew they had to match the Flyers physically for a chance at the Cup. As far as Risebrough was concerned there was no better time to demonstrate Montreal muscle than in a preseason game at the Forum. He took on Dave Schultz, and then the following night in Philadelphia he took on Flyers captain Bobby Clarke. That night the Canadiens dressed a big, tough lineup that featured Pierre Bouchard, Sean Shanahan, Glenn Goldup and Rick Chartraw. The Montreal side pounded out a victory, and they knew right there and then that they could match the

Flyers at their own game. It was no contest in the finals when the two teams met for the Cup: the Habs won in four straight games. The Canadiens repeated as champions in 1977. Risebrough scored the opening goal of the finals that year when he blasted a 25-foot shot past Gerry Cheevers in the Boston net. The Habs won the opening game 7–3 and the Cup in four straight once again!

Risebrough was never a big goal scorer with the Canadiens — his highest total as a Hab was 22 in 1976–77 — but he often reached the 20-goal mark and the 100 penalty minute mark. Risebrough — like Doug Jarvis, Bob Gainey and Lambert — knew he was a role player. Under Scotty Bowman's tutelage, these four players were willing to do their jobs without complaint, much like the role players who excelled under coach Toe Blake in the '50s and '60s. As injuries began to slow Risebrough down, Montreal manager Irving Grundman looked to move the pivot before it was too late to get anything. Risebrough was dealt to Calgary for a couple of draft choices, which didn't turn out well for the Habs. He enjoyed his best goal-scoring year with the Flames (23 in 1984–85) and helped the young team make the finals in 1986 when, ironically enough, Montreal beat Calgary!

He soon became an assistant coach in Calgary (winning a Cup in 1989) and then moved into management where he was only moderately successful. Dismissed as general manager in 1995, he was named to the same position with the expansion Minnesota Wild in 1999. He wisely took a few former teammates with him to Minnesota — Jacques Lemaire as coach, Mario Tremblay as an assistant coach and Guy Lapointe as a scout — and quickly showed he was better prepared for the job than he had been in Calgary. The Wild made it the Western Conference final in just three seasons.

RISEBROUGH'S CANADIENS STATS:	GP	G	A	P	PIM
regular season	493	117	185	302	959
playoffs	74	11	20	31	143
STANLEY CUPS: 4					

Doug Risebrough led the Montreal Canadiens in penalty minutes for three straight seasons between 1974 and 1977. (HHOF)

LARRY ROBINSON

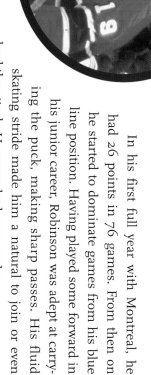

BEFORE THE 1973 Stanley Cup playoffs, few people knew who Larry Robinson was, especially since the Montreal Canadiens were loaded with superstars. But when regular defenceman Jacques Laperriere was injured in the third period of a playoff game against Philadelphia, Robinson was thrown into the fray, and the big blueliner (6'4", 225 pounds) didn't disappoint. The Habs were down one game in the series and didn't want to lose another overtime game at the Forum. The puck came to Robinson just inside the Flyers blue line. He wound up and let go a blast that beat Philadelphia netminder Doug Favell for the game winner and a 4–3 victory. After the game, Robinson told the television audience in an interview that his Montreal teammates had told him, "Philadelphia has their big bird [Don Saleski] and now we have ours." It wasn't the last time Robinson would impose his presence on the ice with predictable results!

Robinson wasn't exactly thrilled when the Habs chose him 20th overall in 1971. The team had just won the Stanley Cup and had plenty of depth. The Kitchener Rangers graduate was sent to Halifax to play for the Nova Scotia Voyageurs for the 1971–72 season. Coach Al MacNeil told him that he had better start using his size if he ever wanted to play in the NHL. A farm boy who grew up in Marvelville, Ontario, Robinson certainly had the physical strength to play a robust game. He quickly got the message. He got a big break when the Voyageurs got veteran defenceman Noel Price to join the club. Price tutored the raw but athletic rookie. The Voyageurs went on to capture the Calder Cup as the first Canadian-based team to win the coveted minor-league championship trophy. Robinson split the next season between Halifax and Montreal. But when he recorded 39 points in 38 AHL games, there was no way the Habs could keep him off the big team.

In his first full year with Montreal, he had 26 points in 76 games. From then on he started to dominate games from his blue line position. Having played some forward in his junior career, Robinson was adept at carrying the puck, making sharp passes. His fluid skating stride made him a natural to join or even lead the attack. He never had a 20-goal season — 19 was his highest — but he produced 10 seasons of 50 or more points while with the Canadiens. (He had a career best 85 in 1976–77.) For most of his years with Montreal, Robinson worked in perfect partnership with Serge Savard, who protected his end while Robinson went on his offensive forays. Robinson could calm things down or lead an exciting rush as required. The Canadiens gave their opponents plenty to worry about but none more so than Robinson, who would come out on top in any game the other team wanted to play. Boston coach Don Cherry warned his players not to wake Robinson up. If they did, they were usually sorry!

Robinson's physical reputation solidified during a couple of encounters with the Philadelphia Flyers. The first came against heavyweight champion Dave Schultz, who made the mistake of seeking out Robinson during a bench-clearing brawl. The Habs rearguard pounded out a decisive victory over the Flyers enforcer and shocked many watching on American national television. The other incident occurred during the 1976 Stanley Cup finals when Robinson pasted Flyer forward Gary Dornhoeffer into the boards at the Forum. The thunderous hit could be heard all over the arena. The game had to be stopped while the damage to the boards where Robinson had delivered his blow was repaired! After that, the Habs took the Cup away from the Flyers and held on to it for the next four years, while Robinson was rarely challenged again.

Larry Robinson scored his first NHL goal by beating former Canadiens netminder Rogie Vachon during a 7–1 win by the Habs over the Los Angeles Kings on February 3, 1973. Frank Mahovlich and Guy Lapointe assisted on the goal. (London Life-Portnoy/HHOF)

"They judge seasons here [in Montreal] in terms of winning the Cup or not winning the Cup. That's just the way it is."

Larry Robinson

When Robinson was selected 20th overall in the NHL entry draft in 1971, the Canadiens also selected Guy Lafleur (1st), Chuck Arnason (7th) and Murray Wilson (11th) in the first round. (London Life-Portnoy/HHOF)

With no agent representing him, Robinson signed his first contract with the Montreal Canadiens in the summer of 1971. Claude Ruel got him to sign for $7,000 in salary and $7,000 in bonus money. [DM]

As evidence of his superior play, Robinson was awarded the Norris Trophy on three occasions and was named a first team all-star three times as well. His playoff performance in 1978 earned him the Conn Smythe Trophy as the fourth defenceman to win the coveted award. As some of his teammates left, Robinson remained the Canadiens' biggest asset on the blue line. He was named to the Canadian squad for the 1984 Canada Cup, his third such selection in his career. He said he felt rejuvenated playing with the likes of Ray Bourque, Paul Coffey and Doug Wilson.

In 1986 he helped the Habs hoist another Cup, the last of his illustrious career.

Robinson went on to play for the Los Angeles Kings for three seasons before he tried coaching. He was an assistant on the staff led by former teammate Jacques Lemaire in New Jersey when the Devils won the Cup in 1995 and was the head coach when they won the Cup again in 2000. Dismissed by the Devils two years later, he will likely find another head coaching position in the near future. He was elected to the Hockey Hall of Fame in 1995.

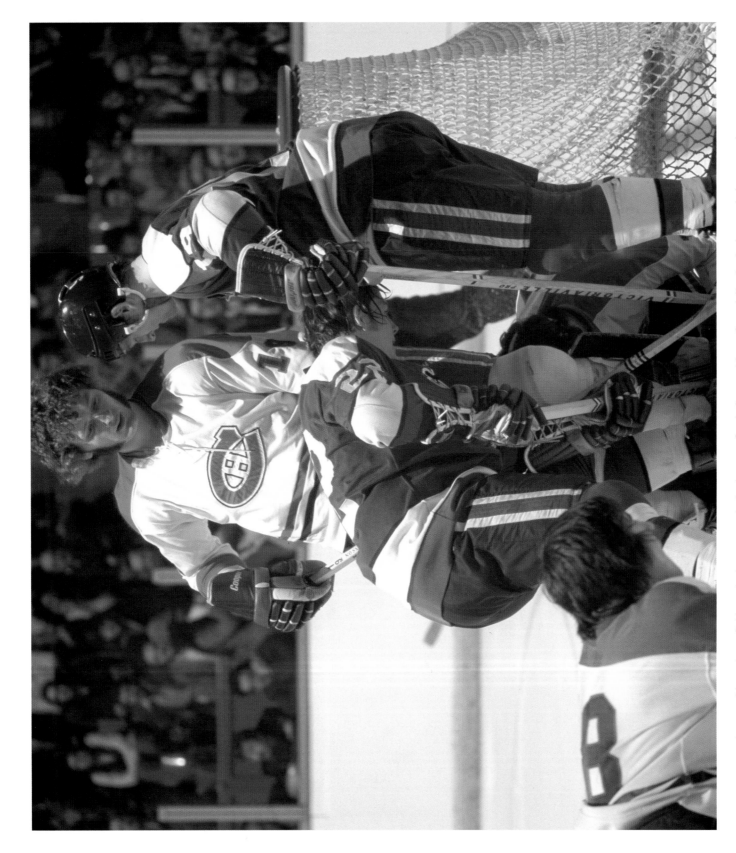

A superstitious player, Robinson had to step on the ice between Guy Lafleur and Serge Savard. He also had to touch the two goalposts of the Canadiens net before the start of each period. (Frank Prazak/HHOF)

ROBINSON'S CANADIENS STATS:	GP	G	A	P	PIM
regular season	1,202	197	686	883	706
playoffs	203	25	109	134	186
STANLEY CUPS: 6					

STEVE SHUTT

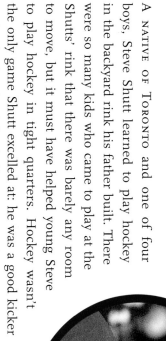

A NATIVE OF TORONTO and one of four boys, Steve Shutt learned to play hockey in the backyard rink his father built. There were so many kids who came to play at the Shutts' rink that there was barely any room to move, but it must have helped young Steve to play hockey in tight quarters. Hockey wasn't the only game Shutt excelled at: he was a good kicker on his high school football team. But there was no doubt that hockey was his first love. As he advanced through the junior hockey system, it was obvious he was destined for the National Hockey League.

Shutt first came to prominence as a member of the powerful Toronto Marlboros junior team. He played on a line with Bill Harris and Dave Gardner, and the trio terrorized the OMHL with an offensive firepower rarely seen, even in junior hockey. Shutt scored 70 goals in 1970–71 and added 63 more in his final junior season. All three players were projected first-round draft choices in 1972. Harris went first overall to the expansion New York Islanders. Shutt was certain that the Vancouver Canucks would select him, but they chose left-winger Don Lever third instead. The Montreal Canadiens then selected Shutt with their fourth choice and took Gardner four picks later. (The Habs took goalie Michel Larocque sixth overall and defenceman John Van Boxmeer with their 14th choice to finish their four first-round selections that year.) Of all the players selected in the first round that year, it was Shutt who would become the star.

It was said that the Canadiens took Shutt because of his touch around the net. He wouldn't disappoint them, but first they had to turn him into a more well-rounded player. Coach Scotty Bowman emphasized to Shutt that he had to play some defensive hockey and that he had to stay in shape. (Weight was a problem early in

Shutt's career.) He didn't play much in his first season as a Hab in 1972–73, scoring eight times in 50 games. He got into only one playoff contest as the Canadiens took the Stanley Cup and played in only six minor-league games that year, scoring four times. He scored 15 goals in his second year, but soon

left-wingers like Frank Mahovlich, Marc Tardif and Rejean Houle moved to the World Hockey Association. Ready to be a regular, Shutt came into the 1974–75 season really focused. He scored 30 goals and totalled 65 points in 77 games. There were no more doubts that he would be an NHL star.

Shutt ripped in 45 goals in 1975–76 and set a record for left-wingers (since broken) with an amazing 60 goals the following year. The Montreal squad won the Stanley Cup in both of those seasons, and Shutt was especially pleased the Canadiens had knocked off the brawling Philadelphia Flyers in four straight games in the '76 finals. The 5'11", 185-pound Shutt wasn't the league's biggest left-winger, but he probably had the fastest hands. Sometimes he wasn't even noticed until the scoring sheet was reviewed at the end of a game. He was highly skilled at pouncing on loose pucks and rapping them home with his accurate shot before anyone knew what happened. It was often suggested that Shutt got "garbage" goals by putting in linemate Guy Lafleur's rebounds, but Shutt knew how to use his speed to get himself in the right places to score. He could dart all over the ice, and his shifty moves caused many headaches for defencemen who also had to deal with right-winger Lafleur and centre Jacques Lemaire. Shutt found himself on another great line!

The Canadiens won two more Cups. In the next few seasons, Shutt never scored less than 30 goals. By 1983–84, however, the team was no longer a league powerhouse, and Shutt only scored

Steve Shutt's best year in the NHL came in 1976–77 when he had 60 goals and 45 assists. (HHOF)

Above: Steve Shutt was a three-time NHL all-star, once on the first team (1977) and twice on the second squad (1978 and 1980). (London Life-Portnoy/HHOF)

Facing page: Only Luc Robitaille has scored more goals as a left-winger in one season (63 in 1992–93 when he was with Los Angeles) than Steve Shutt, who was the first to score 60 in one year. (London Life-Portnoy/HHOF)

14 times in 63 contests. He found losing difficult to accept (the team won only 35 games that year) and didn't like working for new coach Bob Berry. The 1984–85 season saw Shutt score twice in 10 games before he was dealt to the Los Angeles Kings. In a classy move, Montreal general manager Serge Savard assured Shutt that he would guarantee his contract no matter what hap-

pened with his new club, so Shutt found the move to the West Coast easier. As a King Shutt scored 16 times in 59 games, but he decided to retire at the end of the year.

Quick with a quip and a smile, Shutt was named to the Hall of Fame in 1993. During the '90s he was an assistant coach with the Habs.

SHUTT'S CANADIENS STATS:

	GP	G	A	P	PIM
regular season	871	408	368	776	400
playoffs	96	50	48	98	61

STANLEY CUPS: 5

MARIO TREMBLAY

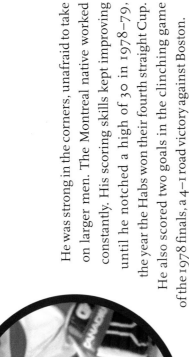

THE MONTREAL CANADIENS had an incredible five selections in the first round of the 1974 entry draft. Shrewd moves by general manager Sam Pollock had secured extra picks. The Habs boss made the most of his choices. Selected with the first pick (fifth overall) was Cam Connor of the Flin Flon Bombers, while Doug Risebrough, a graduate of the Kitchener Rangers, was taken two picks later. Next came Rick Chartraw, also of the Rangers (10th overall). Two slots later the Canadiens took right-winger Mario Tremblay from the Montreal junior team in the QMJHL. Finally, the Habs took Gord McTavish from the Sudbury Wolves (15th overall) to end their first-round feast. With the exception of McTavish, all these selections played for at least one Stanley Cup-winning team in Montreal. The best scorer of the group was Tremblay, who would remain for years in the Canadiens organization and make a lasting impression in his every role with the team.

Tremblay turned professional at the young age of 18 after two good seasons of junior hockey, which included 91 goals. The scrappy 6′, 185-pound Tremblay was sent to Halifax to play for the Montreal farm club in 1974–75 and made such an impression after just 15 games (10 goals, eight assists) that he was called up to the NHL. He never looked back. As the Voyageurs' most popular player, he led the team in scoring. But the Canadiens wanted to shake up their roster. Tremblay was a logical choice for promotion. In the '74–'75 season he proved that he belonged by scoring 21 times and adding 39 points in 64 games. The next season saw him score just 11 times in 71 contests, but the Habs won the Stanley Cup for the first time in three years. Tremblay was proud to be a member of the team. In the dressing room after the game that clinched the Cup, defenceman Larry Robinson spotted Tremblay quietly crying as he hugged Lord Stanley's mug. Robinson put his arm around the youngster and told him that his name would go "right about there."

In fact, Tremblay would have his name etched into the Cup five times before the end of his career. Opposition teams didn't relish playing against him because Tremblay hit anything that moved.

He was strong in the corners, unafraid to take on larger men. The Montreal native worked constantly. His scoring skills kept improving until he notched a high of 30 in 1978–79, the year the Habs won their fourth straight Cup. He also scored two goals in the clinching game of the 1978 finals, a 4–1 road victory against Boston.

But it's probably his spirit that he's best remembered for. Coach Scotty Bowman was actually pleased when Tremblay reacted with disgust when told early in his career that he wouldn't be playing a game against the New York Islanders. On another occasion he fought Bobby Schmatz of the Bruins in a 1979 playoff game at the Forum. That highlighted one-on-one scrap will always be remembered by Canadiens fans — and by Boston coach Don Cherry since Tremblay got the better of Schmatz!

Many players left the Habs after their fourth consecutive championship, but Tremblay stayed to enjoy another Cup win in 1986. (Robinson and Bob Gainey were two other hold-overs.) Due to a shoulder injury suffered late in the regular season, Tremblay didn't play in the '86 playoffs, but he did mange 19 goals in 56 games. His injury ended his playing career, which was spent entirely in Montreal. After retiring, Tremblay became an outspoken broadcaster. In 1995–96 he came out of the booth to coach the Canadiens with Rejean Houle as general manager. The Habs had no cup wins when he took over, but he won his first contest against the Toronto Maple Leafs. Although the team lost to the New York Rangers in the first round of the playoffs, Tremblay finished with 40 wins and 90 points. But Tremblay wasn't a favourite of Montreal superstar Patrick Roy, and an embarrassing loss to Detroit in the Forum led Roy to say that he was through as a Hab. As a broadcaster Tremblay had at times been critical of Roy, and Roy wouldn't forget those remarks. The two kept feuding, even after the netminder was dealt to Colorado. Nevertheless, Tremblay put up respectable numbers as a coach with 71 wins, 63 losses and 25 ties between 1995 and 1997.

Tremblay is now an assistant coach with the upstart Minnesota Wild, who have former Montreal star Jacques Lemaire as their head coach.

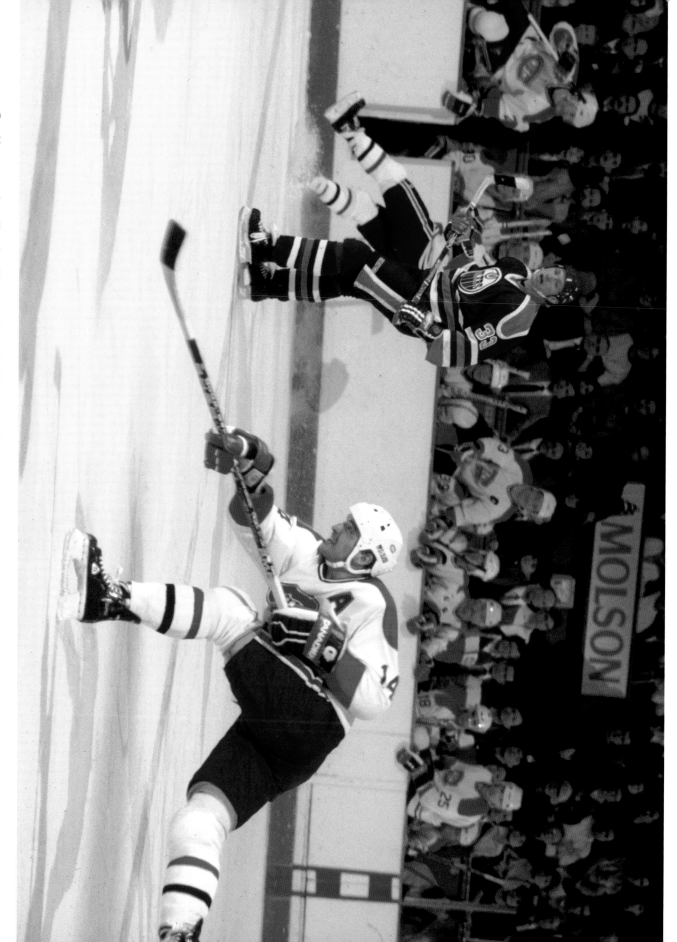

Tremblay gets a shot off against Edmonton. Mario Tremblay scored 30 goals four times in his career, including a high of 33 markers in 1981–82, a year that also saw him record a career best 73 points. (Paul Bereswill/HHOF)

TREMBLAY'S CANADIENS STATS:

	GP	G	A	P	PIM
regular season	852	258	326	584	1,043
playoffs	101	20	29	49	187

STANLEY CUPS: 5

HAPPY NEW YEAR! — THE CANADIENS HOST THE RUSSIANS

by Frank Orr

DEBATED TO this day is where the fabled "New Year's Eve Game" of December 31, 1975, at the Montreal Forum — between the Montreal Canadiens and the Central Red Army of the then Soviet Union — rates on the list of greatest hockey games ever played. That the evening ranks at the top of any tally of great hockey "events" is unchallenged.

Surprisingly, many in the Forum crowd of 18,975 and among the millions who watched the telecast across Canada regard the outcome, a 3–3 tie, as a victory by the Canadiens. Their large margin in play, typified by a 38–13 edge in shots on goal, made the contest seem like a Canadien triumph. But despite the extraordinary goaltending of Army's brilliant Vladislav Tretiak, many feel that the Montreal club's huge territorial edge and the Russians' need for two goals that dribbled by goalie Ken Dryden disqualifies the game from the "great" category.

The game's background lifted it far above the routine category, however. Although the Philadelphia Flyers won the Stanley Cup the two previous springs (1974, '75), they were likely the most scorned kings in National Hockey League history. While the Flyers played with skill and discipline, their nickname, the Broad Street Bullies, summed up their violent, intimidating approach. Even their brilliantly executed 4–1 win over the Red Army team days after the Montreal game was marred by a Russian 20-minute walk-off to protest "the animal hockey" of the Flyers.

The Canadiens, regarded as the NHL's classiest team, continued to focus on skill, not the muscle with which some teams tried to overcome the Flyers sluggers. They had won the Cup in '71 and '73 with a roster of aging stars backed by outstanding young talent slowly fed into the lineup. In the '75–76 season, they rose to the top with a maturing group of highly skilled players. Their ascent to the Cup — they won four consecutive crowns from '76 to '79 — was almost universally viewed as inevitable. Many saw *Les Habitants* — not the actual titleholders, the Flyers — as the champs. The game against the Central Red Army was a supreme test of the promise represented by the Canadiens.

The previous NHL-Soviet test at the Forum was in 1972 when the USSR demolished Team Canada, 7–3, to open the Summit Series. That game was the longest night in a hockey arena or in front of the

television that many fans can remember. Thus, when Russia's perennial club champions with many of the stars of the '72 Nats — notably goalie Tretiak, Boris Mikhailov, Vladimir Petrov, Valeri Kharlamov and Aleksandr Maltsev — played against the Canadiens, many Canadian hockey fans saw those fabled red-white-blue outfits as Team Canada uniforms.

The game was watched by perhaps the best-dressed crowd ever to attend a hockey game. New Year's Eve is a big night out in Montreal, and many spectators came ready for the post-game parties and dinners, women in evening gowns and furs, their partners in tuxedos and dinner jackets. Scalpers outside the Forum got a record high of $200 per ticket. The fans gave the Russians a rousing welcome during the introductions and a standing ovation for Kharlamov, the exceptional little winger.

Coach Scotty Bowman had his team well-prepared for the superbly skilled, ultra-swift, technically sound Soviets. Often in the game the Habs used an early version of the much scorned neutral zone trap — with four defenders cutting off Army's swift rushes before the Soviets reached centre — and alternated with swift forechecking, often by three forwards, a tactic most North American teams hesitated to use against the quick breakouts of the comrades.

But the outcome remains a tribute to Tretiak's superb goaltending and the Red Army's offensive opportunism. Viewed as the pre-Summit weak point of the '72 team, the remarkably athletic 20-year-old goalie stopped at least a dozen glittering Canadien scoring chances. Army managed perhaps six good scoring chances against Dryden, but as Canadian teams had discovered over two decades, the Russians could manufacture scores from little raw material.

Steve Shutt, with an awesome slapshot over Tretiak's shoulder, and Yvon Lambert gave the Canadiens a 2–0 first-period lead. But the Russians scored on innocuous play early in the second, Mikhailov's shot going off Dryden's glove into the net. Halfway through the period, Yvan Cournoyer restored the two-goal lead on a power play.

Of course, it was the magician Kharlamov, materializing from nowhere, who pulled the Russians close with a late score. Petrov lulled the Canadiens defence with slow stickhandling outside the cordon

Central Red Army Goalie Vladislav Tretiak foils Montreal Canadiens captain Yvan Cournoyer, one of 35 saves he made during the famous game on December 31, 1975. The game ended in a three-all tie. (Montreal Gazette)

protecting the net and, all of a sudden, Kharlamov appeared behind the defence to take Petrov's pass and slide a backhand shot behind Dryden.

"Where in hell did he come from?" Dryden said later. "I think he popped up out of a hole in the ice."

The Canadiens had a 16–6-shot edge in the third period. Tretiak made a half dozen highlight saves. But the Russians pounced on one of the Montrealers' few mistakes — a defenceman trapped up-ice — and Boris Alexandrov scored on Army's only two-on-one rush in the game. Dryden appeared to have stopped the shot, but the puck rolled over him and into the net.

The Canadiens, disappointed with losing, felt they had made a strong case for the calibre of NHL hockey, which had been much criticized after the closeness of the '72 Summit.

"I think we proved quite a few things about NHL hockey," said

defenceman Guy Lapointe. "We showed our style of playing is just as good as theirs and we are in as good a physical condition without doing all the stuff they do 12 months of the year. Their skating and passing is strong but our up-and-down checking game is just as effective."

Years later, Bowman reflected on the '75 game.

"In retrospect, it's sort of funny to think that we had more good scoring chances in that game against the Russians than in any game we played in those four Stanley Cup seasons," Bowman said. "That sticks in your craw a little. If we proved anything that night, it had to be that Canada produces some pretty good hockey players, too."

Canadiens defenceman Serge Savard had an often-quoted post-game line on the outcome.

"That game convinced me that God must be a Russian," Savard said. "If He's not, how do you explain a tie when we outplayed them by so much?"

189

return to glory 1985-1995

A s soon as Ronald Corey was hired, he went to work at making the Canadiens a more modern organization. He dismissed some people (such as Irving Grundman and Ron Caron) who had been in the front office for some time, which gave the new general manager,

Serge Savard, a chance to bring in some of his own staff. Corey was a savvy marketing executive who realized that the Forum needed upgrading, as did the entertainment package around the game. He forged closer ties with the alumni who were a valued Montreal tradition. Because the NHL was a much larger league in the eighties than ever before, keeping the Canadiens winning tradition alive — well in front of demanding fans and media in two languages — was very difficult.

The first crisis of the Corey-Savard regime was the sudden retirement of Guy Lafleur, Montreal's superstar of the seventies and a five-time Stanley Cup champion. Lafleur didn't see eye to eye with coach and former teammate Jacques Lemaire. A natural goal scorer, Lafleur found Lemaire's defence-first approach stifling. His attempts to get his view across fell on deaf ears. Early in the 1984–85 season, Lafleur decided he wouldn't just sit on the bench and announced his departure. Scoring 518 career goals as a Hab — second only to Maurice Richard's 544 — he left the club as the all-time leader in points and assists. The Canadiens should have traded the star left-winger to another team, but Savard didn't want to trade away a legend. Lafleur quietly retired to a front-office position, although that didn't work out as well as anybody had hoped.

Flames to win the Cup. It was a remarkable effort by a flashy goalie and youngsters who refused to believe they were too inexperienced to win it all. Quality veterans like Robinson, Bob Gainey, Rick Green and Mario Tremblay gave the team a strong backbone. With so many youthful players on the team that won the Cup, it looked as if the Habs might once again dominate the NHL — but that wasn't to be.

As drafting players became more difficult in the eighties and nineties, the Canadiens collected their share of duds. The Habs had an especially rough time with their first-round selections, including Doug Wickenheiser (first overall in 1980), Alain Heroux (1982), Alfie Turcotte (1983), Jose Charbonneau (1985), Mark Pederson (1986), Eric Charron (1988), Lindsay Vallis (1989), Brent Bilodeau (1991), David Wilkie (1992), Brad Brown (1994)

"You know what I remember most

about that year [1986]? Toe Blake was in our dressing room a lot. After we beat Boston in the first round, he told us, 'You haven't won anything yet.' After we beat Hartford, same thing: 'You haven't won anything yet,' and then he said the same thing again after we beat the Rangers. Finally, we go in and beat Calgary to win the Stanley Cup and afterwards Toe Blake says to us, 'That's just one.' I'll never forget that." Brian Skrudland [Canadiens player, 1985 to 1993]

Just as the 1984–85 season ended, Lemaire decided that he was through with the demands of coaching the Canadiens and offered his resignation. Savard turned to a virtual unknown when he made Jean Perron the team's next coach. A university coach and an assistant with the Canadian Olympic team, Perron stepped into the breach and, with young players who were learning on the job, delivered a 40-win season in 1985–86. Then the team caught fire in the playoffs under rookie goaltender Patrick Roy, knocking off the Boston Bruins, the Hartford Whalers, the New York Rangers and the Calgary

and Terry Ryan (1995). But the news wasn't all bad. In fact, the Canadiens did well in the late seventies, adding good support players and a sprinkling of stars. For instance, the 1978 entry draft saw the Habs land Keith Acton, while the 1979 selections included Gaston Gringras, Mats Naslund, Guy Carbonneau and goalie Rick Wamsley. Defencemen Craig Ludwig and Ric Nattrass were added in 1980 along with Mike McPhee and goaltender Steve Penny, a quick fix in goal for one playoff upset. Mark Hunter, Gilbert Delorme, Chris Chelios, Kjell Dahlin, Steve Rooney and Tom Kurvers were all 1981 picks. David Maley was taken in 1982 and the pesky Claude Lemieux was chosen in 1983 along with grinders like Sergio Momesso and John Kordic.

The Canadiens' two best years at the draft table since the days of Sam Pollock came in 1984 and in 1987. In '84 the team selected Petr Svoboda — to much fanfare for an overrated player — Shayne Corson, Stephane Richer and best of all goaltender Roy. In '87 Montreal took Andrew Cassels, John LeClair, Eric Desjardins and Mathieu Schneider. (All but Cassels made a major contribution to the Canadiens.) Other good role players selected between 1985 and 1990 included Tom Chorske, Brent Gilchrist, Benoit Brunet, Donald Dufresne, Jryki Lumme, Lyle Odelein, Sean Hill, Patrice Brisebois,

Ed Ronan, Pierre Sevigny, Andre Racicot, Gilbert Dionne and Paul DiPietro. As strong proof that the Canadiens were still formidable at the draft table, all of these players were either members of the Habs' Stanley Cup-winning teams in 1986 or 1993 or they were traded in deals to acquire players who were on these championship teams.

Parron left the scene after the team lost in the 1987 and 1988 playoffs. Savard turned to a former Montreal cop as his new head coach. Pat Burns had worked his way up the system — with successful stints in junior and the minors — to take over the team for the 1988–89 season. After a a tough start, the team ended up winning 53 games and totalling 115 points. The team made it to the finals, but the Calgary Flames had a little too much depth for the

Pat Burns pointed the Canadiens in the right direction as soon as he took over in 1988. His coaching record in four seasons (320 games) was 174-104-42 and one trip to the finals. (Paul Bereswill/HHOF)

Goaltender Patrick Roy was the main reason Montreal won the Stanley Cup in 1986 and 1993. (Paul Bereswill/HHOF)

Habs to overcome. The next three seasons saw Montreal with 41, 39 and 41 wins but not enough playoff victories to get near the finals. Pressure mounted on Savard to make a major move, but Burns decided on his own to leave and found himself in Toronto. The Canadiens turned to Montreal native Jacques Demers, a seasoned NHL coach who had enjoyed good years with St. Louis and Detroit. A 48-win season propelled Montreal into the playoffs, and the stellar work of Roy allowed the Canadiens to record 10 straight overtime wins. In 1993 the Canadiens secured the team's 24th Stanley Cup in five games over the Los Angeles Kings.

While considered a strong contender, the 1992–93 team wasn't favoured to win the Cup. Excellent trade acquisitions like Kirk Muller, Vincent Damphousse and J. J. Daigneault gave the team the right mix of veterans and youngsters needed to take the championship in a year with many postseason upsets. But the next two

seasons would show that the '93 run to the Cup couldn't be repeated. The effect on Canadiens management would be severe.

AWARDS SUMMARY 1985–1995

STANLEY CUP: 2 (1986, 1993)

SELKE TROPHY: 3 (Guy Carbonneau, 1988, 1989, 1992)

VEZINA TROPHY: 3 (Patrick Roy, 1989, 1990, 1992)

CONN SMYTHE TROPHY: 2 (Patrick Roy, 1986, 1993)

NORRIS TROPHY: 1 (Chris Chelios, 1989)

LADY BYNG TROPHY: 1 (Mats Naslund, 1988)

JACK ADAMS AWARD: 1 (Pat Burns, 1989)

Jacques Demers took over as Habs coach for the 1992–93 season and won the Stanley Cup. His overall record with the Canadiens was 107-86-27. He was dismissed in October of 1995. (Paul Bereswill/HHOF)

GUY CARBONNEAU

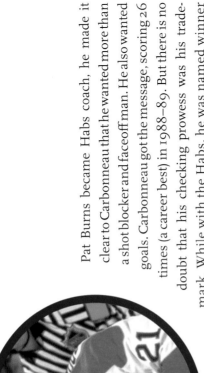

CENTRE Guy Carbonneau, an excellent playmaker in junior hockey, recorded 189 assists in his last 144 contests with the Chicoutimi Sagueneens of the QMJHL. (He left home at 16 to play junior.) He also scored 134 goals over that same period, but it was likely his lack of size (5'11", 186 pounds) that made NHL scouts wary of the smooth-skating pivot. But the Montreal Canadiens knew about him and selected him 44th overall in the 1979 draft, a year when many fine players were available in the first round. Not ready for the NHL in 1980, Carbonneau spent the next two seasons with the Nova Scotia Voyageurs, preparing for a big-league position.

Carbonneau scored well in the American Hockey League: 66 goals and 182 points. He set a team record for most assists (seven) and points (eight) in one game. But when the Canadiens brought him up for the 1982–83 season, coach Bob Berry started using him in a defensive role. The Habs had just traded another young centre, Dan Daoust, to Toronto to make room for Carbonneau. Criticism of Habs management inevitably followed after Daoust made the NHL's all-rookie team. Time, however, would prove that Carbonneau was the better player. For starters, he didn't exactly embarrass himself as a rookie, scoring 18 times and adding 29 assists in 77 games. He also showed another highly valued trait by scoring five short-handed goals in '82–'83 (second only to Wayne Gretzky). For the next three seasons Carbonneau, one of the best two-way players in the game, scored 20 or more goals.

A good skater, able to check the best opposition players, Carbonneau carved out a niche for himself that few if any in the NHL could hope to occupy. A tireless worker on the ice, he was known for his willingness to sacrifice his body to block a shot. A great sense of anticipation always put him in the right position. He thrived on the challenge of making the right defensive play or scoring a key goal. Most often a plus player, he could shift easily from offence to defence. At times he focused too much on his checking role. But when

Pat Burns became Habs coach, he made it clear to Carbonneau that he wanted more than a shot blocker and face off man. He also wanted goals. Carbonneau got the message, scoring 26 times (a career best) in 1988–89. But there is no doubt that his checking prowess was his trademark. While with the Habs, he was named winner of the Selke Trophy as best defensive forward three times. He was considered the heir apparent to teammate Bob Gainey as the NHL's top defensive forward.

During his time in Montreal, Carbonneau experienced many team and personal triumphs. In 1985–86, he won his first Stanley Cup — adding 12 points in 20 playoff games — and was simply outstanding in 1992–93 when he helped shut down Gretzky and lead the Canadiens to a Cup win over the Los Angeles Kings. In the '93 playoffs, Carbonneau scored two overtime winners — one against Buffalo, one versus the New York Islanders — further proof that he could score in the clutch. Carbonneau's heart-and-soul commitment led to his nomination as team captain in 1989, an honour he shared with Chris Chelios for one year. As a result, he accepted the Cup in '93 from NHL president Gary Bettman. Carbonneau showed great class by giving the Cup to longtime NHL veteran Denis Savard — who wasn't even dressed for the final game — out of respect for the former all-star player's achievements.

Not shy about speaking his mind and a tough negotiator at contract time, Carbonneau eventually wore out his welcome in Montreal. In a trade that saw the Habs get Jim Montgomery, Carbonneau went to the St. Louis Blues. After one year in St. Louis, Carbonneau went to the Dallas Stars who were then run by Gainey. In five years with Dallas, Carbonneau never scored more than 10 goals in one season, but he was still very effective on defence. Other members of the Stars found his work ethic infectious. They won a Cup in 1999 and made the final in 2000, a great way to end Carbonneau's superb career, which might one day be recognized with a selection to the Hall of Fame.

Montreal captain Guy Carbonneau played a major role in defeating the Los Angeles Kings in the 1993 Stanley Cup finals. [Paul Bereswill/HHOF]

"In Montreal you've got to win.

You can't even afford a bad practice, never mind a bad game.

You can't come out after a loss and say to the public, 'We're sorry. We're rebuilding right now.' The word 'rebuilding' is not a word you're allowed to say in public."

Pat Burns (Montreal coach, 1988 to 1992)

Guy Carbonneau played in 231 career playoff games and recorded 93 points. (Paul Bereswill/HHOF)

CARBONNEAU'S CANADIENS STATS:	GP	G	A	P	PIM
regular season	912	221	326	547	623
playoffs	161	30	43	73	125

STANLEY CUPS: 2

CHRIS CHELIOS

CHRIS CHELIOS was born in Chicago, Illinois, and grew up in San Diego, California — not a hockey hotbed, but his love of the game remained intact. To progress in hockey, he knew he would have to play in Canada — he left home at 16 — but he was cut by teams at the Junior B level. He persisted and as he grew taller and heavier, he made the Moose Jaw Canucks in the SJHL for two seasons. He then went to the University of Wisconsin for two seasons before joining the United States Olympic team for the 1983–84 season.

In progressing as he did, Chelios caught the eye of the Montreal Canadiens scouts. In the 1981 entry draft, he was selected 40th overall. In spite of his all-star recognition in college hockey, Chelios didn't believe he would make the NHL.

Chelios first joined the Canadiens after the 1984 Olympics, playing 12 games for them in the '83–'84 campaign. He never went to the minors and made the team for the 1984–85 season, scoring nine goals and adding an amazing 55 assists. He was named to the all-rookie team, his first NHL honour. But his next season was just 41 games long (34 points) due to a knee injury. However, the Habs captured a surprising Stanley Cup win in the 1986 playoffs on the strength of Patrick Roy's stellar goaltending and young players like defenceman Chelios (who added 11 points in 20 games). In the 1987–88 season Chelios scored 20 goals and added 41 assists. Montreal general manager Serge Savard, a great defenceman in his own right, said the young blueliner would win the Norris Trophy. By the 1988–89 season — a year that saw Chelios score 15 goals and earn a career high 73 points — that prediction came true. Unfortunately, just as Chelios' playing career was blossoming, his off-ice problems began to annoy his teammates.

Chelios appeared destined for a long career as a Hab, especially after he was named co-captain with Guy Carbonneau in 1989–90. (He was the first American-born player to get this honour.) Not the biggest blueliner around (6'1", 190 pounds) he nonetheless had a solid build backed up by a nasty disposition that made him feared, but also got him lots of unnecessary penalty minutes.

Genuinely frightening was his playoff hit on Brian Propp of the Philadelphia Flyers. It made him a target for the rest of that playoff series. (Chelios was viciously attacked by Flyer goalie Ron Hextall as the series ended.) He could control a game with his skating and puck-handling skills. His shot from the point was low, hard and accurate. Chelios was excellent on special teams and trusted by all his coaches. No matter how good a player Chelios might be on the ice, however, the Canadiens lost patience with his off-ice behaviour. Savard had no choice but to deal Chelios to Chicago (along with a second-round draft choice) for centre Denis Savard, a popular but fading French-Canadian star.

Denis Savard's impact on the Canadiens was minor, while Chelios became the NHL's best defenceman. A Norris Trophy winner twice more, he was a first team all-star another three times while with the Blackhawks. (He made the first team once as a Hab.) Sometimes it seemed that he kept the Chicago club competitive all on his own. Certainly the amount of ice time he got made it look like he was on the ice for the whole game. Chelios matured in the Windy City to play disciplined, although still emotional, hockey. With Chicago for nearly nine years, he was then sent to Detroit, where he finally won another Cup in 2002 with a stellar Red Wings club. Fond of international hockey, he has played for the Americans in three Olympic Games, including the team that won the World Cup of Hockey in 1996.

CHELIOS' CANADIENS STATS:	GP	G	A	P	PIM
regular season	402	72	237	309	783
playoffs	98	16	52	68	186
STANLEY CUPS: 1					

VINCENT DAMPHOUSSE

THE TORONTO MAPLE LEAFS knew they wanted to select Vincent Damphousse with their first choice in the 1986 NHL entry draft. A 6'1" centre, Damphousse was a scoring machine for the Laval Voisins of the QMJHL, recording 155 points (45 goals, 110 assists) in 69 junior season games. Named to the QMJHL's second all-star team in 1985–86, Damphousse was expected to be a high selection. For these reasons, the Maple Leafs didn't think there was any chance they would land the gifted scorer and playmaker. But the unexpected happened after Joe Murphy was taken first overall by Detroit. The Los Angeles Kings picked centre Jimmy Carson second after New Jersey shocked everyone by taking centre Neil Brady third. (Brady played in only 89 NHL games.) The next two selections — defencemen Zarley Zalapaski and Shawn Anderson — allowed the Leafs to get their man sixth overall.

Damphousse and Carson were the only players selected in the first round of the '86 draft to play in the NHL for the 1986–87 campaign. There was no use sending Damphousse back to the Quebec league where he had accomplished everything possible, so the Leafs kept him with the team. (He never played a game in the minor leagues.) He scored 21 goals as a rookie. The Leafs soon realized, however, that Damphousse wasn't a gifted skater, so they moved the excellent playmaker to the left wing to give him less ice to worry about. With remarkable poise for such a youngster, he produced 25 assists to add to his impressive numbers. Like other skilled players able to see the entire ice, Damphousse could make pinpoint passes. He wasn't a physical player, but his puck-possession game made up for any defensive liabilities.

He put in four good seasons with the Maple Leafs, including a

94-point season in 1989–90. But the team kept floundering. Management changes meant players were going to be moved to help the team. New general manager Cliff Fletcher put his mark on the team with a blockbuster trade when he sent Damphousse and a package of players to Edmonton for more experienced players.

Although the Oilers made Damphousse the centrepiece of their trade, he would stay for only one season (an 89-point campaign) before the Montreal Canadiens made an offer for his services. (His contract was up, and the Oilers worried about the cost of keeping him.) Montreal manager Serge Savard sent Shayne Corson, Brent Gilchrist and Vladimir Vujtek to Edmonton and brought Damphousse back to his hometown.

Coming home worked wonders for Damphousse who responded with 97 points in 1992–93 and then led the Canadiens to the Stanley Cup with 20 points in 23 postseason games. Concerns about Damphousse's performance in the '93 playoffs were finally put to rest. A generally consistent performer, he was an offensive force for the next several years and had seasons of 91 (1993–94) and 81 (1996–97) points. His excellent work with the Habs was recognized when in the '96–'97 season he was named team captain.

It looked like he would be a Hab for life, but as free agency loomed and the Canadiens were no longer on top, they decided his contract demands were too high. His performance in 1998–99 fell below his usual standard (only 12 goals and 36 points). After 65 games he was dealt to the San Jose Sharks. He has been a Shark for five full seasons and remains one of the NHL's better players. His name still turns up in trade rumours, which means that hockey managers still regard Damphousse as highly as they did in 1986.

Above: Vincent Damphousse led the Canadiens in goals scored (twice), assists (four times) and points (three times) at various times in his career with Montreal between 1992 and 1999. (Paul Bereswill/HHOF)

Facing page: Chris Chelios holds the Montreal rookie record for defencemen with 55 assists and 64 points. (Paul Bereswill/HHOF)

Montreal moment:

The Canadiens lost the opening game of the 1993 playoffs to the Quebec Nordiques 3–2 in overtime on a goal by Scott Young. But the Canadiens then won 10 straight extra-time games on their way to winning the Stanley Cup. Kirk Muller (two), Guy Carbonneau (two), John LeClair (two), Gilbert Dionne, Stephane Lebeau, Eric Desjardins and Vincent Damphousse scored the overtime winners.

Montreal traded Vincent Damphousse to San Jose in 1999 receiving three draft choices in exchange (one of which turned out to be Marcel Hossa). (Paul Bereswill/HHOF)

DAMPHOUSSE'S CANADIENS STATS:	GP	G	A	P	PIM
regular season	519	184	314	498	559
playoffs	48	19	24	43	48

STANLEY CUPS: 1

ERIC DESJARDINS

It RAISED A FEW eyebrows when defenceman Eric Desjardins was named to Team Canada for the 1991 Canada Cup tournament. After all, Team Canada was supposed to gather hockey's elite. Some felt that he was named to the squad because his coach with the Montreal Canadiens, Pat Burns, was an assistant coach for the Canadian side. The truth was that he made the team on merit. Though not as well-known as other NHL defencemen, he soon gained recognition with five points in seven games that helped to secure a Canadian win. The entire league, and the Canadiens in particular, came to learn just how valuable Desjardins could be.

The Canadiens drafted Desjardins 38th overall during the 1987 entry draft and never lived to regret selecting the native of Rouyn, Quebec. A top defender for the Bisons for two seasons, he played junior hockey in Granby. Desjardins' final year of junior, the 1987–88 campaign, saw him score 18 goals and add 49 assists in 62 games. He finished that year by playing three games with the Montreal farm team in Sherbrooke. That was the extent of his minor-league career. Desjardins joined the Canadiens for the start of the 1988–89 season. He got into 36 games, recording 14 points. He then played in 14 postseason games during which the Habs fell just short of the Stanley Cup. Brought along slowly, he played in 55 games the next year and totalled 16 points. By the 1990–91 season, Desjardins was a full-fledged team member and developed a style that would make him one of the NHL's top blueliners. In serious need of a leader on the blue line after trading away many fine, developing defencemen, the Habs were lucky to have Desjardins.

Desjardins had good size (at 6'1", 205 pounds) but never tried to play an overly physical game. Excellent at getting the puck out of the Montreal defensive zone, he was capable of handling traffic in his own end. (He was good at using his stick to check effectively.) Desjardins was a strong skater with a great ability to read the play and join the attack judiciously. On offence, he displayed a low drive from the point, which was usually on the net. He could quarterback a power play with ease and twice recorded 32-assist seasons as a Hab. His all-round game was clearly on display during the 1992–93 season when he had 13 goals and 45 points as well as during Montreal's remarkable playoff run to the Cup. In the second game of the final against Los Angeles, Desjardins scored all three goals in a 3–2 overtime win that evened the series at one game each. His last two goals — one to tie the game late on the power play and the other to win it in extra time — were clutch markers that only a cool customer like Desjardins could produce. If the Canadiens had lost that game, they would have had trouble bouncing back to win the Cup. Thanks to Desjardins' great performance, they were on their way to sweeping the next four contests.

Only two years later the Canadiens fell upon hard times and needed to shake up their roster. The Philadelphia Flyers dangled scoring forward Mark Recchi in front of them. Desperate for offensive talent, the Canadiens took the bait. Desjardins was included in the deal that also sent John LeClair to the Flyers. The Habs were never the same again. Montreal fans bemoaned the loss of a future 50-goal scorer in LeClair, but the real loss was Desjardins as the Canadiens' blue line brigade couldn't recover from the loss of their best defender. Soon Montreal missed the playoffs regularly, while Desjardins became an all-star defender — twice making the second end-of-season squad — in the City of Brotherly Love. You can bet that Montreal general manager Serge Savard would have loved to reverse that deal, which helped to bring down his previously successful regime.

Since joining the Flyers, Desjardins has produced six seasons of 45 or more points. With an appearance in the 1997 finals, Philadelphia has been a perennial playoff contender. Montreal hasn't enjoyed such success ever since the departure of the reliable Desjardins.

Eric Desjardins scored the 15,000th goal in Canadiens history when he beat goalie Vincent Riendeau on February 25, 1990, during a game against the St. Louis Blues at the Forum. (Paul Bereswill/HHOF)

When the Habs gave up defencemen Chris Chelios and Craig Ludwig — blueliner Rick Green left the team one year earlier — it was up to Eric Desjardins to lead Montreal's rearguard brigade. (Paul Bereswill/HHOF)

DESJARDINS' CANADIENS STATS:	GP	G	A	P	PIM
regular season	405	43	136	179	351
playoffs	71	9	20	29	55
STANLEY CUPS: 1					

JOHN LECLAIR

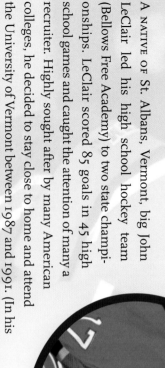

A NATIVE OF St. Albans, Vermont, big John LeClair led his high school hockey team (Bellows Free Academy) to two state championships. LeClair scored 85 goals in 45 high school games and caught the attention of many a recruiter. Highly sought after by many American colleges, he decided to stay close to home and attend the University of Vermont between 1987 and 1991.

A Montreal Canadiens scout first noticed LeClair during a high school tournament. The Habs selected the left-winger with second choice (33rd) overall in the 1987 entry draft. The Canadiens had found another diamond in the rough.

As soon as his university career was over, LeClair joined the Canadiens at the end of the 1990–91 season, recording seven points in 10 games. He split the next season between Montreal (59 games, 19 points) and Fredericton (eight games, 14 points) of the American Hockey League before becoming a full-time regular with the Habs in 1992–93. His first full NHL season saw LeClair score 19 times and total 44 points. But he saved his best for the playoffs. Although he scored only four goals in the postseason, two of them came on consecutive nights of overtime contests in Los Angeles during the Stanley Cup final. The double game winners crushed the Kings, and the Habs went back home to clinch the Cup on home ice in five games. LeClair might have been at the right spot at just the right time, but it was an incredible feat nonetheless, considering the pressure of overtime in the finals. As a result, even bigger things were expected of LeClair in the future.

LeClair's most noticeable ability was to move well despite his large size (6'3", 226 pounds). A smooth skater with a good understanding of the game, he could use his long reach effectively to

scoop up loose pucks. With his terrific shot, he was good around the net, especially when he used his size to tie up a defenceman. Montreal teammate Mathieu Schneider predicted LeClair would become a 40-goal scorer.

But in 1993–94 LeClair scored only 19 again, and the next season saw him languishing on the bench. For all his great attributes, LeClair simply couldn't find his game with the Habs. The team also struggled, and so in February 1995 the Canadiens dealt the inconsistent LeClair to Philadelphia for scoring winger Mark Recchi. As soon as LeClair arrived in Philadelphia, he became a different player. Teamed with budding star centre Eric Lindros and winger Mikael Renberg to form the "Legion of Doom Line," LeClair began to score as expected, finishing the '94–'95 campaign with 25 goals in his last 37 games.

The Flyers were ecstatic with LeClair's progress. Over his next three seasons, he produced 50, 51 and 50 goals. If he had produced anywhere near these numbers in Montreal, the Canadiens would never have traded him away. They could only watch as LeClair became the prototypical power forward all NHL teams love. Easily one of the best wingers in the game, he was a four-time league all-star with the Flyers. He also had two more seasons that saw him score 43 and 40 times before injuries finally slowed him down. Never an overly physical player with lots of penalty minutes, he nevertheless took a beating for being one of the most feared goal scorers in hockey. The Flyers wouldn't let him escape when free agency loomed for LeClair, but he has slowed down considerably due to back surgery. Philadelphia general manager Bob Clarke made it clear that he was unhappy with LeClair's recent playoff performances. LeClair may soon find himself in another uniform.

LECLAIR'S CANADIENS STATS:	GP	G	A	P	PIM
regular season	224	49	69	118	91
playoffs	38	7	8	15	26

STANLEY CUPS: 1

John LeClair was first called up to the Canadiens on March 9, 1991. He scored a goal in his first NHL game against the Vancouver Canucks. (Paul Bereswill/HHOF)

CLAUDE LEMIEUX

ONE OF THE main reasons for the Montreal Canadiens' storied history is that they have rarely made bad trades. But there are always exceptions: the deal that sent pesky right-winger Claude Lemieux out of Montreal qualifies as one of them. Not seeing eye to eye with the coach is often a reason why a player finds himself on the move. Lemieux had clearly pushed Pat Burns too far by the end of the 1989–90 season. During a Stanley Cup final broadcast on national television, Burns let Lemieux roll around on the ice in pain and told the trainer to stay put because he felt that Lemieux was exaggerating his injury! The New Jersey Devils, always on the lookout for strong wingers, put in a bid for Lemieux. All they gave up was Sylvain Turgeon, a one-time valued prospect but a bust as an NHL player. Turgeon would only play in 75 games for the Habs, while Lemieux would rack up Stanley Cups as a valued member of championship teams.

A native of Buckingham, Quebec, Lemieux played junior hockey in Trois-Rivieres and Verdun where he was noticed by the Canadiens who selected him 26th overall in the 1983 entry draft. He had a good season in 1983–84, his second year of junior hockey, with 41 goals and 86 points (scoring once). He got promoted to the Habs for eight games that year and 124 points, he didn't perform well at training camp in the fall of 1985 and found himself playing with Sherbrooke of the AHL. Adjusting well to the professional game, he had 21 goals in 58 games before the Canadiens brought him to Montreal to finish the '85–'86 season. With no hint of what was to come in the postseason, Lemieux scored 10 goals in the playoffs and helped the Canadiens — a team comprised of mostly young players and a few key veterans — win the Cup. Lemieux scored perhaps the two most important goals, two overtime markers, of the

playoffs. The first came in the seventh game of the series against the Hartford Whalers (a 2–1 win) while the second came versus the New York Rangers in the semifinal for a 4–3 victory. The once unknown Lemieux forged a well-deserved reputation for scoring clutch playoff goals.

Another aspect to Lemieux's well-earned reputation wasn't nearly as pleasant. He had a way of getting under the skin of his opponents, often resorting to personal comments. (To his credit, he eventually stopped using that tactic.) Soon Lemieux was hated in every opposition rink, infuriating fans and coaches alike for starting trouble and skating away. He was physically strong (6'1", 226 pounds) but rarely dropped the gloves to back up his words. Lemieux could play the agitator role to perfection. While that style rubbed many the wrong way, he was really much more than just a pest. He had a good shot that netted him many goals — 27 or more in three of his years with Montreal — and his drive to the goalmouth earned him the attention of opposing defencemen. His strong skating stride would get him to where he wanted to go, and his work in the corners was superior to most.

Lemieux won the Conn Smythe Trophy in 1995 when the Devils won their first Cup. Among his 13 markers in 20 playoff games were many important goals. A contract dispute with the Devils forced another trade, this time to Colorado where he won another Cup with the Avalanche in 1996. A deal back to New Jersey — the Devils wouldn't let past problems stand in the way of reacquiring the veteran player — gave Lemieux another Cup win in 2000. He has also played for Phoenix and Dallas.

Mostly because of an ugly hit from behind on Kris Draper of Detroit during a playoff series, Lemieux remains one of the most hated players in hockey. But even those who despise Lemieux would admit that he's a proven winner.

LEMIEUX'S CANADIENS STATS:	GP	G	A	P	PIM
regular season	281	97	92	189	576
playoffs	77	22	23	45	225

STANLEY CUPS: 1

After being called up to the Habs in the 1983–84 season, Claude Lemieux scored a goal in his first NHL game when he beat goalie Tom Barrasso of the Buffalo Sabres. [Paul Bereswill/HHOF]

KIRK MULLER

On the topic of the 1984 entry draft, hockey people invariably discuss Mario Lemieux, the first overall selection. (Other great players selected in this draft include Patrick Roy, Brett Hull, Gary Roberts and Luc Robitaille.) The Pittsburgh Penguins — challenged during the 1983–84 season by the New Jersey Devils for the worst record in hockey — made one of the most talked about picks in the draft's history. With the second choice the Devils were pleased to select centre Kirk Muller from the Guelph Platers of the Ontario Hockey League. The Devils knew that no available player was as good as Lemieux, but they also knew Muller's great work ethic and style of play would become a cornerstone for the franchise they hoped to rebuild.

Born in Kingston, Ontario, Muller played junior hockey there until he was selected first overall by the Platers in the 1982 OHL draft. He went to Guelph for the 1982–83 season, and although the team he played for had little support, Muller still managed 52 goals and 60 assists on an expansion team with only 14 points! Muller developed a strong two-way style of play, despite his poor squad, believing that this would make him a good NHL player. At the Devils camp in the fall of 1984, he made the team on his first attempt. Showing that he was going to be a leader, he scored 17 goals and added 37 assists in 80 games. Muller kept improving his scoring totals: he put in impressive 25, 26, 37, 31 and 30 goals over his next few seasons in New Jersey. He was named team captain, and his relentless approach to playing the game quickly became his trademark. Muller wasn't the biggest player (6', 205 pounds) nor the swiftest skater, but he was dangerous on the attack and

as a penalty killer. Always giving his best, he wasn't afraid to get physical.

Despite some good years with the Devils — nearly making it to the finals in 1988 — Muller got into a contract squabble with management, which led to a trade with the Montreal Canadiens in September 1991. Muller found the change of scenery to his liking; he recorded a 77-point season in '91–'92. The 1992–93 season saw him score 37 times and total 94 points. But he saved his best for the playoffs when he scored two overtime winners. Muller's winning tallies — one versus Buffalo and one against the New York Islanders — helped the Habs to a Stanley Cup win. His 17 points in 20 postseason games were impressive, but he was just as valuable on defence against other top centres like Pat LaFontaine and Pierre Turgeon. Ultra-competitive yet modest and down-to-earth, Muller shut down the opposition and outscored them. He was a deserving champion.

Two years later, as the Canadiens struggled, the New York Islanders dangled Turgeon in front of their eyes. The Habs couldn't resist bringing a French-Canadian star back home. The price was a heavy one: the Islanders coveted Muller, but the Habs were in dire need of the offence that Turgeon could supply. The deal wasn't to Muller's liking. He was soon moved to Toronto, where he had a 20-goal season. As he got older, Muller slowed down considerably, but he was still willing to stick his nose in wherever he could get a loose puck. He soon started to play a strictly defensive game, carrying on in this role with Florida and then with Dallas. He was with the Stars when they made it to the 2000 finals.

MULLER'S CANADIENS STATS:	GP	G	A	P	PIM
regular season	267	104	143	247	292
playoffs	38	20	12	32	53

STANLEY CUPS: 1

On April 5, 1995, Montreal traded Kirk Muller, Mathieu Schneider and Craig Darby to the New York Islanders for Pierre Turgeon and Vladimir Malakhov. (Paul Bereswill/HHOF)

MATS NASLUND

As Canadiens great Guy Lafleur slowed down in the early eighties, Montreal fans wondered who would provide the needed offence. Many of the forwards — Steve Shutt, for example — who played with Lafleur during Montreal's glorious Stanley Cup years of the late seventies were also fading. Others, like Jacques Lemaire, had retired. Eventually, the Habs discovered an unlikely source of attack after selecting — 37th overall in the 1979 draft — little (5'7", 160 pounds) Mats Naslund, an unknown Swedish-born left-winger. Although Naslund's arrival was much anticipated, he didn't get to Montreal until the 1982–83 season. A new star in the making, he quickly showed that a small man could still have a large role to play in the NHL.

First noticed as a hockey player when he was just seven years old, Naslund was born in Timra, Sweden. In a photo that appeared in all the Swedish newspapers, the youngster posed with Russian hockey great Vyacheslav Starshinov. He began playing competitive hockey in his hometown and then went to play for the Brynas club in the Swedish first division. The smallish Naslund reminded Montreal scout Ron Caron of Henri Richard and Yvan Cournoyer. While in Europe former Canadiens goaltender Ken Dryden sent back glowing reports on the competitive Naslund. In 1978 Naslund tied Wayne Gretzky for the scoring lead at the World Junior Championships. After being selected by the Habs in '79, Naslund stayed in Sweden for three more seasons before deciding to come to North America.

Naslund made the team and showed he could play in the world's best league by accumulating 26 goals and 45 assists in 74 games. Driven to succeed to prove that Swedes could earn the regard of North Americans and play tough, Naslund got a helping hand from team-mate Bob Gainey while adjusting to life in Montreal. So that Naslund could focus on hockey, Gainey helped him find housing and a doctor for his children. Adjusting well to his new home, Naslund scored 29 goals in his second season and then 42 goals in 1984–85. The high point of the season came on December 3, 1984, when Naslund scored four goals in one game against the Hartford Whalers in a 9–3 Habs win. A quick skater, he could dart around the ice easily, always hustling. His fast hands helped him to score many goals. His clean style helped him to become a fan favourite in Montreal. Naslund became the first European-born player to have a major impact on the Canadiens.

The 1985–86 season was a great one for Naslund, who scored 43 times and totalled 110 points, both career highs. Easily Montreal's most dangerous forward, he kept up his fine performance (19 points in 20 games) in the postseason when the Canadiens won the Stanley Cup. He scored a key goal in the final versus the Calgary Flames: his tally broke a 2–2 tie in the third game of the series. The Habs went on to a 5–3 win and took the Cup in five contests. Naslund continued to perform well for the Canadiens, scoring 25, 24, 33 and 21 goals over his next four seasons. But he never again reached the heights of '85–'86 when he was named to the NHL's second all-star team. The Habs reached the final again in 1989. Naslund had 15 points in 22 playoff games. But the Flames took the Cup on Forum ice. His final season in Montreal, 1989–90, saw him record 41 points in 72 games. Naslund left to play in Switzerland for the next season before returning to Sweden.

Naslund surprised the hockey world by returning to the NHL for the lockout-shortened 1994–95 season with a reasonable performance of 22 points in 34 contests playing for the Boston Bruins.

NASLUND'S CANADIENS STATS:	GP	G	A	P	PIM
regular season	490	225	196	421	399
playoffs	77	36	21	57	51

STANLEY CUPS: 1

Mats Naslund is one of only two Canadiens in team history to win the Lady Byng Trophy, awarded to the leagues most gentlemanly player. The other recipient was Buddy O'Connor. (Paul Bereswill/HHOF)

STEPHANE RICHER

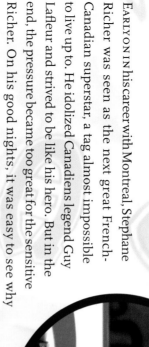

Early on in his career with Montreal, Stephane Richer was seen as the next great French-Canadian superstar, a tag almost impossible to live up to. He idolized Canadiens legend Guy Lafleur and strived to be like his hero. But in the end, the pressure became too great for the sensitive Richer. On his good nights, it was easy to see why the fans pinned their hopes on the native of Ripon, Quebec.

Blessed with a great shot and good size, the 6'2", 215-pound Richer was an exciting performer to watch, especially early in his Habs career when he gave his best performances at the Forum. But each of his goals further raised expectations. It soon became obvious Richer had to leave Montreal to continue his career.

In his youth Richer was a good baseball player, but he was exceptional at hockey and soon devoted all his efforts to it. He went to Hull, Quebec, to play for a high-profile midget team, and then at 16 he played for a Triple-A midget team in Laval. He was selected by the Granby Bisons to play major junior hockey for the 1983–84 season. His 39 goals in 67 games got him drafted by the Canadiens 29th overall in the 1984 entry draft. He returned to Granby for the 1984–85 season to score 30 goals in 30 games. Traded to Chicoutimi for the next 27 games, he added 31 goals to his total. Montreal then sent him to Sherbrooke of the American Hockey League for the playoffs, which brought the team the Calder Cup. Richer scored six goals in nine games, including the one that clinched the championship. He seemed ready for the NHL.

The 1985–86 season saw the NHL rookie score 21 goals and earn 37 points in 65 games. Richer also contributed four goals in their 6 playoff games when a group of young Canadiens jelled at just the right time to win the Stanley Cup. Although Richer's contribution to Montreal's surprise championship wasn't considered vital, he was certainly seen

as an up-and-comer. Unfortunately, because of a rocky relationship with coach Jean Perron, he split the 1986–87 season between Montreal and Sherbrooke. Richer later patched that rift by working harder, and the next season saw him explode with 50 goals in 72 games. Certainly not a physical player, he displayed a great natural instinct for goal-scoring, his potential seemingly limitless. He had a nose for the net. However, the next year Richer slumped to just 25 goals in 68 games. Suspended 10 games for a slashing incident in November of 1988, he struggled for consistency under new coach Pat Burns.

Burns' faith in Richer had positive results: 51 goals and 91 points made 1989–90 Richer's best season. Richer was back on track, but the next season saw him score only 31 goals, enough for most players, except that the demanding fans and media wanted Richer to maintain a 50-goal pace year after year just as Lafleur had done. It was too much for Richer, who one day cried in Burns' office, to handle. Clearly the Habs had to move Richer. A deal sent him to the New Jersey Devils in September of 1991.

Playing in New Jersey, out of the limelight, proved to be a great tonic for the enigmatic Richer. He became a consistent goal scorer and a better all-round player for the Devils, posting seasons of 29, 38, 36, 23, 20 and 22 goals. He helped the Devils to their first Cup ever in 1995 with 12 points (including seven goals) in 20 games. Never the superstar once expected, he nevertheless became a solid hockey player coaches could rely on.

The Canadiens reacquired Richer briefly but then sent him to Tampa Bay where he played for more than two years. He also played for St. Louis before retiring for a short while to deal with personal problems. Pittsburgh signed him as a free agent for the 2001–02 season, and the Devils took him back in a trade-deadline deal at the end of the year. He totalled 14 goals in 68 games with both clubs.

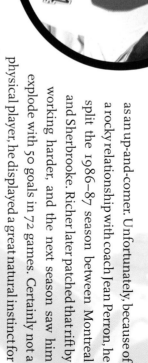

RICHER'S CANADIENS STATS:

	GP	G	A	P	PIM
regular season	490	225	196	421	399
playoffs	77	36	21	57	51

STANLEY CUPS: 1

PATRICK ROY

At his official retirement press conference in May 2003, Patrick Roy was asked if there was any shooter he feared. The confident netminder looked his questioner straight in the eye and said there was no one who came to mind. Some critics said this was proof that Roy was a cocky, arrogant player who never admitted to being wrong. It wasn't the first time Roy showed his brash side. When he was traded by the Montreal Canadiens to the Colorado Avalanche in the middle of the 1995–96 season, he predicted he would win the Stanley Cup, which he did a few months later. As an old baseball sage once said, "It ain't braggin' if it's the truth." It was the truth with Roy.

Hockey didn't always come so easily to Roy. At the tender age of 15 he was cut from a midget team and had to play house league. But he had great bloodlines: his mother was a synchronized swimmer and his father was a good tennis and baseball player. Eventually his athletic ability would win out. He made the local squad the next season, winning a league best 27 games. Then the native of Quebec City found himself playing junior hockey for the Granby Bisons. Roy didn't play for a great club in Granby, often facing 50 shots a night. His goals against average ranged from 4.44 to 6.25 during his three seasons with the team. But he worked hard at developing his skills because he didn't like to lose. Noting Roy's athleticism, the Canadiens selected him 51st overall in the 1984 entry draft in spite of the poor numbers.

As a youngster Roy wanted to be in the NHL. He collected the hockey cards of goalie legends like Ken Dryden and Gerry Cheevers and really admired French-Canadian netminders Rogie Vachon and Daniel Bouchard. In fact, Roy's father once drove peewee-aged Patrick to the Montreal Forum so that the youngster could see Vachon, then a member of the Los Angeles Kings, play against the Canadiens. Before making it to the big league, Roy was assigned to Sherbrooke of the American Hockey League and thrust right away into the 1985 Calder Cup playoffs. He won his first game. The coach, liking what he saw, wouldn't take him out. The team went on to win the championship.

By the start of the 1985–86 season, Roy was the Habs' number one netminder, playing in 47 games, winning 23. Although the Canadiens weren't favoured to win the Stanley Cup, the rookie goalie was simply incredible. He took his team all the way to the finals, during which the Habs bested the Calgary Flames in five games. In a fitting end to the playoffs, Roy made an unbelievable save on Flames defenceman Jamie Macoun to preserve a 4–3 Montreal lead in the game's dying seconds. A legend was born. The unknown Roy won his first of a record three Conn Smythe Trophies as the best player in the playoffs.

Soon Roy became known as the best clutch goaltender in the game. Ultra-competitive as well as a student of the game, he relished the pressure that came with recognition. A big help to his defencemen, he wasn't shy about directing traffic or letting his teammates know when they weren't playing well. To an entire province he became a hero. Many young French-Canadian goaltenders copied his goaltending style. After years of no one goaltender dominating, Roy became the new superstar of the twine hut. Some of the better athletes — like Martin Brodeur and Jean-Sebastian Giguere — found goaltending fashionable again. Roy had figured out that shooters had a hard time putting shots in the top part of the net, and his butterfly style was copied by just about everyone. His size (6'2", 185 pounds) allowed him to cover the bottom of the net. Roy perfected the technique of going down at just the right moment, but he wasn't a flopper. He focused on being at the right spot just as the shooter unleashed a blast. Roy's style revolutionized netminding and the game itself.

Over the years as a Hab, Roy remained a consistent 25 or more game winner. The Canadiens enjoyed many good seasons under

Patrick Roy's first game as a Canadien came on February 23, 1985, in Winnipeg against the Jets. Surprised to get the call, he went out and won the game 6–4. (Paul Bereswill/HHOF)

When Patrick Roy first joined the Canadiens, he had the odd habit of talking to his goalposts because, as he said,
"They are my friends." (Paul Bereswill/HHOF)

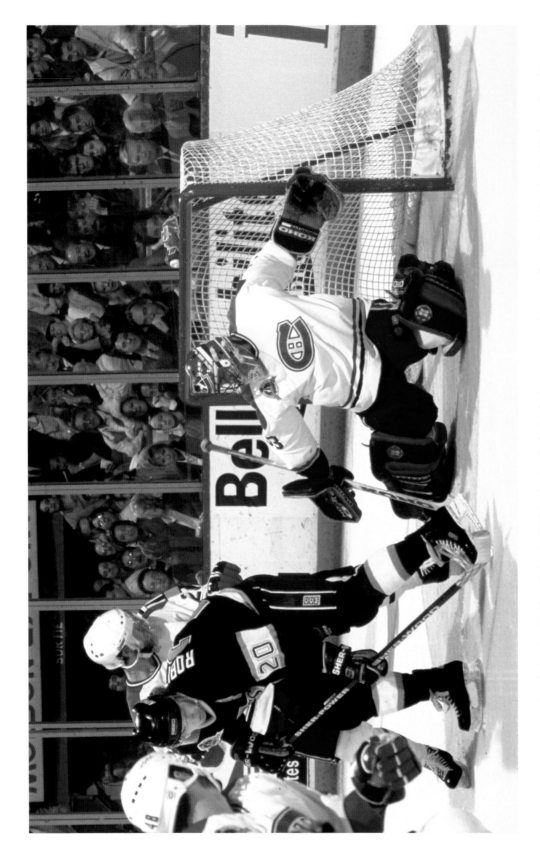

Patrick Roy makes a save against the Los Angeles Kings during the 1993 Stanley Cup finals. Roy had many great performances in overtime during the playoffs, but perhaps his greatest came against the New York Rangers in the 1986 playoffs when he made 13 saves in the extra session before the Habs scored to win the third game of the series. (Paul Bereswill/HHOF)

his goaltending leadership. In 1989 Montreal was back in the finals, but the Flames took the Cup away with a six-game series win. Not until the 1992–93 season did the Habs regain the Cup, when once again they weren't favoured to win. As in 1986, Roy was the outstanding performer in the postseason, winning an NHL record 10 consecutive overtime games. Roy wasn't going to be beat in extra time. A new hero emerged as night after night the Habs knocked off Quebec, Buffalo, the New York Islanders and the Los Angeles Kings to take their 24th Stanley Cup. It was Roy's last great moment with the Canadiens.

After their Cup win, the team fell apart when a winning coach (Jacques Demers) and a stellar general manager (Serge Savard) were let go. Roy wasn't pleased to see former teammate Mario Tremblay behind the bench. It was soon obvious that the two couldn't live in harmony. A December 2, 1995 meltdown against the Detroit Red Wings saw Roy stomp off the ice in disgust after allowing nine goals.

In front of a national television audience, he told team president Ronald Corey that he had played his last game in a Canadiens uniform. Perhaps everyone overreacted, but Roy nonetheless went to Colorado a few days later. The change couldn't have worked out better for Roy.

As a rising NHL power, the Colorado Avalanche needed a goalie to solidify their chances of winning the Cup. Roy did just that, although he didn't have to be as dominating with Colorado as he had been in Montreal. Before his career ended, Roy won two more Cups (1995 and 2001), added his third Smyth (2001) and became the NHL's all-time leader for goalie wins (551) and the all-time leader in games played (1,029). All things considered, Roy may well have left the game as the best goalie of all time.

Facing page: Patrick Roy holds up the Stanley Cup in 1993.
Roy finished his career with an NHL record 60,227 minutes for goaltenders.
He once played in a playoff game for the Canadiens just a few days after having his appendix removed! (Paul Bereswill/HHOF)

ROY'S CANADIENS STATS:

	GP	Wins	Losses	Ties	Shutouts	GA
regular season	551	289	175	66	29	2.77
playoffs	114	70	42	–	5	2.46

STANLEY CUPS 2

DENIS SAVARD

THE MONTREAL Canadiens had the first overall pick — acquired in a deal with the Colorado Rockies — in the 1980 entry draft. Meanwhile Quebec native Denis Savard wanted nothing more than to join the team of his boyhood dreams. But the Canadiens chose a much larger centre — Doug Wickenheiser. Wickenheiser was the star of the Western Junior League with the Regina Pats, while Savard was clearly the best player available for the top junior circuit in Quebec. Normally the Canadiens, following tradition, would have chosen the French-Canadian star. However, the Montreal scouts were convinced Wickenheiser was potentially a dominating NHL player. They couldn't have been more wrong.

Born in Pointe Gatineau, Quebec, Savard grew up playing hockey in Verdun. He played hockey every chance he got and admired the Canadiens, especially Yvan Cournoyer and Guy Lafleur. He played three years of junior hockey in Montreal and put up remarkable offensive numbers — 146 goals and 309 points in 214 games. Not a big player at 5'10", 175 pounds, he was a dynamo on skates. His spinning and turning presented nightmares for defencemen trying to check him, and he was always in the right spot to score goals. Savard's shot wasn't overpowering but it was deadly accurate. He was a dominating centre who could outskate any would-be checker. His drive for the net and feisty nature set him apart from other smallish players. He would have loved to become a Hab, but the Chicago Blackhawks selected Savard third overall. They would never live to regret it.

Savard was undeniably the Blackhawks' offensive leader with five years of 100 or more points and six seasons of 35 or more goals. During Savard's time as a Blackhawk, Chicago was a good team but not a great one. The hiring of new coache Mike Keenan made Savard

vulnerable to being traded. In the summer of 1990 the Canadiens were on the lookout for some help on the attack. They also wanted to peddle defenceman Chris Chelios who had fallen out of favour. The Blackhawks took on Chelios. Montreal general manager Serge Savard thought the Canadiens could match Savard with winger Stephane Richer for a deadly duo. It was reported that the Habs, to take Savard, passed on a chance to acquire Dale Hawerchuk. But how could they pass up an opportunity to correct a wrong committed 10 years earlier?

Soon the critics were out in full force as it became evident that the Canadiens had acquired Savard 10 years too late! The pairing with Richer never did work out, and Savard produced only a disappointing 59-point season. (To add insult to injury, Chelios had 64 for the first-place Blackhawks!) In 1991–92, however, Savard bounced back somewhat with 28 goals and 70 points in 77 games. But the Habs could do nothing in the playoffs. The 1992–93 season saw Savard slump to 18 goals, his lowest total since joining the NHL, and 50 points. At least the team was a contender for the Stanley Cup. Savard played in only 14 postseason games, but after the Canadiens won the Cup, captain Guy Carbonneau handed the silver mug first to Savard, who was in street clothes! The gesture told Savard that he was an important team member, highly respected for his NHL accomplishments. It was the only championship of Savard's career.

The Canadiens didn't re-sign the freewheeling pivot, who inked a deal with Tampa Bay. The Lightning then shipped him to Chicago where Savard had one last hurrah in the 1995 playoffs with 18 points in 16 playoff games. Retiring after two more years, he was elected to the Hockey Hall of Fame in 2000.

SAVARD'S CANADIENS STATS:	GP	G	A	P	PIM
regular season	210	72	107	179	215
playoffs	38	5	25	30	47
STANLEY CUPS: 1					

When the Canadiens acquired Denis Savard in a trade with Chicago, two French-speaking radio stations took out newspaper ads to welcome him to Montreal. (Paul Bereswill/HHOF)

BOBBY SMITH

Back in 1978 the National Hockey League's entry draft was limited to players 20 years of age or older. But there was no doubt that centre Bobby Smith of the Ottawa 67s was going to be the top choice. In his last year of junior, Smith won the Ontario Hockey Association's scoring title with 192 points (69 goals, 132 assists).

His excellent size (6′4″, 210 pounds) made him even more appealing. He made it clear that he had no interest in signing with the World Hockey Association, which was on its last legs. Looking for a cornerstone on which to rebuild, the Minnesota North Stars had the first choice in '78 and didn't hesitate to take Smith. Time would prove that the North Stars made the best choice, as Smith was easily the best player to come out of that draft.

Smith made a smooth transition to the professional game and won the Calder Trophy for his performance in the 1978–79 season when he had 30 goals and 44 assists. The next year saw Smith raise his point total to 83. The North Stars pulled off a great upset in the playoffs when they knocked off the Montreal Canadiens who were trying to win their fifth straight Stanley Cup. (The Philadelphia Flyers beat the North Stars in the next round.) Smith kept improving, as did the North Stars, and he recorded 93 points in 1980–81. The North Stars had finally started to reap the benefits of merging with the California Seals. They now had a young but formidable squad. The Islanders who were then in the middle of their dynasty. Smith enjoyed his finest NHL season in 1981–82 when he recorded 114 points (43 goals, 71 assists). The North Stars, however, couldn't get close to the Cup again, in spite of fine talent with unlimited potential. Just two years later Smith — who didn't like new coach Bill

Mahoney — fell out of favour with the North Stars. Smith asked general manager Lou Nanne for a deal. Nanne was willing to accommodate the slick pivot since he had concerns about Smith's skating and leadership abilities. At the same time the Canadiens wanted a big centre.

Montreal general manager Serge Savard remembered playing against Smith and being impressed with his abilities. The Habs didn't hesitate to make a high-profile deal, sending Mark Napier and Keith Acton, plus a third-round draft pick, to the North Stars. It was a high price to pay, but Smith was the strong playmaker the Canadiens wanted. Smith was thrilled to join the Montreal squad. In fact, he scored 12 goals in his first 13 games with the team!

After a good start with the Habs — 26 goals, 37 assists in 70 games in the 1983–84 season — Smith slumped the next season (as did the entire team) and produced only 15 goals and 40 assists. But in 1985–86 he came back to score 31 times and add 55 assists. He was especially strong in the playoffs when, with 15 points in 20 games, he helped the Habs take the Cup by knocking off Boston, Hartford, the New York Rangers and Calgary. Smith had found his game again and put in four more excellent seasons for the Habs, including a 32-goal season in 1988–89 when the Habs made it to the finals but lost the Cup to the Calgary Flames.

The rangy centre with the long reach stayed one more year in Montreal, but the slowed down a little, so the Habs moved him back to Minnesota in a deal that saw the Canadiens land an insignificant fourth-round draft choice. Smith showed he had lots left by helping the North Stars get back to the finals in 1991. He produced 16 points in 23 playoff games. He retired two years later with 357 career goals and 1,036 points.

SMITH'S CANADIENS STATS:	GP	G	A	P	PIM
regular season	505	172	310	482	430
playoffs	107	38	46	84	139

STANLEY CUPS: 1

Bobby Smith scored the Stanley Cup-winning goal in the fifth game of the 1986 finals against the Flames to give Montreal a 4–3 victory. (Paul Bereswill/HHOF)

THE BATTLE OF QUEBEC: THE GREAT CANADIENS-NORDIQUES RIVALRY

by Dave Stubbs

POLITICAL SCIENTISTS will tell you that, as battles in Quebec go, the French versus the British on the Plains of Abraham in 1759 is the grandest of them all.

But hockey fans will beg to differ. They'll tell you that greater wars were fought two centuries and two decades later, on the ice of the Montreal Forum and Le Colisée in Quebec City. Their logic is this: hostilities on the Plains of Abraham lasted barely 15 minutes, roughly the penalty time doled out in just a single period of any decent game between the Canadiens and the Quebec Nordiques.

Theirs was a wonderful hockey rivalry born of geography and necessity, between two cities separated by a couple hundred kilometres, different outlooks on life and more than 20 Stanley Cups — all of them won by Montreal. In its prime, it was bitter and worse, each game another salvo in a long-running war, its cannons volleyed by players, coaches and management, and the rowdy fans who dared show up in the enemy's rink.

The Nordiques arrived in the NHL in 1979–80 after seven seasons in the World Hockey Association, giving the Canadiens their badly needed rival. Montreal's long-simmering feud with Toronto had cooled — the Maple Leafs no match for the Canadiens dynasty of the late '70s.

It's a given that a hard-core Canadiens fan signs a pact declaring a disgust for Toronto. But this same fan was torn between loyalties when it came to the Nordiques. A love-hate relationship existed for many reasons, notably the following:

- The Nordiques' base was the cradle of French Canada, by extension the spiritual home of its language and culture.
- Montreal hockey owed much to Quebec City, which had long been a fertile junior- and senior-league training ground for Canadiens-in-waiting, including legends like Jean Béliveau and Guy Lafleur. Canadiens icon Maurice Richard was the Nordiques' first coach in the WHA, if only for two games (one win, one loss).
- Lafleur, the pulse of the Canadiens' glorious clubs of the 1970s, wore the Nordiques fleur-de-lys for 98 games, even on Forum ice, in the twilight of his career. How could they jeer the wondrous Flower?

In all, the Canadiens played the Nordiques 113 times in 16 seasons, winning 62, losing 39 and tying 12. They won 17 of 31 playoff games and three of the five series, twice gaining momentum to win the Stanley Cup.

But this rivalry wasn't just one of goals for and against. The feud between the two cities traces its roots to the 17th-century fur trade of New France. In the 1980s, it was Montreal, the province's vibrant economic engine, versus Quebec, its cobble-stoned, romantic soul. Their game statistics included an invisible column for civic pride won or lost.

The Canadiens grew ordinary as the 1980s wore on, winning just one Stanley Cup in that decade. Soon, crafty signings, shrewd draft picks and a powder keg coach named Michel Bergeron had the Nordiques at their heels, and in their faces.

The battle lines had been drawn in 1981–82 when NHL realignment put both teams in the Adams Division. Fuelled by an atmosphere just this side of a circus, players raised their game to a higher level, now meeting more frequently. Canadiens forward Mario Tremblay, never a choirboy, remembers Bergeron leaning over the boards during Montreal's game-day skate, bellowing threats.

But never was the feud uglier than at the Forum on April 20, 1984, in the sixth game of the divisional playoff final. Even before the match, Bergeron and his Canadiens counterpart, Jacques Lemaire, were at their provocative, passion-stoking best, fanning the flames in the press.

The short fuse was lit and perhaps the explosion was inevitable — a huge brawl at the end of the second period spilling past the intermission into the third. As part of a violent, bench-clearing rumble not seen before or since on Montreal ice, Nordiques strongman Louis Sleigher sucker-punched Canadiens defenceman Jean Hamel, knocking him cold.

The Canadiens' Mark Hunter and his Nordiques brother, Dale, squared off, just before Montreal backup goaltender Richard Sevigny chased Dale around the rink. On the undercard, Mario Tremblay broke the nose of Nordiques sniper Peter Stastny. The game report read like a police blotter: 21 minor penalties,

16 fighting majors, three misconducts, 10 game misconducts. It added up to 252 penalty minutes — enough time to re-enact the Plains of Abraham battle more than 16 times. The Canadiens scored five straight goals to eliminate the Nordiques from the playoffs. The game is still remembered as the "Good Friday Massacre."

The rivalry would fade in time, with Quebec missing the playoffs from 1987 to 1992. In 1993, the Nordiques' first NHL coach, Jacques Demers, would steer Montreal to its 24th Stanley Cup. Two years later, unable to keep financial pace in the aging Colisée, short of reliable revenue and unsuccessful in convincing the city to build his club a new arena, Nordiques managing partner Marcel Aubut abruptly sold the club.

The Nordiques became the Colorado Avalanche, winning the Stanley Cup their first spring in Denver. Starring in goal was Quebec native Patrick Roy, recently arrived from the Canadiens, to complete the nightmare. It was on Canada Day 1995, with a whimper unworthy of a rivalry that once screamed from the rooftops, that the Battle of Quebec had come to an end. Hearts were broken in Quebec, also in Montreal.

Seven years later, the Canadiens and Avalanche played a training-camp exhibition at Le Colisée, the first NHL game in Quebec since the Nordiques pulled up stakes. It was an emotional event — 7,000 fans watching the morning skate, a sellout of 15,399 on hand for the game. Many wept openly when Avalanche players Joe Sakic, Adam Foote and Peter Forsberg, all former Nordiques, tugged on vintage Quebec jerseys during the introductions.

A little of the magic was rekindled for one night, but it was clear this rivalry had forever been laid to rest. In Quebec City, the ceremonial cannons guarding the old town were silent, and on the ice, not a single punch was thrown.

Amid the chaos, a goal is scored: a classic game between arch-rivals the Canadiens and the Nordiques. (Bruce Bennett/BBS)

B y the start of the 1995–96 season the club had changed. It had traded away two vital players in John LeClair and Eric Desjardins without getting enough in return (although Mark Recchi was a good player). After a start that saw the team go 0–5, upper management panicked and dismissed Savard and Demers in one fell swoop. Their replacements were a couple of inexperienced former Habs: Rejean Houle as general manager and Mario Tremblay as coach. The Canadiens made the playoffs with a 40–32–10 record but lost to the New York Rangers in the first round.

An even bigger loss to the organization occurred when Patrick Roy demanded to be traded. The hiring of Tremblay as coach wasn't to his liking. After being left in too long during a disastrous game against Detroit, Roy expressed his feelings on national television. The trading of Roy marked the end of that era when the Canadiens were always considered contenders for the Cup.

217

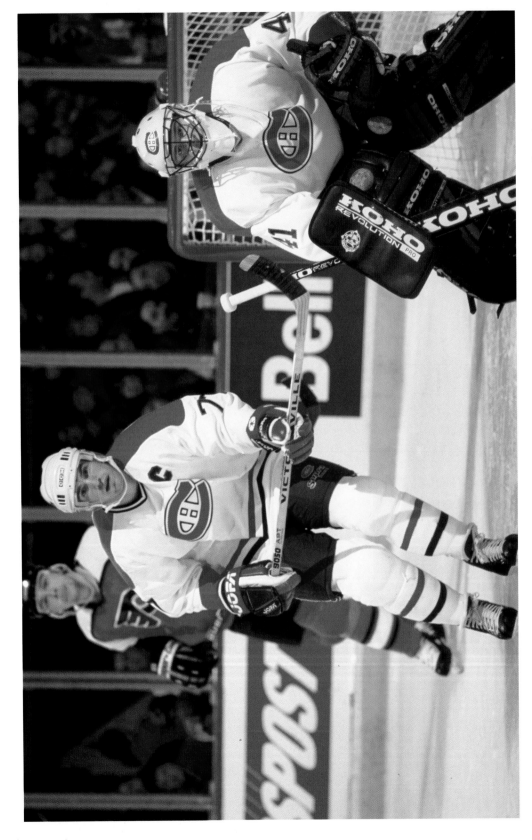

Pierre Turgeon had one excellent season in Montreal when in 1995–96 he scored 38 goals and totalled 96 points. [HHOF]

Another major change was the team's move from the Forum to a new facility. The last game at the Forum took place on March 11, 1996, when the Habs said farewell to the building in style with a 4–1 win over the Dallas Stars. After the game the beautifully presented closing ceremonies tugged at the heart of every fan in attendance or watching on television.

Ground was broken for the new arena on June 22, 1993. The Habs played their first game at the Molson Centre (as it was first known) on March 16, 1996. Before a sellout crowd, the Canadiens won the opening game 4–2 over the New York Rangers. Vincent Damphousse scored the first goal in the new building. But in its first years the new arena wouldn't prove to be friendly as the Habs struggled just to make the playoffs. The team went through a variety of managers, coaches and captains, ending their trademark stability at the top of the organization. The most successful sports team in Canada even got sold to an American owner.

As a general manager Houle was inexperienced, and the trading of Roy was a major crisis thrust upon him. He did his best to diffuse an explosive situation, but the Canadiens simply didn't get enough in exchange for one of the NHL's truly great goalies. In the 2000–01 season Andre Savard replaced Houle as general manager. The former director of player personnel and scout for the Ottawa Senators tried to focus on good drafting as a way to rebuild the team. Tremblay didn't last long as coach: in the 1997–98 season he was replaced by Alain Vigneault. Vigneault took the Canadiens to one playoff appearance but was dismissed and replaced by Michel Therrien in the 2000–01 season. The Habs reclaimed some of their former glory in 2001–02 when they upset the Bruins in the first round of the playoffs (and should have won the second series). That success was short-lived: the team missed the playoffs again in 2002–03, the fourth time in five years.

Defenceman Stephane Quintal (#5) was acquired twice in trades made by the Canadiens — in 1995 from Winnipeg and in 2001 from Chicago. He was dealt away in June of 2004. (Jim Leary/BBS)

Claude Julien replaced Therrien in the '02–'03 season and got the club back into the playoffs in 2003–04. In spite of his good reputation while coaching the Habs farm club in Hamilton — 33–9 when he left for Montreal — many expected Julien to be replaced after the arrival of a new general manager. As it happened, the Canadiens made the best possible move before the start of the 2003–04 season by choosing experienced and successful hockey man Bob Gainey to lead their team as general manager. In his first season the former Hab and Hall of Famer made few moves — a trade for Alexei Kovalev was one of them — but Montreal fans can rest assured that he will do what's necessary in the years to come. With a man of Gainey's experience in charge, the Canadiens have regained their respectability and now stand a chance to recapture their glory.

Claude Boivin's appointment as team president to succeed Ron Corey is another big reason for the Habs' return to contender status. Boivin's sports marketing background will undoubtedly serve him well in positioning the Habs for the future. The biggest change of all, however, concerns the team's ownership: no longer in the hands of Molson Breweries, the team now belongs to George Gillett, an American businessman from Colorado. (The arena was included in the deal completed on January 31, 2001.) While it shocked many Canadians to learn that the team is no longer in Canadian hands, Gillett has proven to be a reliable owner who understands what the Canadiens mean to hockey and to Quebec in particular. One of hockey's quieter owners, he lets the hockey people (like Gainey) and local business managers (like Boivin) do their jobs. After Molson passed on the right to name the arena, it became the Bell Centre when the phone company spent an estimated $100 million for the privilege. The unthinkable seems to be working. The fans of Montreal are right to be excited about *Les Glorieux.*

Montreal Canadiens president (1982 to 1999) Ronald Corey. [HHOF]

During these difficult years the Canadiens tried many approaches to staying competitive. Free agents — like Andy Moog, Doug Gilmour, Mariusz Czerkawski, Joe Juneau, Randy McKay, Stephane Quintal and Yanic Perreault — were signed with varying degrees of success. Trades that netted players like Richard Zednik, Jan Bulis, Chad Kilger, Niklas Sundstrom, Jeff Hackett and Donald Audette had a limited impact on the team's success. (Zednik may be an exception.) But the Canadiens did start to develop their own players like Craig Rivet, Jose Theodore, Andrei Markov, Saku Koivu, Michael Ryder and Mike Ribiero. This group of young players now forms the team's nucleus. The Canadiens lack some size and a superstar forward, but they have good speed and a top netminder in Theodore, enough talent around which to build until management can find bigger players. The team saw a variety of captains during these years — including grinder Mike Keane, the disappointing Pierre Turgeon and the now departed Vincent Damphousse — but now seem to be firmly settled behind Koivu, whose triumph over cancer is nothing less than inspirational.

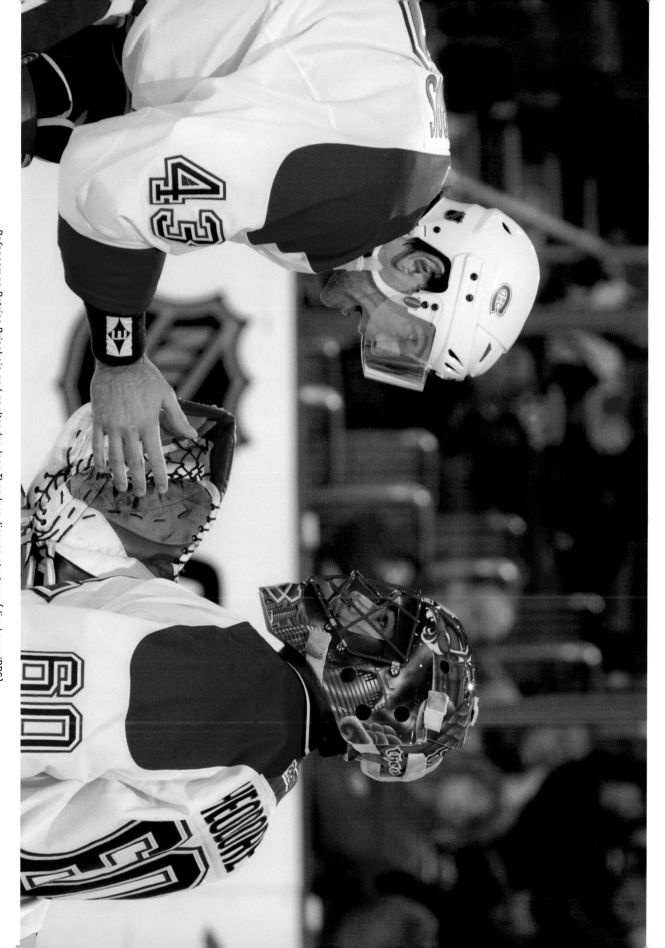

Defenceman Patrice Brisebois and goaltender Jose Theodore discuss strategy. (Jim Leary/BBS)

PATRICE BRISEBOIS

As a youngster, Patrice Brisebois worked at hockey all the time. A native of Montreal, he would even practise his shot with a ball whenever the opportunity arose. The Canadiens were his heroes, his favourite player the legendary Guy Lafleur. At 10 or 12 years of age Brisebois saw his first game at the Montreal Forum. Lafleur scored two goals in a 5–2 Habs win over the Buffalo Sabres. It's quite likely that as Brisebois watched Lafleur he imagined himself playing for the Canadiens one day.

As a relatively small defenceman, Brisebois understood in his junior days that he would have to rely on his attacking and puck-handling skills to get noticed. An admirer of top offensive NHL blueliners like Paul Coffey and Ray Bourque, he tried to imitate their style. Brisebois made two trips to the Memorial Cup while playing hockey in Laval. In the 1988–89 season he produced 65 points (20 goals, 45 assists) for his junior club. The NHL teams were certainly aware of him by this point. The Canadiens selected the hometown prospect 30th overall in the 1989 entry draft but let him play one more year in Laval where in 1989–90 he recorded 88 points. Brisebois split his next season between the Canadiens — in 10 games he recorded two assists — and Drummondville of the QMJHL, winning junior hockey's defenceman of the year award. In 1991–92 he divided his time between Montreal and the Habs' farm club in Fredericton where he earned 39 points in 52 games.

By the 1992–93 season the Habs were convinced the flashy defenceman was ready for full-time work on the big team. He scored a respectable 10 goals and added 21 assists in 70 games, earning an additional four assists in 20 playoff games when the Habs

won the Stanley Cup. Since then Brisebois has been a regular for the Canadiens, posting 10 seasons of 20 or more assists. In spite of his success as a homegrown player, Brisebois hasn't always found it easy in Montreal. Being a local French Canadian can add pressure to playing for the Canadiens, and when a soft defensive zone is as noticeable as the offensive talent, evenings at the rink can be long. Brisebois' strength is his ability to move the puck and make a good, crisp pass. Able to join the attack at any time, he also has a low, hard drive from the point, useful on the power play. His defensive play isn't always as strong as it should be, given that he filled out to be 6'2" and 203 pounds. (He has trouble handling some of the league's larger forwards.) Moreover, his decision-making in his own end can get him into trouble.

His defensive shortcomings secured him as the NHL's worst plus/minus player in the 2000–01 season when he was a minus 31. (However, he did record 15 goals that season, a career high.) He rebounded in 2001–02 to post a plus nine rating but only scored four goals. The Canadiens rewarded their longtime defenceman with a new contract for $4 million a year. But it seemed that as soon as the deal was done, the Habs tried hard to trade him away. He soon became the target of Montreal boo-birds, but injuries and his sizeable contract made dealing him away nearly impossible. When Bob Gainey became the Habs general manager in 2003, he defended the beleaguered player, admonishing Montreal fans for booing a loyal soldier. Gainey's outburst was refreshing and may have given Brisebois — who has played close to 800 games as a Hab — a new lease on life in Montreal.

BRISEBOIS' CANADIENS STATS:	GP	G	A	P	PIM
regular season	791	79	263	342	501
playoffs	78	8	17	25	66
STANLEY CUPS: 1					

Patrice Brisebois was a two-time all-star in the QMJHL and played on two Canadian junior teams that won gold medals at the World Junior Championships. (Bruce Bennett/BBS; inset photo: Lisa Meyer/BBS)

SAKU KOIVU

News in September of 2001 that Saku Koivu had cancer shocked the hockey world and Koivu's Montreal teammates. No one was more stunned than the feisty Koivu himself. How could such a thing happen to a young, healthy hockey star? Luckily, Koivu was in excellent condition and able to endure the difficult medical procedures that killed the cancer. Koivu was back for the final three games of the 2001–02 season, recording two assists. He then played in 12 playoff games, notching 10 points to help the Habs upset the Eastern Conference first-place Boston Bruins. Although the Canadiens lost in the second round of the playoffs to Carolina, the good news was that Koivu was back to stay. His struggle to play hockey again was recognized in June of 2002 with the Masterton Trophy, less than one year after the devastating news. There was never a more deserving recipient of the award, which recognizes dedication to hockey. After his experience of great pain and doubt, Koivu reacted with joy to the award.

At the 1993 entry draft, the Canadiens selected Koivu 21st overall, pleased to take the Finnish-born star with their first selection. He spent the 1993–94 season playing at home for TPS Turku in the Finnish elite league, scoring 23 goals and 53 points in 47 games. Koivu played for the same team in 1994–95, earning 74 points in 45 contests. Named player of the year, he joined the Habs for the 1995–96 season. As a rookie he scored 20 goals and totalled 45 points, playing in all 82 games. After that season Koivu struggled to stay healthy, but whenever the slick centre played he

justified being selected in the first round. Not large at 5'10" and 180 pounds, Koivu nevertheless plays a fearless game. Early in his career he tended to run at larger opponents — perhaps trying to prove that he belonged in the NHL — but the Habs coaching staff wisely steered him away from doing that regularly. He plays an intense but smart brand of hockey; his game built

around strong skating and good speed. Koivu can dish the puck off to his linemates very effectively — 43 assists in 1997–98 marked a career best — and he shows good hands when close around the net. With good vision on the ice, he'll dart all around the rink for a loose puck. His excellent snap shot gets him goals. His chances of staying off the injured list — he has had shoulder and knee problems — will ultimately determine how well his career progresses.

Since the Canadiens aren't a deep squad offensively, Koivu has had to assume the first-line centre role when he might have made a perfect second-line pivot. If Koivu acknowledges his physical limitations, he'll be an effective player for many years to come. Koivu faced his first controversy in 2003–04 when fans and a few in the media briefly turned on him. He weathered the storm easily and posted a 55-point season to help the Habs return to the postseason. He was terrific in the 2004 playoffs when he led the Habs with 11 points. No player is more inspiring than Koivu. Named captain in 1999, he should serve well in that prestigious position for many years to come.

KOIVU'S CANADIENS STATS:	GP	G	A	P	PIM
regular season	497	120	278	398	342
playoffs	40	13	21	34	34

Saku Koivu scored his first NHL goal on October 23, 1995, against Los Angeles Kings goalie Bryon Dafoe. (David Kaye/BBS)

Montreal moment:

In 2002 Saku Koivu became the fourth Canadien to win the Masterton Trophy, awarded to the NHL player who best exemplifies the qualities of perseverance, sportsmanship, and dedication to hockey. The other Habs to win the award were Claude Provost, Henri Richard and Serge Savard. The New York Rangers are the only other team with four Masterton winners.

Above: *Koivu returns to the Montreal ice after his battle with cancer. (Andre Pichette/BBS)*

Right: *In the 2004 playoffs, team captain Saku Koivu led the Habs with 11 points in 11 games played as the Canadiens knocked out Boston before losing to Tampa Bay. (Lisa Meyer/BBS)*

CRAIG RIVET

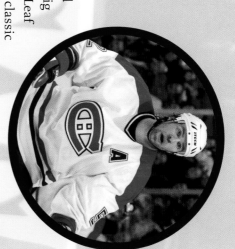

ON FEBRUARY 21, 2004, at the Air Canada Centre, the Montreal Canadiens, in the middle of a slump, were doing poorly against the Toronto Maple Leafs. The Leafs jumped out to a quick 3–0 lead. Defenceman Craig Rivet got into a fight for a full minute with Leaf defenceman Bryan Marchment. It was a classic hockey fight: both players knew they had been in a tussle when it was over. Rivet's involvement showed that the Canadiens weren't about to quit, and they came close to tying the 5–4 contest. Rivet's actions pulled the Habs out of their lethargy. They went on to clinch a playoff spot, which seemed doubtful that night in Toronto.

A blueliner with good size (6'2", 207 pounds) Rivet isn't a fighter but won't shy away when he or his team is challenged. That distinction makes Rivet valuable to the Canadiens. Selected by the Habs 68th overall in the 1992 entry draft, he was by no means assured an NHL position. After completing his junior career with Kingston of the Ontario Hockey League (164 points in 191 games), he joined the Habs' farm team in Fredericton to close out the 1993–94 season. The next season he played 78 games in Fredericton where he recorded 32 points and 126 penalty minutes. In 1995–96, when the Fredericton club made it all the way to the American Hockey League finals, he was named team captain. Rivet split the next season between Montreal (35 games) and the farm team (23 games). His minor-league training was finally over when he became a full-time Hab in 1997–98. As a rookie in the NHL, Rivet got into 61 games and recorded two assists, making his mark, however, with 93 penalty minutes.

Rivet's main strength is his all-round game. Physical when necessary and an excellent team leader, he blocks shots, jumping to help a teammate without any hesitation, and plays hard every night. Using muscle effectively, Rivet finishes his check with authority to keep the opposition honest. He missed much of the 2000–01 season with a shoulder injury, but he recovered well enough to play 82 games back to back for each of the next two seasons. While not very gifted offensively, Rivet has occasionally contributed to the attack, posting his best output of 25 points (eight goals, 17 assists) in 2001–02. He had a 22-point season in 2002–03. Although he has the ability to contribute more on the attack, Rivet concentrates on defending in his own end. The Canadiens recognized the value of Rivet's stay-at-home style with a new contract for $2.5 million per season.

Firmly in place on the Canadiens club as a highly valued member for close to eight seasons, Rivet could one day emerge as a captain. Solid once again in 2003–04 when the Canadiens made it back to the playoffs, he'll be a reliable Hab for a long time to come.

Craig Rivet led the Canadiens with 137 blocked shots in the 2001–02 season. (Andre Pichette/BBS; inset photo: Andy Marlin/BBS)

RIVET'S CANADIENS STATS:	GP	G	A	P	PIM
regular season	517	26	75	101	629
playoffs	33	1	8	9	22

SHELDON SOURAY

THE NEW JERSEY Devils are one of the NHL's best at selecting new talent at the entry draft. They have used the draft to insert new assets into their lineup or store up trade material. Their selection of defenceman Sheldon Souray — 71st overall in 1994 — is a classic example of how the Devils can turn a player into an NHLer and later move him on if necessary. A native of Alberta, Souray played junior hockey in western Canada with Tri City, Prince George and Kelowna of the WHL. Known for his high penalty minute total, he scored 16 times in his last junior year. There is little doubt that the New Jersey club liked Souray for his size (6'4", 223 pounds) and his aggressive game.

As they are apt to do with many mid-level prospects, the Devils assigned Souray to their farm club in Albany, New York, where he played in 70 games in the 1996–97 season, recording 13 points and 160 penalty minutes. He played most of the next three seasons with New Jersey, developing slowly and showing little on offence (only four goals in 182 games) while taking care of his own end. He learned a great deal from his childhood idol, New Jersey teammate Scott Stevens, and coaches like Jacques Lemaire and Larry Robinson. But in March of 2000, the Devils wanted a more offensive-minded defender and found their man in Vladimir Malakov, who was then with Montreal. The deal between the two clubs meant that Souray missed out on the Devils' second Stanley Cup. Souray played in 19 games for the Canadiens to finish the 1999–2000 season and notched three points, all goals. He had looked forward to more ice time in Montreal, but injuries began to

take their toll on him. He played in 52 games for the Habs in 2000–01 but in just 34 games over the next two years because of a serious wrist injury. He missed the entire 2002–03 season.

With his wrist back in working order after surgery, Souray dedicated himself to becoming a better player. By his own admission, he wasn't the most disciplined of athletes, but he returned to the game, now a married man, with a strong sense of purpose. Souray's name was bandied about in 2003–04 for the Norris Trophy until a knee injury cut his season short. At the time of the injury Souray led all defencemen with 15 goals scored, which included his first hat trick in a game against Nashville. He also tied a club record for blueliners with six points, including five assists, in a contest against the Pittsburgh Penguins. Souray's willingness to jump into the rush gave the Canadiens a more varied attack with which to worry the other teams. His good play earned him a spot on the Eastern Conference all-star team, and he played in the game staged in Minnesota. Souray was now using all his skills, the most noteworthy being his hard, accurate shot from the point, which earned him power-play time. Willing to use his size to take on opposing players, Souray is difficult against the opposition when he goes into the corners.

If Souray plays a disciplined game, stays healthy and keeps his confidence high (he had a difficult time in the 2004 playoffs), the Canadiens may have a defenceman who will merit all-star consideration on a yearly basis.

Sheldon Souray had his best offensive year in 2003–04 when he scored 15 goals and added 20 assists in 57 games played.
(Jim MacIsaac/BBS; inset photo: David Kaye/BBS)

SOURAY'S CANADIENS STATS:	GP	G	A	P	PIM
regular season	168	24	33	57	265
playoffs	23	0	5	5	55

JOSE THEODORE

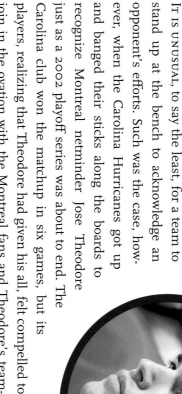

It is unusual, to say the least, for a team to stand up at the bench to acknowledge an opponent's efforts. Such was the case, however, when the Carolina Hurricanes got up and banged their sticks along the boards to recognize Montreal netminder Jose Theodore just as a 2002 playoff series was about to end. The Carolina club won the matchup in six games, but its players, realizing that Theodore had given his all, felt compelled to join in the ovation with the Montreal fans and Theodore's teammates. Theodore was sent back into the game — which turned into an 8–2 romp by the Hurricanes — so that he could be acknowledged. It was a rare moment — especially in today's competitive sports world — but one that proved great performances in hockey are still valued. Theodore would never forget it.

That moment at the end of the Carolina playoff series was the culmination of Theodore's rise to a dominant position in the NHL. Very competitive as a youngster even at road hockey, Theodore was a hometown kid who rose through the ranks to assume the Habs' number one netminding job. Drafted 44th overall by Montreal in 1994, Theodore only began to play the majority of games for the Canadiens in the 2000–01 season. Before that he split his time between Montreal and Fredericton of the American Hockey League. Essentially a .500 goalie, he got thrown into a playoff series in 1997 against New Jersey to replace a faltering Jocelyn Thibault in goal. He made an impression by recording a 4–3 victory in overtime, edging out Martin Brodeur in the Devils net. But it wasn't until the 2000–2001 season when Theodore got into 59 games that he started to show his potential as a number one netminder.

Working on his technique with former NHL goaltender Roland Melanson helped Theodore the most. Melanson's suggestions — turning properly on his skates, standing up straighter, moving his

hands back — got Theodore on the right track. His good positional play allows Theodore to use the popular butterfly style of netminding. He has the agility to move laterally to get to many shots. He recovers quickly on shots when he gives up a rebound and doesn't mind sprawling to make a save. His incredible save on Bill Guerin of the Boston Bruins in the first round of the '02 playoffs is a classic example of how Theodore can scramble to make a spectacular stop. Since he isn't the NHL's biggest goalie (5'11", 182 pounds) Theodore's quickness is essential. He also handles pressure well and can bounce back from a bad goal with greater ease than most.

The 2001–02 season was a dream year for Theodore, who won the Hart and Vezina Trophies with a 30–24–10 record. He also earned a spot on the second all-star team. His performance was the main reason the Habs made it back to the playoffs. He was also outstanding in the first round of the postseason when the Canadiens defeated the ancient rival Bruins in six games. As the top seed in the Eastern Conference, the Bruins were heavily favoured to win the series, but Theodore played like a stone wall, and Montreal scored just enough to win. Theodore was worn down by the end of the second round, but the Habs certainly had their new superstar.

Perhaps Theodore enjoyed the adulation a little too much in the off-season because his 2002–03 campaign (20–31–6) wasn't what he or Montreal fans expected. The Habs missed the playoffs once again. Moreover, Theodore faced added pressure when the police began to investigate the immediate members of his family. But he overcame the negative attention and got the Habs back to the playoffs with a 35-win season in 2003–04 and another first-round upset of the Bruins! His star is shining brightly once again. The Habs have a chance to win every night he starts a game.

For the record:

In 2002 Jose Theodore became the second Montreal netminder to win the Hart Trophy, awarded to the player judged most valuable to his team. Jacques Plante was the first. Only the Canadiens have had two different goalies win the award. The only other goalies to win the Hart are Roy Worters, Chuck Raynor, Al Rollins and Dominik Hasek.

Montreal moment:

Goaltender Jose Theodore became the 28th Montreal netminder to win the Vezina Trophy, based on both methods of awarding it. At first the award recognized fewest goals allowed, and then in 1982 it acknowledged the league's best goalie. No other NHL team comes close to this mark. Chicago has won it six times, Buffalo and Boston seven times each, Toronto six times and Detroit five times. The Canadien netminders whose names appear on the award include George Hainsworth, Bill Durnan, Jacques Plante, Charlie Hodge, Gump Worsley, Rogie Vachon, Ken Dryden, Michel Larocque, Richard Sevigny, Denis Herron and Patrick Roy.

Left: Goaltender Jose Theodore stretches to make a great save against the Bruins Sergei Samsonov. (Andre Pichette/BBS)

Below: Theodore celebrates after scoring a goal. He shot the puck into an empty New York Islanders net on January 2, 2001. (Jim MacIsaac/BBS)

Jose Theodore has led the Canadiens to two playoff upsets against the Boston Bruins (in 2002 and 2004). (Jim Leary/BBS)

THEODORE'S CANADIENS STATS:	GP	Wins	Losses	Ties	Shutouts	GA
regular season	315	124	143	30	23	2.43
playoffs	28	11	15	–	1	2.52

RICHARD ZEDNIK

RIGHT-WINGER RICHARD ZEDNIK is one of those European-born players who get drafted very late by a team hoping to capture some lightning in a bottle. Such was the case in 1994 with Zednik, a native of Czechoslovakia, selected 249th overall by the Washington Capitals.

The Washington scouts didn't have much hard data to go by — nine points in 25 games that Zednik played in his homeland — but they must have seen or heard something they liked. Zednik left home for the 1994–95 season to play for Portland of the western junior league, hoping to develop his skills against better competition. He proved he could play with the best juniors by recording 86 and 81 points during his two seasons with the Winter Hawks. He was even named to the second all-star team in 1996. It did seem that the Capitals had indeed stumbled upon something special.

Although Zednik played 11 games and scored two goals for the Washington club in 1996–97, he wasn't quite ready for the NHL. Sent to the Capitals' farm club in Portland, Maine, he put up a respectable 35 points in 56 games. Full-time employment with Washington followed in the 1997–98 season with 17 goals in 65 contests. The next year he slumped to nine goals but rebounded to score 19 in 1999–2000. At the trade deadline in March of 2001, however, Zednik found himself on the move to the Montreal Canadiens. The Habs gave up the highly regarded Trevor Linden, along with another young player Dainus Zubrus, to acquire Zednik. (Montreal also got Jan Bulis in the exchange.) Clearly the Canadiens had some expectations for the speedy winger.

Zednik wasn't a disappointment in the goal-scoring department, notching 22 in his first full year in Montreal. In 2002–03 he had a team best 31.

Since his arrival in Montreal Zednik has displayed soft hands, which all good goal scorers need. In addition to speed, Zednik has many shifty moves and drives to the net very well, despite the fact that he isn't a large man (6', 200 pounds). In the 2002 playoffs, Zednik was enjoying a superb first round versus Boston (four goals, four assists in eight games) when he was viciously hit on the head by Bruins defenceman Kyle McLaren. He couldn't return for the next round against Carolina when the Canadiens could have used his goal-scoring skills. Carolina made it all the way to the finals.

He has strong legs, and his shot is an effective weapon. Zednik has all the skills to be a consistent 25- to 30-goal man. In fact, he lived up to that level in 2003–04 with 30 goals. In the playoffs he scored the winning goal in the seventh game of the first round series which saw Montreal eliminate Boston once again. With new additions to the Habs offense, the opposition can no longer focus on Zednik alone.

Zednik has a way of getting under the skin of the opposition with his chippy style. Often run at, he seems to relish letting other teams know when he has scored a goal. Even though his play can be irritating, Zednik is undoubtedly one of the Habs' most dangerous forwards.

ZEDNIK'S CANADIENS STATS:

	GP	G	A	P	PIM
regular season	255	82	71	153	211
playoffs	15	7	7	14	8

Richard Zednik led the Canadiens in goals scored in the 2003–04 season with 20 markers. (Jim Leary/BBS)

A CHANGE OF VENUE:
THE FORUM AND BELL CENTRE

by Dave Stubbs

Today, hockey fans walk a few blocks southeast of the Forum to the Bell Centre, a cavernous multi-purpose building that since 1996 has been home. Through the decades, the Canadiens have passed their traditions of excellence from one team to the next. So it is with arenas, too.

The Bell Centre is 50,000 tons of foundation concrete, 4,000 tons of steel in the roof and considerable history in between. In the Canadiens dressing room, modelled after the one in the Forum, photos of Hall of Famers gaze down from above on today's players, on walls bearing the inspirational words of John McCrae's poem "In Flanders Fields": "To you from failing hands we throw the torch, be yours to hold it high."

Perhaps more than any other NHL team, the Canadiens celebrate their heritage. Never was this clearer than at the Forum's closing ceremony on March 11, 1996, an emotional evening of both joyful reflection and tearful farewell. Later that week, then captain Pierre Turgeon held a symbolic flaming torch to centre ice at the new address, completing the historic move.

Four years later, more than 115,000 mourners streamed silently into the darkened arena to view the mighty Maurice Richard one last time, in his open casket. His body was at one end of the rink, appropriately in the high slot he ruled throughout his illustrious career. It was an eerie reminder of another Canadiens great, Howie Morenz, whose funeral was held before thousands at the Forum in 1937.

The Rocket was at his incandescent best playing in the Forum, which like every other "original six" rink is no more. Though it still stands, it has been refitted as a movie theatre and entertainment complex, its only hockey played in the arcade.

It was built in 1924 on the site of a former open-air roller skating palace. Erected in just 159 days for $1.5 million, the Forum was to be the home of the NHL's expansion Montreal Professional Hockey Club, known the following season as the Maroons.

But the Canadiens, lacking ice at their own Mount Royal Arena, opened the Forum that November 29. They whipped the visiting Toronto St. Pat's 7–1, on three goals by Billy Boucher. A sellout crowd of 8,500 was in the stands, almost 12,000 including

ITS FOUNDATION was poured at Atwater and Sainte Catherine streets, but in the hearts of many Canadiens fans, the Montreal Forum stood at the corner of History and Legend.

On Forum ice between 1930 and 1993, the Canadiens won 12 of their NHL-record 24 Stanley Cups. Banners hung in the rafters celebrated the seven retired numbers worn by its grandest players: Jacques Plante, Doug Harvey, Jean Béliveau, Howie Morenz, Guy Lafleur and the two Richards — Maurice and Henri. No fewer than 42 Hall of Fame Canadiens were showcased in the arena.

The Beatles performed there, as did almost every singer, circus act, figure skater, boxer and wrestler worth the ticket price. The Forum was a perfect 10 — so said the scoreboard three times for Romanian gymnast Nadia Comaneci, the queen of the 1976 Olympic Games.

The Forum redeemed a few points every season for the Canadiens. So hostile was the arena to the opposition that at least one team executive said that only an exorcist could drive away its many ghosts.

These phantom players didn't occupy much space, in fact. Still, the Canadiens inevitably outgrew their home of seven decades. If the club was to survive the financial game of a 30-team NHL, it needed the extra revenue that only a larger, more modern arena could offer.

the general-admission spectators who paid 50 cents for a ticket, urged on by a Montreal press that fanned the flames of excitement with their Underwoods.

"A more up-to-date building for sporting events could hardly be imagined," the *Gazette* enthused. "New seating arrangements eliminated discomfort to the players, who have been frequently ragged and aggravated until they would lose their tempers, which results in arguments between spectators and players."

Montreal Herald sports editor Elmer Ferguson looked at more than just the Canadiens' new uniform, a globe temporarily replacing the CH crest in honour of the team's 1924 Stanley Cup "world championship" victory, to praise the wife of the Montreal coach and manager: "Mrs. Léo Dandurand looked charming in a new squirrel coat," he wrote. "Léo has done his Christmas shopping early."

The Canadiens played only that one game in the Forum until they settled in for good in 1929. The rink was viewed as hockey's cathedral, expanded in 1949 and again in '68 to accommodate almost 18,000 faithful.

But as the costs of running a franchise spiralled, the team needed more cash. Ground was broken in June 1993 for the $230-

million Molson Centre, so named for the brewery that owned the club and financed the arena. It featured 135 corporate loges, 3,300 more seats and four restaurants.

Renamed the Bell Centre in 2002, it has become the cash register the Forum never could be. In 2003, it played host to 98 non-hockey events, ranking it number one in North America for entertainment tickets sold. The current owner of both the team and arena, George Gillett Jr., presumably can dip into this deep pocket to improve the Canadiens on the ice, surely the most important issue for those fans who claim that the Bell Centre is too big, too loud, too expensive and woefully short of the intimacy that used to be.

But then, it should also be argued that the expanded, big-money NHL isn't what it was for the Rocket, Béliveau or Lafleur. For this reason the Bell Centre is the Canadiens' home for the 21st century, and it's here that they must conjure up new ghosts to enact their history of tomorrow.

Though gone, the Forum is hardly forgotten. Like a weathered photograph, its sepia-tone memories will live as long as they're cared for, a glorious past too rich to discard.

Above: *A look inside the Canadiens new home, now called the Bell Centre. (Charla Jones/Montreal Gazette)*

Facing page: *One of hockey's greatest buildings: the Montreal Forum. (HHOF)*

The Future of the Canadiens

A new group of young players, including Craig Rivet and Michael Ryder (above), now forms the nucleus of the Montreal Canadiens. (Phil McCallum/BBS)

t hasn't been easy for the Montreal Canadiens since they last won the Stanley Cup in 1993.

The general manager has changed three times — Serge Savard, Rejean Houle and Andre Savard — and coaches have come and gone — including Alain Vigneault, Mario Tremblay and Michel Therrien — with varying degrees of minor success. The Habs missed the playoffs four out of five years between 1999 and 2003. Canadiens fans have developed an awkward indifference to the team's plight.

Sure, they hoped the team would recover from their tailspin. But Hab supporters no longer seem to *expect* the Habs to dominate.

" 'I have never doubted this province's passion for the sport, nor for this team."

George Gillett (current majority owner of the Canadiens)

Defenceman Andrei Markov had 13 goals and 37 points for Montreal in the 2002–03 season, his third year with the team. (Jim McIssac/BBS)

235

An uneven record of trading and drafting cost the Canadiens dearly in the 1990s. Management was no longer the best in the league as it had been for many years. Inexperienced general managers like Houle and Andre Savard tried their best to improve the team, but their moves served only to keep the team competitive, on the edge of a playoff spot but not quite there most of the time. Replacing stars — like Patrick Roy, Eric Desjardins, John LeClair, Kirk Muller, Vincent Damphousse and Mark Recchi — who leave the team is difficult.

Passing the torch has become much more difficult in the bloated 30-team NHL. Montreal went through four captains between April of 1995 and March of 1999, unusual for a team that in the past chose its leadership with perfect logic and timing. The long reigns of captains like Maurice Richard and Jean Béliveau are now things of the past. Even Montreal-born star Pierre Turgeon, named captain in 1995, couldn't find happiness in his hometown, despite seeming to be a perfect fit. The term once given to the Habs to describe their attacking style of play — the "Flying Frenchmen" — can be tossed out. The team hasn't had a player finish in the top 10 of league scoring since the 1985–86 season when Mats Naslund finished eighth with 110 points. The Canadiens became a plodding defensive squad that hoped to scrape into the playoffs, fingers crossed.

For one season, 2001–02, that formula seemed to work as the Habs rallied around a great year's performance by goaltender Jose Theodore. They sneaked into the playoffs in the season's last week and then pulled off a major upset of the Boston Bruins in the first round. They should have won the second, but they faltered as a worn down Theodore finally buckled. What happened off the ice was no more

encouraging than the failure on the ice. Nobody in Quebec or anywhere in Canada stepped forward to buy the team when Molson Breweries sought to unload their major share. It was a humbling moment for one of the world's greatest sports franchises.

American George Gillett bought 80.1 percent of the team and 100 percent of the arena in 2001. Thankfully, the new majority owner of the Habs understands what the Canadiens mean to the city and the province. In many ways an ideal owner, he has kept his distance but remains far from indifferent to the team's needs. Losing a capable team president like Ronald Corey was certainly a blow, but the installation of Pierre Boivin in that job seems to have stabilized the club at the boardroom level. The need for new management was obvious after the Habs missed the 2002–03 playoffs. The team signed the best man available. Former Habs star Bob Gainey, experienced at putting together a winning team, was the perfect choice for the *bleu, blanc et rouge*. Gainey won six Stanley Cups as a Hab and managed the Dallas Stars to another championship in 1999. (Dallas also made the finals in 2000.) Gainey's hiring sent a clear signal to the league that the Canadiens were now in the hands of a highly regarded winner. Just as importantly, Gainey understands the team's history and the expectations of Canadiens fans.

Gainey could have made a loud noise in his new role by firing the coach, but he realized that the recently hired Claude Julien had something good to offer his team. He also wanted to take advantage of Andre Savard's top work as a scout and his ability to develop players. Savard became assistant general manager, giving the front office needed experience. It all seemed to work like magic in 2003–04 when the Habs recorded 96 points — a surprise to just about everyone — and returned to the postseason.

A big reason for the turnaround was the use of young players like Michael Ryder, Mike Ribiero, Andrei Markov, Jason Ward and Mike Komisarek. Add in good seasons by veterans like Saku Koivu, Richard Zednik, Sheldon Souray and Craig Rivet, and the Canadiens had a good balance between youth and experience. The return of Theodore to his MVP status of 2002 was also a big help. In addition, the front office sent a clear message by acquiring Alexei Kovalev at the trade deadline in exchange for prospect Jozef Balej. In a March 2004 interview, Koivu told the *Globe and Mail* newspaper, "We feel that we've done something well, that management believes in us and wants to bring another high-level guy [Kovalev] in and make our team better." The Habs had been "sellers" at the trade deadlines in previous years, but Gainey let it be known that he now expected his team to perform.

If certain prospects develop, the long-term future will also look promising. The 1990s produced some forgettable first-round selections — Terry Ryan, Matt Higgins and Eric Chouinard come to mind — but the team did a decent job in the second round of the entry draft and beyond. Rivet, Theodore, Ribiero and Markov were all selected in the second round or higher. The Habs have high hopes for developing youngsters Komisarek, Andrei Kastsitsyn, Chris Higgins, Alexander Perezhogin, Marcel Hossa and Ron Hainsey. The lack of young quality players has hindered the team's success during recent seasons, but with Gainey and Savard now in charge, the Habs might once again become one of hockey's best drafting teams. Every team needs to draft well in today's NHL but none more so than the "small market" Canadiens. Younger, less expensive players are the best way that teams like the Canadiens will survive. Paying outrageous salaries to aging veterans and unrestricted free agents isn't a viable option.

Although the Canadiens improved on the ice in the 2003–04 campaign, a secure financial status was by no means assured. The Canadiens have lost money every year since 1996. In June of 1998, then president Corey warned that profits were indeed declining at an alarming rate and that Molson, the owner at the time, wasn't at all happy. In February of 2004, Boivin said that the team needed to go three playoff rounds — a daunting task given the Eastern Conference's competitive nature — to make a profit. "A well-managed organization would strive to not lose money on the regular season," Boivin told The Canadian Press during a February 2004 interview. The Canadiens — unlike a team such as the Toronto Maple Leafs — have to be careful about raising ticket prices too high in a volatile marketplace, particularly if the team is losing.

Most draining on the team's finances is the $8.2 million paid yearly to the local government for property taxes on the Bell Centre. (Estimates are that the Canadiens have paid $64 million in taxes since

Mike Ribiero
(Andre Ringette/BBS)

Michael Ryder
(Jim Leary/BBS)

the arena opened in 1996.) The team needs some tax relief as well as lower player costs, a tax on visiting players and a strong Canadian dollar over the long term. (These are the hopes for most teams based in Canada.) Team management chooses to work quietly with the local and provincial governments to make their case, but it shouldn't come as a shock if the Canadiens resort to more drastic measures if their concerns aren't met.

The best way for a sports team to handle just about any issue is to win. In '03–'04 the Habs seemed to recover their old ways. There was an excitement about the team that has been lacking for years. Sellouts were common again as Montreal fans rediscovered their pride in the fabled team. Scrutiny of the team remains as high as it was in the glory years. The players, especially team captain Koivu, feel the heat of the media spotlight. They can't simply take their skates off and go home. But this attention is good: it means the team is once again relevant to the city. Souray told the *Toronto Star* in a March 2004 interview: "Now when I go for a coffee, everyone is reading the sports pages, checking out how we're redoing. We've got people's interest a little perked. Everyone wants to talk to you, shake your hand and pat you on the back. It's like we've restored this city's pride. It feels like we're the city's team again."

The club now has few French-Canadian players and more European-born ones. Nine Quebec natives skated for the team in at least one game during the '03–'04 campaign. But that's the reality of competing for talent against 29 other teams. The Canadiens are anchored by their stellar goaltender and a stout defence. Julien has incorporated more attack into the game plan. He isn't afraid to bench players who don't perform, giving the team a sense of accountability that has been lacking. At a delicate moment in their history, the Canadiens need to build on their performance of '03–'04. It will be up to Gainey to make the right moves. Already he has added Radek Bonk to the line-up and has finalized a contract with Julien. Montreal fans have every reason to be hopeful that management can turn the club into a serious Cup contender. A return to glory may not be far off for *Les Canadiens*.

Index

Page numbers in **bold** refer to illustrations

Aitkenhead, Andy, **8**
Armstrong, George, **116**
Art Ross Trophy, 45, 88, 154
Awery, Don, **91**

Backstrom, Ralph, **40**, **90**, 90–91, **91**
Balon, Dave, 86
Barkley, Doug, **128**
Baun, Bob, **120**
Begin, Steve, 236
Béliveau, Jean, 7, 10, **54**, **84**, **92**, 92–95, **93**, **94**, **95**, **81**
Bell Centre, 220, 232–33, **233**. *See also* Molson Centre
Berenson, Red, 88
Big Three, 171
Blake, Hector "Toe," **40**, **96**, 96–99, **97**, **98**, **99**, 192
Boivin, Claude, 220
Bonin, Marcel, 42
Bouchard, Emile "Butch," **46**, 46–47, **47**
Bouillon, Francis, 236
Bower, Johnny, **66**, **78**, **95**, **101**, **126**, **139**
Bowman, Scotty, 148–49, **149**, 152, 153
Brisebois, Patrice, **221**, 222, **222**, 236
broadcasters, Canadiens, 38–39
Bronfman ownership, 88
Burns, Pat, 193, **193**, 197

Calder Trophy, 45, 88
Campbell, Clarence, 76, 82, **83**
Carbonneau, Guy, **196**, 196–97, **197**
Cattarinch, Joseph, 19
Central Red Army–Canadiens Game (1975), 188–89
Chadwick, Ed, 67
Chelios, Chris, 198, **198**
Clarke, Bobby, **173**
Cleghorn, Sprague, 22, **22**, 26
Connolly, Wayne, 68
Conn Smythe Trophy, 88, 154, 194
Corey, Ronald, 153–54, 191–92, 220
Cournoyer, Yvan, **85**, **94**, **100**, 100–103, **101**, **102**, **103**, **189**
Crozier, Roger, **107**, **128**
Curry, Floyd, 48, **48**

Damphousse, Vincent, **199**, 199–200, **200**, 218
Dandurand, Leo, 19, 22
Demers, Jacques, 194, **195**
Desjardins, Eric, **201**, 201–2, **202**
Dryden, Ken, 87, 151, 156, **157**, 157–59, **158**, **159**
Duff, Dick, **89**, 104–5, **105**
Dupont, J. Arthur, 38
Durnan, Bill, **49**, 49–50, **50**

Engblom, Brian, **155**
expansion, NHL, 87, 164

Ferguson, John, **84**, **106**, 106–7, **107**
Fleming, Reggie, **117**
Flying Frenchmen, 35
Forum. *See* Montreal Forum
Foster Hewitt Memorial Award, 138
Frank J. Selke Trophy, 154, 194

Gainey, Bob, 14–15, **150**, **160**, 160–63, **161**, **162**, **163**, 220, 222, 236
Gallivan, Danny, 38
Gardner, Cal, 75
Garneau, Richard, 38
Geoffrion, Bernie "Boom Boom," **40**, **51**, 51–54, **52**, **53**, **54**
Giacomin, Eddie, **130**
Gillet, George, 220, 235, 236
goalie masks, 74
Good Friday Massacre, 214–15
Gorman, Tommy, 41–42
Goyette, Phil, **43**
Grundman, Irving, 153

Hainsworth, George, **16**, 23, **23**
Hall, Joe, 24, **24**, 26
Harmon, Glen, **41**
Harper, Terry, **108**, 108–9, **109**
Harris, Ted, **110**, 110–11, **111**
Hart, Cecil, 19, 21
Hart Trophy, 21, 45, 88, 154, 220
Harvey, Doug, **55**, 55–58, **56**, 57, 58

Henry, "Sugar" Jim, **1**
Hodge, Charlie, **112**, 112–13, **113**
Horton, Tim, **139**
Houle, Rejean, 164, **164**
Hull, Bobby, **133**

Irvin, Dick, Sr. 38, 41–42, 46, 59, **59**
Irvin, Dick, Jr. 38

Jack Adams Award, 154, 194
Jarvis, Doug, 165, **165**
Jeffrey, Larry, **113**
Johnson, Tom, **60**, 60–61, **61**
Joliat, Aurel, **17**, 25, **25**

Keane, Mike, **191**
Kelly, Dan, 38
Kennedy, George (Kendell), 19
Keon, Dave, **111**
Koivu, Saku, **216**, **223**, 223–24, **224**, 237

Lach, Elmer, **62**, 62–63, **63**, **97**
Lady Byng Trophy, 45, 194
Lafleur, Guy, 12, **12**, **166**, 166–70, **168**, **169**, **170**, 192
Lalonde, Edouard "Newsy," 25, **26**, 26
Lambert, Yvon, 170, **170**
Langway, Rod, **153**
Laperriere, Jacques, **114**, 114–17, **115**, **116**, **117**
Lapointe, Guy, **171**, 171–74, **172**, **173**, **174**
Larose, Claude, 118, **118**

Larouche, Pierre, **154**

Laviolette, Jack, 18, 19, 35

Lecavalier, Rene, 38, **38**

LeClair, John, 203, **203**

Lemaire, Jacques, 119, 119–22, **120**, **121**, **122**, 154, 192

Lemieux, Claude, 190, 204, **204**

Lepine, Alfred "Pit," 27, **27**

McDonald, Ab, 40

McNeil, Gerry, 47, 64, **64**

Mahovlich, Frank, 123, 123–24, **124**

Mahovlich, Peter, 175, **175**

Maki, Chico, **145**

Malone, Joe, 28, **28**

Mantha, Georges, **20**

Mantha, Sylvio, 29, **29**

Markov, Andrei, **235**

Marshall, Dan, **43**

Masterton Trophy, 88, 154, 220

Molson Centre, 218, 233. *See also* Bell Centre

Molson family, 87, 153

Molson, Hartland, **10**, 20

Mondou, Pierre, **154**

Montreal Canadiens: first team, 19; 1958–59, **44**

Montreal Forum, 13–14, 21, 218, **232**, 232–33

Moore, Richard "Dickie," **54**, 65, 65–67, **66**, **67**, **68**

Morenz, Howarth William "Howie," **8**, **10**, **17**, 21, 30, 30–33, **31**, **32**, **33**

Mosdell, Ken, 69, **69**

Muller, Kirk, 205, **205**

Naslund, Mats, 206, **206**

National Hockey League (NHL), 19, 87, 164

Nesterenko, Eric, **74**

Norris Trophy, 12, 45, 88, 154, 194

O'Brien, J. Ambrose, 17, 19

O'Connor, Herbert "Buddy," 34, **34**

Olmstead, Bert, 70, **70**

Parent, Bernie, **91**

Perron, Jean, 192

Pitre, Didier, 35, **35**

Plante, Jacques, **71**, 71–74, **72**, **73**, **74**, 136

Pollock, Sam, 86, 138, 165, 176–77, **177**

Pronovost, Andre, **54**

Provost, Claude, **89**, **125**, 125–26, **126**

Punch Line, 42, 62, 76, 97

Quebec Nordiques, 214–15, **215**

Quintal, Stephane, **219**

Reardon, Ken, 75, **75**

Redmond, Mickey, **89**

Ribiero, Mike, **237**

Richard, Henri, 84, **127**, 127–30, **128**, **129**, **130**

Richard, Maurice "Rocket," **1**, **5**, **9**, **10**, 42, 76, 76–80, **77**, **78**, **79**, **80**, 82, **97**, 232

Richard Riot, 82

Richer, Stephane, 207, **207**

Risebrough, Doug, 178, **178**

Rivet, Craig, 225, **225**, **234**

Roberts, Jimmy, 131, **131**

Robinson, Larry, 179, 179–82, **180**, **181**, **182**, 186

Rousseau, Bobby, **132**, 132–33, **133**

Roy, Patrick, 186, 194, **208**, 208–11, **209**, **210**, **211**, 217

Ruel, Claude, 87

Russian Central Red Army, 188–89

Ryder, Michael, **234**, **237**

S Line, 36

Salming, Borje, **167**

Samsonov, Sergei, **229**

Savard, Denis, 184, 191–92, 212, **212**

Savard, Serge, **134**, 134–35, **135**

Sawchuk, Terry, 86

Selke, Frank, **40**, 42–43, 45, 81

Selke Trophy, 154, 194

Shutt, Steve, **183**, 183–85, **184**, **185**

Siebert, Albert "Babe," 36, **36**

Skrudland, Brian, 192

Smith, Bobby, 213, **213**

Souray, Sheldon, 226, **226**

Stanley Cup wins, 14; 1909–1939, 19, 21, 22; 1940–60, **42**, **44**, 45, 80; 1961–73, 88, **89**; 1974–1984, **150**, 154; 1985–1995, **15**, **190**, 192, 194, **211**

Talbot, Jean-Guy, **136**, 136–37, **137**

Tardif, Marc, **152**

Theodore, Jose, **217**, **221**, 227, 227–30, **228**, **229**, **230**, 236

Tremblay, Gilles, 38, 39, 138–39, **139**

Tremblay, J.C., **140**, 140–41, **141**

Tremblay, Mario, 186–87, **187**

Tretiak, Vladislav, 189

Turgeon, Pierre, **218**

Turnbull, Ian, 163

Vachon, Rogie, **142**, 142–43, **143**

Vezina, Georges, 37, **37**

Vezina Trophy, 21, 45, 88, 154, 194, 220

Watson, Harry, **64**

Worsley, Lorne "Gump," **117**, 144, 144–47, **145**, **146**, **147**

Zednik, Richard, 231, **231**

Acknowledgements

ABOUT THE ESSAY CONTRIBUTORS

Hockey Hall of Fame journalist **Red Fisher** has been covering the Canadiens for 49 years — first with *The Montreal Star* until it closed in 1979, since then with the *Montreal Gazette*. He has twice won the National Newspaper Award for sportswriting.

Veteran sportswriter **Frank Orr** was inducted into the Hockey Hall of Fame in 1989. A longtime reporter for *The Toronto Star*, Orr covered many Canadiens games.

Dave Stubbs is a feature writer with the *Montreal Gazette*. His biggest regrets in life are not having been born 15 years earlier, so he could have enjoyed the magnificent Canadiens teams of the 1950s — and not knowing better than to put a Jean Béliveau rookie card through the spokes of his bike.

ACKNOWLEDGEMENTS

Thanks to the following for use of photos in this book: Harold Barkley Archives (HB), Bruce Bennett Studios (BBS), Dennis Miles (DM) and The Hockey Hall of Fame (HHOF).

The author would like to thank the following writers for their invaluable works on the Canadiens and on hockey in general that were used to complete the research for this book: Michael Berger, Ross Brewitt, William Brown, Roch Carrier, Stephane Cole, Charles Coleman, John Devaney, Dan Diamond (editor), Gerald Eskenazi, Shirley Fischler, Stan Fischler, Red Fisher, Ed Fitkin, Trent Frayne, Chris Goyens, Zander Hollander (editor), Bruce Hood, Hugh Hood, Jim Hunt, Douglas Hunter, Dick Irvin, Brian Kendall, Geoffrey Kent, Craig MacInnis, Ron McAllister, Brian McFarlane, Tim Moriarty, Claude Mouton, Andy O'Brien, Frank Orr, Raymond Plante, Andrew Podnieks, Jim Proudfoot, Dean Robinson, Sherry Ross, Dave Stubbs, Allan Turowetz, Michael Ulmer, Sheila Wawanash (editor), Charles Wilkins.

The author would like to thank the following Canadiens legends for their books that were also used in completing the research for this book: Jean Beliveau, Ken Dryden, John Ferguson, Bernie Geoffrion, Guy Lafleur, Maurice Richard, Frank J. Selke, Sr. and Gump Worsley.

Record books used to compile statistical information: *Official NHL Guide and Record Book*, *Total Hockey* (Second Edition), *Total Hockey* (2003 Edition), *Stanley Cup Playoff Guide* (various issues), *Hockey Almanac* (issued by *The Hockey News* in 2000), *Sporting News Player Register* (various editions). Three issues (1993-94, 2002-03 and 2003-04) of the Montreal Canadiens media guide were also referred to extensively.

Magazines used to complete research: *Les Canadiens*, *Macleans*, *Goal Magazine*, *The Hockey News*, *The Hockey News – The Top 50*, *The Hockey News – The Best of Everything in Hockey*, *Inside Hockey*, *Hockey Digest*, *Hockey Illustrated*, *Hockey Pictorial*, *Hockey Scene*, *Hockey World*, *Superstar Hockey*, *Sports Illustrated*. Newspapers consulted: *Montreal Gazette*, *Toronto Sun*, *Toronto Star*, *Globe and Mail*.

The author also wishes to thank the following people for their invaluable assistance in helping to put this book together: Paul Patzkou, Tyler Wolosewich, Craig Campbell, Derek Fairbridge, Doug McLatchy, Phil Pritchard and Dennis Miles.

A special word of thanks to my wife, Maria, and to my son, David, for their patience and support while this book was being put together.